The End

of

Mine

PAUL BLESSINGTON

Kona Epub Hui

Kailua Kona, Hawaii

Special thanks to Mary Blessington who, out of the kindness of
her heart, edited this book.

Printed by CreateSpace, An Amazon.com Company.

E-Book ISBN: 978-0-615-79466-2
Print ISBN: 978-0-615-84875-4

Published in the United States
by Kona Epub Hui.

This book is dedicated to Dr. John T. Watabe along with countless other health care professionals who perform uparalleled feats of courage on a daily basis.

Chapter 1

There will come a day when all of humanity lives in harmony with one another. There will come a day when every person will be well nourished, living in a good home without fear of poor health or old age. There will come a day when every person will be an asset to their community, with time to pursue their own happiness, goals, desires, education and religion. There will come a day when nations no longer defend themselves against each other and war will be a thing of the past. There will come a day when all people will truly be equal in each other's eyes...this day is coming sooner than you think.

Speeding down the highway, Saul Beckman was dreaming of a world powered by wind.

Saul wasn't dreaming of the kind of wind that powers windmills, or even ferocious, seventy mile per hour hurricane wind that tear roofs off buildings. The wind Saul Beckman dreamed of can only be found five miles overhead.

Saul's quest was to harness the power of the heavens. To capture a mere one percent of the jet stream's power is enough energy to fuel the planet. And now, after years of engineering prototypes, Saul finally had enough proof to get a meeting with Simion Ruzart, the world's second most wealthy person.

Getting closer to Simion Ruzart's home with each passing mile, Saul's tension grew a little more intense.

With 56 billion to his name, Simion did not lavish upon himself unimaginable riches. Simion Ruzart had a much higher calling. Simion wanted nothing less than to save the planet.

It takes much more than good luck, excellent timing, or even a great product to build the world's largest fortune. It was Simion's supernatural ability to look into the depths of the numbers and perceive the future that enabled him to amass the second largest fortune the world has ever seen. After peering into thousands of carbon emission numbers, Simion discovered that all of them lead to just one number: fifty.

In just fifty years, carbon emissions must be brought down to zero or Armageddon becomes a reality.

Saul could feel blood pulsing in his neck as he pulled up to the gate to inform the guard that he had arrived. In an attempt to slow his heart rate Saul attempted to breath deep calming breaths as he made his way up the long winding driveway.

Parking along the circular driveway, he was surprised to see Simion waiting at the bottom of the wide white travertine steps leading into the sprawling mansion. Like sunshine breaking through dark clouds, Simion's warm smile and extended hand washed away the most of fear building inside of him. While shaking his hand Simion said with conviction, "Welcome. It is good that we can finally meet. I have heard so many good things about your work."

Entering the foyer, Saul couldn't help being impressed by the rough-honed Angkor sandstone veneer walls set against sun-bleached mahogany trim. The light washing down from the skylights high above sharpened Saul's senses. Walking down the hall that lead to the study, Saul began to feel himself. An impressive tall glass wall along the back of the study looked out onto the bay.

Wasting no time, Saul described the recent test flight in Maui as he addressed his lap top to sync with the huge flat screen TV against study's southern wall. Once connected, Saul began, "The Maui kite generator exceeded our expectations."

The screen filled with an image of what looked like a huge paraglider tracing a figure-eight pattern against a perfect blue Hawaiian sky.

"You are looking at a thirty-meter kite flying one-hundred and twenty-four feet off the ground in twenty-six mile per hour winds. This kite is producing half a megawatt...enough energy to power two-hundred and fifty homes."

Clearly intrigued, Simion watched the kite strain against its cables as it dove, banked then curved upward before repeating the looping sequence. Over and over Simion watched the kite fly in a flawless figure eight pattern before observing, "This kite changes shape during its dive."

Undoubtedly in his element, Saul said, "Precisely. This kite's ability to change its shape mid-flight constitutes a new generation of intelligent kites. We call it a Flexwing. You see, conventional kites are ripped from their harness lines if their width exceeds twenty square meters when flying in winds over eighteen miles per hour. We were able to overcome this hurdle by mimicking the wing control of a hawk. Watch as the Flexwing contracts its wings during a diving loop and unfurls them when climbing.

"We broke the size-to-wind speed barrier. You are looking at the most efficient wind-based energy-producing machine in existence."

Musing, Simion said, "So, by expanding its wings it generates power as it gains altitude, like a roller coaster being hoisted up a ramp before taking a dive. But the kite, or rather, the Flexwing, is made of fabric. How can fabric change shape?"

"Intelligent textiles. Electronic monofilament fiber cable is woven into each seam. Thrust, tensile strength, flight pattern along with wind speed is instantaneously fed electronically along the Flexwing's monofilament fibers leading to the main tether cable. Acting like an umbilical cord, the cable conducts a constant stream of data both to and from the kite, along with enough electricity to power dozens of micro-pulleys that contract and expand, enabling the Flexwing to change shape."

"Impressive. But why go to all the expense? Why not use conventional ridged materials?"

"We learned what happens with rigid materials from hurricane Katrina. Katrina had no damaging effect over water, but once Katrina hit land it tore apart everything in its path. Just imagine a solid object tethered to a cable flying in jet stream winds that have three times the power of Katrina. A rigid aircraft would be ripped to shreds."

Still not convinced Simion said, "But commercial aircraft are constantly flying in the jet stream and they aren't ripped apart."

"Yes, buy they are not tethered to a cable powering a ten megawatt generator. If that was to happen, their wings would instantly be torn off."

In disbelief, Simion said, "Did you say ten megawatts?"

Simion knew that even the largest wind turbines in existence, towering 538 feet off the ground, can only produce 7.5 megawatts of power. Feeling the prize within his grasp, Saul said, "The jet stream Flexwing is four times larger than the Maui Flexwing. Our 120-square meter Flexwing is capable of generating ten megawatts of power. With a wingspan as wide as a commercial jumbo jet's, a single Flexwing can generate enough power to fuel 6000 homes."

As if the numbers just appeared in his mind Simion replied, "So, you're telling me that sixty of these Flexwings are capable of producing the same amount of energy as a 600 megawatt coal-burning electrical plant?"

Looking like he could not be more pleased with himself, Saul exclaimed, "Yes. Replacing coal-burning electrical plants with wind driven energy is now within our grasp."

"But if you're looking at replacing hundreds of coal-burning electrical plants, you'll need thousands of Flexwings in the air. How do you keep commercial aircraft from running into them?"

"There are millions of square miles of airspace. One Flexwing only needs a quarter mile to run its horizontal figure eight pattern. Accordingly, a full scale Flexwing plant only needs 15 square miles. Coordinates for Flexwing plants need to be programmed into commercial jet airliner computer systems to prevent them from accidentally entering Flexwing airspace."

"That still amounts to hundreds of square miles of land. How do you keep those below safe?"

"While it's inadvisable to position Flexwings above a city, they can be safely deployed over agricultural land. Due to monofilament seam lines constantly monitoring their stress, we can slowly fly down a Flexwing if it's showing signs of fatigue. Should the Flexwing experience a catastrophic event, it automatically detaches from its cable by deploying two jet helium balloons, allowing for a safe descent of both the cable and the Flexwing."

The screen changed from an image of the flying Flexwing to a rather unimpressive drab olive metal box. Saul said, "This is our thrust generator. It doubles the energy-transfer by incorporating two modes of power generation. The first uses the same regenerative break-recovery energy found in hybrid cars. The second is the kinetic-thrust energy that drives its pistons. The Flexwing reaches its maximum kinetic-energy force just as it pulls out of its dive. At that point, the Flexwing engages the regenerative break-recovery component of the thrust generator. As the Flexwing climbs again, the kinetic energy drives the pistons that power the thrust component of the generator."

Simion was impressed, but he still had one major concern. As Saul neared the end of his presentation, Simion posed his last question: the multi-billion dollar question.

Perhaps better than anyone, Simion Ruzart understood that a product must be economically competitive to be viable. Even with huge cash reserves, a company is destined to fail if it cannot compete in the marketplace. In the short run, he could subsidize any number of zero-emission energy ventures, but in the long run coal will be burned until the day when it is no longer economically viable.

"One of my requirements for meeting with you today was for you to compare your costs with those of a coal-burning electrical plant generating 600 megawatts. How economically viable is your high-altitude Flexwing?"

Saul's heart skipped a beat as he quickly answered, "When real estate laws were written, no one placed a value on the air above the land. So, although you don't necessarily own the mineral rights under your land, you always own the air above the land. Therefore, our raw material is free. We don't need to dig it up out of the earth and ship it hundreds of miles away to fuel some towering inferno. What's more, the flight path of the Flexwing is fully automated, so our operational costs are lower. That leaves the cost of the plant itself. Our generator costs are about the same, but our cable and Flexwings costs are significantly lower than those created by building furnaces and smokestacks."

"I understand. But to put it simply, are your kilowatt-per-hour costs lower than nuclear?"

Saul felt as if the wind had been knocked out of him. Dejected, lost for words, he stared at Simion and stammered, "What?"

"If there is one thing I've learned it's that economic laws are steadfast. Conventional wind turbines run at eight cents per hour; coal, at four point five cents; nuclear, at four cents; and hydro, at two point five. Prove to me your Flexwing can produce electricity equal to the cost of nuclear power and I will give you whatever funding you need."

Still trying to regain his composure, Saul asked, "Why nuclear?"

"You may have heard of Tectonic Power. I'm providing them seed money to get their traveling wave-reactor functioning. Their management tells me they are close to being able to burn depleted uranium. Once they crack that nut, we should have a good supply of cheap, clean energy to last another 100 years. Hopefully, we will have figured out the fusion problem by that time, or found some other low-price green energy solution."

Saul felt a giddy shock pulsate through his body as he realized his holy grail was slipping through his fingers. Feeling blood rush to his head and sounding like he was about to laugh hysterically, Saul said: "So. I get the funding to build my prototype. All I need to do is demonstrate that I can produce high-altitude wind power at four cents per kilowatt hour."

Reaching out his hand, an optimist to the end, Saul said, "Do I have your word on that?"

Shaking Saul's hand, Simion said, "Prove to me your ten megawatt Flexwing can produce energy at four cents per kilowatt hour and I will give you your prototype funding".

Walking back to his car in the gentle light of mid-afternoon, Saul felt like he had just gone eight rounds with the Heavyweight Champion of the world With a newly tempered enthusiasm, he braced himself for the Ninth.

Chapter 2

Clearly exasperated, Bert Stockton said, "Saul, everyone knows that clean energy costs more. I know you don't want to weave the fibertronic fabric in China, but if we do, we can come down from eight to six point seven cents."

Saul made an involuntary clicking noise as his tongue struck the roof of his mouth, an audible signal that he did not like what he was hearing. Pulling his eyes from some unknown spot on the ceiling, he faced his Controller and said, "Bert, China is not an option."

Saul would never forget the day his father's knitting mill sold off the last of their machinery to China. Saul had spent a large chunk of his adolescence forming bonds with his co-workers at that modest knitting factory on the outskirts of Los Angeles. Not too long ago, the garment industry was one of the largest industries in Los Angeles, generating billions in revenue and employing thousands of workers.

Saul would be dammed if he would hand over the keys of yet another industry to China.

"It doesn't matter how close we get to five cents. I know Simion. He will not give us the funding unless we can produce electricity at four cents or less. What are your cost predictions based on us producing Zylon?"

Sighing as though he'd said it a thousand times before, Bert replied, "Toyobo will not sell their Zylon fiber division. The only way to obtain that technology is to buy the entire company for three point nine billion dollars. Even if we could buy Toyobo, manufacture the fiber, spin the cordage and weave the fabric, our costs would still not come close four cents per kilowatt hour.

"With a tensile strength of two-million-four-hundred and thirty-thousand pounds per square inch, Zylon is one of the few materials capable of withstanding hurricane-force winds. Sixty percent stronger than Kevlar, Zylon is also electronically conductive, enabling Flexwings to change their shape as they enter and exit dive loops. Structural shape changes, flight patterns, stress alarms and safety mechanisms all rely on real-time programming, made possible by Zylon's fibertronic capability. Without realizing it, Toyobo could very well have the most valuable patent on the planet and it's a bargain at three point nine billion dollars. Without a doubt, the team at Stanford Research Institute must be wishing they never sold Zylon to Toyobo."

As Bert's words ricocheted off his brain, Saul was busy searching for a solution. Throughout Saul's adult life he had heard these words: "You can't. We can't. It's impossible." Yet every time, Saul found a way to make it happen. With smiling eyes he leaned over to Bert and said, "You're wrong, Bert. There is a way. We just don't know what it is yet."

Like so many times before, if Saul didn't have the answer, he sought out someone who did. Picking up the phone, he dialed Chris Anderson.

Being the curator of TED conferences had its advantages. Many of the world's leading minds shared their ideas at TED conferences. If anyone knew the person who could help solve Saul's conundrum, it was Chris Anderson.

After a few tries Saul got Chris on the phone.

"Chris, I need your help. Simion put the brakes on my project until I can get my costs competitive with nuclear energy. Do you know anyone who can help me solve this problem?"

Inwardly, Chris thought, "It always comes down to money." Cautiously he asked, "How much lower do you need your costs to go?"

"Roughly? 50%."

"Really? I have no idea if such a feat is possible, but if you want an innovative mind to help you make it a reality, you need to get a hold of Thomas Quinn. For years now I have been trying to get Thomas to participate at TED. He is the most forward-thinking economist I have ever known. His graduate paper on Politics & Corporate Megaliths from Texas A & M is the best work I've seen on the subject. He's a recluse, though. He's living off the grid somewhere near Wichita. If anyone can help solve your financial problem, it's Thomas Quinn."

"What's his phone number?"

"It took me considerable effort just to locate him, let alone discover his phone number. The only way you're going to talk to him is to visit him on his farm. I'll send you his address."

On the flight to Wichita, Saul read what little Chris could provide on Thomas's background. Thomas Quinn was born in 1978 in Los Alamos, New Mexico. In 1977, Thomas's father, Gabriel Quinn, a ranch hand from Chihuahua, married his mother, Maria Antos. Gabriel worked as a gardener and Maria, who received her training in Cebu, worked as a nurse's aide. Thomas was employed at various odd jobs until his high school graduation in 1995. Thomas received a full scholarship to Texas A & M where he received a Masters in Economics. After graduating, Thomas worked as a CEO for a southern California aerospace manufacturer until 2010, at which point he paid cash for a twelve-acre farm outside of Wichita, Kansas. Thomas had just recently turned thirty-five.

Driving his rental car out of the airport, Saul did his best to convince himself that he was not spending what little money the firm had left on some wild goose chase. After driving close to two hours, Saul stopped on the dirt road in front of the address, staring in astonishment at what must be Thomas's home. It was surrounded by a colorful mosaic of connecting vegetable gardens. It looked like a living, meandering canvas. Rivers of bowl-shaped leafy red cabbages flanked by tall celery flowed into stalks of Brussels sprouts gave way to valleys of potatoes and leeks.

Stopping his car at the end of the driveway, Saul spotted Thomas making his way along a hedge of snap peas with a huge grin on his face. As Saul got out of the car he thought Thomas looked so happy he might actually burst into laughter.

"That's quite a garden you have."

"Thanks!"

Thomas's ever present smile was unusual for such a big man. Standing just under six feet, he gave the impression of being much taller. His boxy, bull dog chest, square shoulders and thick hands made him appear formidable. His almond-shaped eyes protruded like a fantail gold fish's. A burgundy birthmark emerged like a floating island from the thick black hair along the left side of his neck. While Thomas would never find himself on the cover of a men's fashion magazine, his compelling features and calm demeanor was attractive.

With a warm smile Thomas exclaimed, "Pulling weeds is a lot more fun when you are working with a pallet. Come, we'll talk out back on the veranda."

Walking around the south end of the aging modest home they came to a flagstone patio. A raw black walnut table and benches stood under a gazebo shaded by wisteria.

Taking a seat, Saul got right to the point: "How can I get my price below nuclear?"

With a pleasant smile on his face, completely at ease, Thomas said, "The information I am about to give you must be carefully managed to prevent it from being corrupted. I need your word that you will get my permission before you divulge this information to anyone, even your wife."

If there was one thing Saul could relate to, it was protecting intellectual property. Jetstream Energy needed to announce their breakthrough technology in order to sell investors on the practicality of high-altitude wind energy while keeping that same technology protected from its competitors.

"No problem; absolutely confidential. Just hand me a Confidentiality Agreement and I will sign it."

With a solemn look Thomas said, "There's no need for an Agreement. If you breach my confidence the damage would be greater than any court could award. You need to understand that my motivation is not monetary. Before I give my report to you, I need to know what you plan to do with this information."

"For twelve years I have thrown my heart and soul into providing a viable clean energy source. Now, on the verge of making high-altitude wind energy generation possible, I am unable to continue my work because the projected costs are too high. So, I know what it's like to have one's vision jeopardized; I would never compromise your information."

With that, Thomas's smile returned. "Good. I told you in my letter that there's a way to reduce your costs. What I didn't tell you is that a new economic model is needed to make your cost be competitive with nuclear energy."

Saul didn't know whether to be thrilled that there was an answer or deflated by the prospect of facing yet another monumental hurdle.

"Okay, what's this new economic model?"

Thomas simply said, "You don't pay your workers."

Saul flinched.

Years ago Saul gave up a great-paying hydro-turbine engineering job to pursue his dream of harnessing the power of wind by creating the first vertical-thrust hydraulic generator. Being his own boss cost him dearly.

Suppressing his frustration, Saul said, "My work has been a labor of love for me, but I hardly think I can convince hundreds of people to work for free."

"I never said the employees of Jetstream Electric will work for free; I said they won't be paid, not in cash."

Skeptical, Saul folded his arms across his chest and asked, "How so?"

"Jetstream employees will not define wealth in relation to their net worth, but rather in terms of their quality of life. Dedicated Jetstream employees are free from worry. Housing, retirement, healthcare, entertainment, along with all the other elements that are important to us will be provided by Jetstream."

"Are you talking about converting Jetstream Electric into some kind of commune?"

"Hell no. An commune is the most inefficient institution devised by man. I'm not talking about changing the way we produce products; I'm talking about a new way of rewarding people for their work. This new method is what I call 'huinomics.'"

"Huinomics?"

"In Hawaiian, the word hui means to form a partnership, an organization, a society; to join together, to unite.

"Jetstream will function very much like a conventional corporation. But, unlike a conventional corporation that disperses a percentage of its profits to its workers, shareholders and executives, a hui corporation will use profits to provide for the needs of its members.

Feeling off-balanced, Saul said, "Employees work to get paid a salary so they can survive."

"That is what takes place in a conventional company, but in a hui company an employee's reward for work takes on an entirely different form. A hui employee lives debt-free. They do not have the nagging fear of earning enough money to pay rent or being burdened with a life-long mortgage payment. Not to mention, they are free from the stress of saving for retirement or paying for medical expenses. Living a worry-free life gives you tremendous sense of freedom. When you consider that hui employees have more leisure time than conventional workers, the benefits of working for a hui company becomes all the more inciting.

"How so?"

"A hui employee is only obligated to preform his task at work. Domestic work is performed by other members of the hui. Meals, laundry, up keep on the home, and other domestic chores are performed by other members of the hui. Conventional employees typically have eight hours of leisure time per week; hui employees have eight hours of leisure time every work day."

"How could a hui company provide all of these things for their employees and still have lower cost?"

"By sharing resources. Our conventional economy stipulates that we own one of everything we desire. A hui economy stipulates that the hui owns enough of everything to supply the desires of its employees. A conventional company of 3000 employees expects all 3000 of its employees to all own their own car. A hui company owns enough cars to supply the needs of its employees. When you begin to stack all of the other things deemed necessary for our lives, from washing machines to lawn mowers, you begin to understand just how fewer resources you need to for a group of people rather than each individual.

"Do you have any idea how hard it will be to sell Simion on this idea? 'Simion, I can get our costs under four cents, but I can't pay my workers.' He'll think I'm nuts."

"It can be difficult to get your head around it at first, but if anyone can understand the efficiency of huinomics, it's Simion Ruzart. But even if Simion doesn't become your sponsor, social evolution has already begun to shift mankind toward the path of huinomics. Change is all around us. If Jetstream isn't the first company to convert to a hui corporation, some other company will be. Change is inevitable."

"Why?"

"We either change how we function as a society by creating a sustainable economy that allows balanced wealth for everyone or the bulk of humanity will perish."

"We all know what will happen if global warming is not stopped, but what does that have to do with how the economy functions?"

"First, an economy that strives to generate an infinite amount of wealth is fatally flawed because the earth has a finite amount of resources. The earth does not have enough resources for each of its seven billion people to own their own car, and home stuffed with kitchen appliances along with all the other objects each of us strive to own. So the more successful our economy becomes, with more third world countries like China becoming wealthy, the closer we come to destroying our environment by depleting what little natural resources we have left. With seven billion people competing to consume more and more of the earth's resources, we're taking more than the earth can provide. We are living on borrowed time.

"People like Simion Ruzart represent the second fatal flaw of our economy. The more wealth an individual has, the greater that individual's ability is to generate more wealth. Perpetual wealth-generation leads to a very small number of individuals having vast sums of money. Today the combined wealth of the richest four hundred people in America is equal to the amount of wealth of one-hundred and fifty million people. Unbalanced ownership of wealth stifles economies and corrupts governments. Wealth inequality is not just confined to America. Nations around the globe are facing the same problem. Inequality of wealth will inevitably lead to social upheaval.

Pleadingly, Saul exclaimed, "I don't want to change society. Isn't saving the planet from the catastrophic effects of global warming enough?"

"You can't have one without the other. Just as the plants on my farm are competing with one another, so too must you compete to be cheaper than nuclear. Your competitive advantage of converting into a hui corporation will enable you to produce energy at three point two cents per kilowatt hour."

Saul felt his heart lift and the concerned lines above his eyebrows vanished. "Cheaper than nuclear! My God. But I don't have the time to wait for this social evolution to take place. We need to act now, or in fifty years there will be nothing left to save."

"If you can get your funding there is nothing stopping you. The growth of Jetstream and the spread of high-altitude wind power will be unmatched."

Saul had a deeply contented look on his face as he gazed out over the blue horizon, and like so many times before, he pictured hundreds of Flexwings generating vast quantities of energy from the upper atmosphere. Like giant circling manta rays feeding on plankton, Saul imagined his Flexwings transferring the power of the heavens down to the earth.

A sense of euphoria spread through Saul; his dream was within reach. Coming down to earth, Saul focused on his holy grail: a sponsor that would contribute the millions needed to allow Jetstream to prove that high-altitude wind generation is viable.

Saul asked, "Do you really think Simion Ruzart will support huinomics?"

Standing up and stretching, Thomas answered, "It is entirely because Simion Ruzart has such a keen understanding of economics that he will support converting Jetstream into a hui corporation and provide you funding.

"You need to understand that Huinomics works within the same economic principles as our current economy. To put it simply, the operational costs of a hui corporation will be a fraction of those for a conventional corporation."

"What is this I hear about Simion Ruzart?" Thomas's wife appeared at the sliding door leading to the veranda. Jackie had a lean athletic build, sharp features and impossibly straight lush brown hair accenting her smooth tan skin. Walking over to Thomas and placing both of her arms affectionately on his shoulders while looking Saul squarely in the eyes, she said with a smile, "You are not going to send me and Thomas packing off to the city, no matter how handsome the prize."

Affectionately, Thomas craned his neck to look into Jackie's eyes and with flushed cheeks said, "You know it will take more than money to get us off the farm."

Saul felt uneasy seeing the warmth between Jackie and Thomas. "After listening to Thomas, my whole world seems upside down. I don't know where to start."

Jackie's piercing eyes darted to Saul: "He has a way of doing that. But don't worry, once you find your footing, you'll feel better."

"I hope so. Look, I'm going to drive back to the hotel in Wichita. I could sure use the drive and I want to leave before the sun sets. I'll be back in the morning."

Jackie, taking on a more serious tone, said, "I hope you don't mind getting a bit dirty tomorrow. We have tomato and eggplant picking to do in the morning. We start at five, so get a good night's rest. As Thomas says, a little physical labor in the morning is the brain's tonic."

As Saul made his way down the driveway, he felt utterly transformed. For almost twenty years, Saul struggled to obtain a solution to global warming. Now, on the brink of being able to bring sustainable clean energy to the world, he must somehow convince Simion to create a new type of corporation. It was too much to take in. Needing the peace provided by the dancing wheat fields on either side of the road, Saul let his mind drift as he wound his way back into town.

Finding it hard to sleep, Saul rolled back and forth under his sheets. Like pesky flies that keep coming back, Saul couldn't stop worrying. Would his workers be willing to commit to a hui life-style on just a promise? What if his dreams fail? What if his team's technology is just not sophisticated enough to withstand jet stream winds? Will Simion sponsor his company? What fame and fortune will come? Is huinomics the only solution?

One by one, waves of euphoria collided with nagging doubts until Saul finally placed his hand on top of his diaphragm and listened to his breathing until his nerves began to unravel and he drifted off to sleep.

Waking, Saul felt a bit stiff and cleared his head with a hot shower. Quickly grabbing two bananas from the complementary breakfast counter, Saul left the hotel and headed down the road.

Turning into the gravel driveway again, Saul noticed how beautiful the colors of the garden were against the rising sun. At the end of the drive stood Thomas, looking as content as ever, making Saul wonder what it must be like to be happy all the time. Warmly greeting Saul, Thomas said, "It's nice to see you're wearing tennis shoes and jeans. Let's get started."

Saul's habitual tension seemed childish next to Thomas's easy nature, but he couldn't help himself. "We don't have time. I have a list of reasons why huinomics will not work for Jetstream. First and foremost is the fact that it sounds a lot like communism to me."

Without the slightest hint of concern, Thomas smiled and said, "As far as the picking goes, my tomatoes will not wait, but don't worry, in about three hours we will be finished and we'll have the whole day to ourselves. But I'll give you something to think about while we work: huinomics is about as far away from communism as you can get. Before communism morphed into what it is today, comrades were not fired no matter how little they worked. Although noble in principle, people simply have no motivation to work for the benefit of their brother, let alone their nation. Communism failed because people are basically selfish."

"Hui employees must be productive or they get fired. This actually creates harmony among these opposing forces. On one side of the coin, a person is naturally self indulgent and is inclined to do as little work as needed to get by. On the other side of the coin, a company must have hard working, dedicated employees in order to be competitive. To align these two opposing forces, hui members must be productive in order to retain their job." Before Saul could reply, Thomas said, "I know you have more questions, but they can wait for now."

Holding back, Saul smiled and asked, "So I'm going to work on your hui farm now?"

"That's right, and if you're not productive, hit the road, Jack."

As Saul filled his basket with tomatoes he thought about how impressed he was by Thomas. Here was an unpretentious, happy young man calmly stating that society as we have known it is going to disappear. Change is inevitable because without it, our current economy will lead to mankind's demise. With hundreds of thoughts swimming in his mind, Saul kept drifting back to how his engineers and managers could ever be content to work without pay. Pulling him back to reality, Saul heard Jackie say, "Not bad for your first day of picking Saul. We might keep you on."

Jackie loaded the last basket into an old boxy sun-bleached pickup truck and said, "You boys have an early lunch waiting for you on the table. There are clean towels in the bathroom."

Thomas looked as if he'd be happy to work in the garden all day, but he turned to Saul and said, "I'll let you shower first and meet you at the table."

Refreshed after his shower, Saul walked to the front porch and sat on the rough- honed hickory swing overlooking the garden. Observing how the lush shades of green blended into each other, Saul heard the cry of a raven and thought about his chances with Simion Ruzart. As Thomas made his way through the screen door with a large tray of sandwiches, Saul asked, "Do you think Simion Ruzart will really buy into huis?"

On into the hot quite afternoon they talked, until at last the sun began to set and Saul rose to make his way back to the airport.

Chapter 3

With the same crystalline clarity he used to envision the bulk of humanity using cell phones so many years ago, Simion again looked into the future and envisioned a world where people lived in harmony with one another.

Gazing out over the bay, watching the wind send shivering ripples across the azure water, Simion smiled with the realization that once the first hui was successful, it would proliferate rapidly causing an irreversible avalanche of corporations converting into huis for their own economic survival. Breathing in the crisp cool air, Simion felt an indescribable pleasure knowing that he would be the founder of the first hui, setting the pendulum in motion.

Bringing Simion out of his trance, his phone vibrated with the message, "Phillip Brownstein has arrived."

Phillip's aging copper skin sank into deep frown crevices, making him appear like a battered bronze sculpture incapable of smiling. Walking his rickety tall stick-man walk, he held out long bony fingers for Simion to shake.

Phillip swam against the tide when he admonished economic policies that foster the accumulation of wealth for a select few. His recent socioeconomic work won him a Nobel peace prize.

Foregoing pleasantries, Simion looked directly into Phillip's eyes and said, "As we discussed in your contract, I want your unbiased opinion."

In a voice that sounded like a deep brass drum, Phillip said, "I am biased. On all accounts, I am biased; even resentful, perhaps, that this work is not mine. Do you realize that huinomics will have a shattering effect on world economics? The entire way we perceive our world is about to change. Nothing can stop its cascading effect."

"But is the math sound?"

Phillip shifted in his chair and pulled at the end of his chin in deep thought. "Theoretically, yes. As long as huis don't horde their profits and actually invest them into establishing new huis, the feasibility and growth projections are on target. Within ten years, US coal-burning electric plants will cease to exist. However, should huis siphon off profits, it's anyone's guess if hui-run nonpolluting electric plants will ever dominate the market."

Shifting uneasily, Simion asked, "Do you believe simply exempting coal-burning electric companies will be effective?"

A critical element of Thomas's theory stipulates that only

nonpolluting entities can be allowed to form hui corporations. Should a polluting corporation try to form a hui, all other huis would refuse to do business with that entity and the general public would be informed to boycott its products.

Phillip laced his fingers together around his mid section and pressed his rickety spine even further into his chair and said, "Imagine being a coal producer squeezed out of business because another, far cheaper producer has undercut your price. The only way you could compete with a hui corporation is to convert into one. In so doing your company would need to invest a considerable amount of capital to build housing facilities for its workers, as well as investing into all the other facilities a hui offers. After which, you would need to persuade your workers to keep working for a polluting company. On top of this you gamble that your customers will defy the boycott.

"You see, the risk-to-reward is far too great. Considering that China alone is scheduled to build over one thousand large scale coal plants over the next few years, it would be far more prudent for you to sell-off your factories overseas."

With deep concern, Simion said, "Our goal is to reduce carbon emissions to zero, not to transplant carbon emissions to Asia."

"During the first few years it will be economically viable to make such overseas investments. However, once hui corporations begin to dominate the market, all polluting entities world-wide will begin to calculate the long term risks of doing business the old way. Even in the poorest countries, the prospect of buying a polluting factory like a coal plant will be seen as a bad investment."

Simion could not help but smile as his confidence in huinomics grew. "Thomas predicts that twenty percent of US based corporations will convert into huis within five years. What is your projection?"

"Despite all the postulation, there are simply too many unknown variables. As with the weather, we have a good idea what will take place in the short run, but we have little knowledge of what will happen in the future. No one would have guessed that within twenty years China could have advanced so quickly."

"Postulating that huis do proliferate at this projected growth rate, what will happen to China?"

"China will falter. The 'world's manufacturer' will be forced to close its doors. Steamships will cease to traverse the oceans as manufacturing reverts back to domestic production. Before China became the world's factory, the citizens of China had far less wealth than they do today, and although they will suffer in the short run when they stop exporting, they will not be impoverished. After all, they still have a market of one point three billion." Clearing his throat, Phillip leaned closer to Simion and said, "Have you considered these socioeconomic factors?"

"That is precisely why I called you."

"It is too early to predict, but Quinn's estimate of reducing manufacturing by seventy percent is not unrealistic. A world where manufactured objects are shared by a group instead of being owned by individuals will shrink our work week by half. Work will cease to be at the center of our lives. Our work-life balance will be similar to that of Bali's golden era, when people spent as much time enjoying life as working. Huinomics will allow humanity to enter a new era where academics, arts and athletics will flourish."

Simion got up, strolled over to the window and looked out over the bay. In the distance, sea gulls were playing in the thermals. Several minutes passed before either spoke again. It was as if Phillip's words opened the door to a new reality for Simion.

Like an alarm awaking one from a deep sleep, Phillip abruptly said, "The rest is in the report. I shall take my leave now."

"Yes, thank you Mr. Brownstein, your work means a great deal to me."

After seeing Phillip out, Simion quickly went to his desk and hit the speaker phone.

"Please get Saul on video."

Seconds later, looking into Saul's face with solemn reserve, Simion said, 'I have confirmed Thomas Quinn's findings with Phillip Brownstein. I will provide the funding to see if high-altitude energy generation is possible. If your prototype generator produces eight megawatts consistently for thirty days, I will provide funding for a 600,000 megawatt power plant."

Saul's eyes glassed over as he stammered, "I am lost for words."

"Before you get all emotional, realize that you have competition. As you know, I have been funding Tectonic Power's traveling wave reactor and they tell me they are getting close. If Tectonic Power gets a working prototype first, they will get the funding."

"No one has successfully built a continuous thrust generator. Who knows how long it will take."

"Time is definitely not on your side this time, Saul. Tectonic Power is not the only player."

"But we're going to have to fabricate a ten meter loom, not to mention producing a lightweight single strand e-textile cable five miles long. This is pioneering work. It takes time to develop new technologies."

After being so elated, Simion felt let down. He sighed and said, "You have the designs for the thrust generator. Just contact you pals at GE to build it for you. Contract out your air jet loom work to Tsudakoma, and have Toyobo manufacture your cable. But keep in mind, you don't have a blank check on this, I'm sending you one of my finance managers to keep track of expenses."

"It will be the best money you ever spent."

"I'm not confident about that. I take it you are aware of the Leipzig report, claiming that high-altitude power generation is not possible because the jet stream exists in a frictionless environment?"

Saul's heart raced as he considered all the unknown elements plaguing any groundbreaking discovery. "We are traveling in uncharted waters with many uncertain factors. All the same, we cannot dismiss the fact that jumbo jets travel faster and use less energy when they're in the jet stream."

In recognition of Saul's point, Simion said, "I'm going to give you the funding to build your Flexwing prototype. You have real promise. But you need to realize you also have stiff competition. In addition to Tectonic Power, I am providing prototype funding for another wind-based electric company by the name of Vorbine."

A wave of confidence spread through Saul as he said, "Our analysis of fixed ground-based wind turbines confirms the fact that you generate far less energy with fixed rooter turbines than with flying turbines. What makes Vorbine different?"

"Like you, Vorbine has a radical new approach for generating wind-driven energy. Although Vorbine will publish the entire schematics of their operation in time, I cannot divulge any information until they have proved that their system works. The only reason I'm letting you know about Vorbine is to help you realize your time is limited."

"I appreciate that. We will do whatever is necessary."

Wishing Saul the best of luck, Simion hung up and paged his pilot.

"Fuel the jet. We're going to Wichita."

Simion reflected on the last time someone didn't jump when he called; was it twenty-five years ago? Thirty? For decades, Simion passively accepted that people would do his bidding based on the simple fact that you don't say no to those with extreme power. So at first, Simion thought Thomas's refusal to fly out to Mercer was a veiled insult. Thomas insisted that flying is antithetical to his beliefs and traveling the distance by bus or train to meet for a day or two was simply too wasteful. After a bit of soul-searching, Simion realized that his feeling of being slighted by Thomas was simply his ego getting the best of him.

Thirty minutes later, Simion was sitting in the cockpit next to his long time friend and pilot, Hank, taxiing to take off. Even after countless flights, Simion still felt exhilarated, watching the land whiz by as the

Gulfstream rose into the air.

As usual Hank offered to drive Simion to his destination. Simion replied by saying, "Thanks for offering, but on this trip, I don't need you to drive. Just have a car waiting for me when we land. I don't want to stand out, so make it a compact." Impressed by Simion's zeal, Hank called ahead to have a car waiting at the hanger.

Driving out to meet Thomas, Simion reflected on how dramatically his life had changed over the short period of time since being introduced to huinomics. Two weeks ago, Simion would not have considered going anywhere without a security team arriving days in advance to scope out the location. Humming along in the Ford Escort watching the wheat dance to the rhythm of the wind, Simion felt exhilarated by a sense of freedom he hadn't known since he was a boy. A sense of pure bliss came over him.

Pulling into the driveway after his pleasant drive, Simion saw a willowy young woman walking up to him as he got out of his car. Entranced by the strong yet peaceful expression in Jackie's amber eyes, Simion took a good look at her. She was a tall, shapely woman wearing a baseball cap over her chestnut hair pulled back in a ponytail.

Feeling right at home, Simion said, "Saul was right, you have a beautiful garden."

Seeing Simion's eyes trace her figure, Jackie briefly wondered if Simion was flirting with her. Shaking off this train of thought, Jackie smiled and said, "Thomas has been waiting for you."

Simion felt such freedom being out in the country he asked without reservation, "Where is he? I want to meet the man that turned my world upside down."

"He is around here somewhere. Let's go see if he's out back."

With that, Jackie turned and headed into rows of snap peas. Simion felt a flash of frustration, thinking to himself, "She wants me to go searching for him?" But seeing Jackie's slim athletic legs walk briskly along the variegated rows of plants, Simion was instantly embarrassed by his gut-reaction. It dawned on him that he has entered a new world; a world where people are not at his beck and call.

A welcome new sensation reverberated inside of Simion. Feeling like he was shedding a heavy cloak, he let go of all expectations. The resulting lightheartedness made him giddy.

From the rise of a small gully, they spotted Thomas weeding with a hoe. Jackie quickened her pace and called, "Hey, Thomas, Simion's here." Thomas dropped his hoe and hurried over.

Grasping Thomas's hand, Simion smiled deeply and said, "At last we get to meet in person. There is so much I want to discuss with you."

"First things first," Thomas said, and, turning to Jackie, asked, "How about lunch?"

"Sounds good. You two go ahead, I'll get it ready and bring it around back."

Thomas and Simion walked along the narrow pathway leading to the back patio where a large pitcher of fresh lemon water was perspiring on the walnut table. Sitting down and pouring them both a tall glass, Simion enjoyed the tangy water as it cooled his chalk-dry throat. The shade of the wisteria vine cast shadows on their faces. In the distance a meadowlark sang a song to its lover.

Simion turned to Thomas and said, "This morning I gave Saul the green light to build a Flexwing prototype."

"I know, it was in the information you sent with currier about an hour ago."

"Saul's Flexwing has potential, but we actually know very little about the jet stream. Not to mention what it will be like to send a kite the size of an airliner into the upper atmosphere. The cable alone weighs over a ton.

Pausing to reflect a moment, Simion continued, "Cliff Higgins with Vorbine is a new player on the scene, also using wind energy but in a much different way. Cliff has redesigned ground-based wind turbines to be four times more efficient at a fraction of the cost. Although Cliff has fewer variables to contend with than Saul, you can't escape the fact that wind corridors average eighteen miles per hour while the jet stream averages eighty-four miles per hour.

"There is also a company I have been funding for quite some time by the name of Tectonic Power. Tectonic has been perfecting a technique that produces nuclear energy with very little waste. It is estimated that in sixty years Uranium 235 will be completely depleted. If Tectonic is successful, we can get upwards of 100 years from our existing Uranium 235."

"How soon do you think one of these companies will be ready?"

"Tectonic Power's nuclear reactor is feasible in theory, but they're experiencing containment issues that won't be resolved anytime soon. Vorbine and Jetstream will be testing their turbine generators in three to four months. I will fund a full scale electrical plant producing 600 megawatts, enough to supply 150,000 homes, for the first company that is successful."

Just then, Jackie called from the window, "It's ready."

Getting up Thomas said, "I'll give Jackie a hand."

Thomas returned with a loaf of dark earthy bread on a plank cutting board and Jackie followed with a large wooden bowl filled with a colorful salad tossed with raspberry vinaigrette.

Delighted in serving a salad made fresh from the garden, Jackie asked, "What have you two been talking about?"

"Simion will be providing Saul with funding to build a prototype."

Smiling at Simion Jackie said, "That's wonderful. Do you think it will work?"

"Simion's not sure now, but there are two other companies working on the same problem." Thomas said,

Following the light conversation, Simion wondered if Thomas had any idea what was being proposed. It seemed incongruent to speak of vast sums of money in such a humble environment. And yet, here they were: two vastly different people with the same goal.

Sensing the time was right, Simion said, "For years now, my only goal in life has been to use my resources to reduce carbon emissions to zero within fifty years. Now that goal has become two goals. Along with providing clean-energy, I want to introduce the world to huinomics. I'll use the second goal to achieve the first. Bringing a clean energy source to the world will be the conduit for launching huinomics."

Jackie asked, "What do you have in mind?"

"Do you remember when you were a little girl waiting for Christmas morning to arrive? The buildup was tremendous. Decorations, Christmas songs, TV shows and presents under the tree. All these little things representing Christmas would build and build until finally Christmas morning arrived. Everything you ever hoped for was wrapped up in those presents under the tree; it was pure bliss opening them up.

"That's what I want to capture. I want Americans to believe that there is something out there that will make their lives better without telling them what it is. I want to build their hopes and desires until they yearn for the day when we announce the opening of the first hui corporation."

Thomas chimed in, "I know what you mean. It's like smelling something delicious, but you don't know what it is."

"That's it. The secret lies in creating a viral phenomenon. With support from some of the world's most prominent movie stars and sports heroes, we will bombard the air waves with the message that there is a better way. We will plant a seed in the hearts of Americans that there's a better way to live, that humanity can prosper without destroying the planet. This message will infiltrate our media-driven social network to such a degree that only the lost tribes of Borneo won't know about the event I call Quasar."

"Quasar?"

"Quasar will be what everyone is waiting for. The opening of the world's first large-scale zero carbon emission electric plant will be the platform for the Quasar."

Focusing on Thomas's eyes, Simion said, "We'll show the world huinomics' potential. We'll build a vertical manufacturing facility employing three thousand workers. It will be like a small town with its own housing facilities, shops, restaurants and school."

"A project that size will take billions," said Thomas. Where will the money come from?"

Simion felt a familiar surrealistic power flow through his being as if abstract thought in his mind created our physical reality. But unlike the past when the world's wealth flowed to him, Simion envisioned his wealth flowing out to all of mankind.

"As we speak, I am quietly liquidating my fortune to launch the first hui."

Simion's words hung in the air like thick molasses. The song of a meadowlark drifted up from the garden until, like a dream, Simion said, "Wealth found its way to me of its own accord. It is time for me to let it go. With half the world's population living in squalor, it's obscene to do otherwise. Now is the time for us to lift each other up."

With the sun drifting into their space, Simion felt a deep sense of emptiness. Relinquishing his wealth felt like part of his consciousness was being amputated. As if waking from a trance, Simion said, "And you, Thomas, will be huinomics spokesperson. You will be the face of huinomics."

A look of concern came over Thomas, "My skill lies with numbers, not public speaking."

Eager to get his mind off liquidating his wealth, Simion said, "Despite what you've heard, no one is a natural born public speaker. Even seasoned news veterans get the jitters before going on stage. But like anything else, with the proper training you will learn to control your stage fright and excel at public speaking. My public relations specialist, Phillip Brownstein, will set you up with an acting coach."

"An acting coach? Jackie is right, before long I won't be able to recognize myself."

With resolve, Simion said, "All great accomplishments require sacrifices. Take a moment to consider what I am willing to give up. Besides, one's personality changes in positive ways when one learns new skills. You will always be the same person no matter what new talents you learn."

"I really appreciate that you think I'm up to the task, but I hardly think I'm your best choice."

"No one can step in front of the media without proper training. It would be like handing a tennis racket to someone who has never played before and having them play a pro. But just like learning a sport, learning to speak in front of an audience is a skill that can be learned."

"Once you get to know me better, you'll realize I'm not the person you think I am. No famous person is really who you think they are. Behind every famous person is a crew of people who guide them along. In all modesty, I am one of the most famous people on the planet. Do you think my fame is based solely on my talents? I have had the aid of hundreds of people to get me to where I am today. Huinomics needs a founding father and you are him."

With conviction Jackie said, "We are happy with our lives the way they are. We have just what we always wanted. We can't just give it up."

"Yes, but you can't have it both ways. You can't expect to change the world without having your personal life affected. I can help you along the way, but your lifestyle is going to change."

Feeling the rug being pulled out from under him, Thomas asked, "What about the farm?"

"For the time being, I will send people here to get you prepared. You need to be ready by the time we launch the Quasar."

Thomas's ever present smile left his face. A silent remorsefulness washed over him as he imagined how everything will change. His quiet, peaceful days of loving life with Jackie will evaporate. Silently accepting what he's always known would happen, Thomas slowly stood up and, with glassy eyes, held out his arms to Simion who silently accepted his embrace.

Chapter 4

The bone-chilling winds of Marietta Washington flattened the back of Saul's pants as he walked through tall wet weeds under a dark starry sky. High winds always excited Saul. With sweaty palms and a pounding heart, Saul leaned backwards against the howling thirty-eight mile per hour wind as he slowly made his way toward the launch site.

Elated, Saul scanned the clear predawn sky, convincing himself that the wind would hold long enough to launch his Flexwing into the jet stream. More times than he liked to remember, strong wind forecasts proved to be wrong. Unconsciously, Saul repressed his fear that the wind might die down as he watched his crew work in the distance.

For months, the crew worked endless hours to be the first to generate high-altitude wind energy. Spending money just as fast as Simion could write checks, the days rolled by like freight train cars until at last the prototype was ready to be tested.

From tip to tip the Flexwing was over 195 feet wide. Spanning the better part of a football field, it resembled a giant flag. To stand out against the blue sky the Flexwing was woven entirely of red fabric.

A crane was used to hoist the Flexwing off a flat-bed semi. Fourteen men on either side of the Flexwing slowly unfolded the Flexwing into position. The men did their best to keep the Flexwing as close to the ground as possible while other team members quickly attached the bridle lines to the deployment pistons.

In theory the deployment pistons were a safeguard against the Flexwing launching prematurely and causing an accident. In practice, Saul hoped to hell they worked. Saul nearly got his shoulder ripped out of his socket when helping to launch a thirty meter kite in twenty-three mile per hour winds in Maui. Still unable to move his arm above his head without pain, Saul pledged not to have a repeat of the Maui accident.

After numerous test runs, the team discovered that the safest launch method was to position thirty-eight deployment pistons along the length of the Flexwing. Once all of the bridle lines were attached to the pistons, the pistons would rise off the ground allowing the Flexwing to inflate. Once inflated, the pistons would simultaneously release the bridle lines allowing the Flexwing to take flight.

After nearly two hours of tension-filled work, Saul used the walki-talki app on the teams smart phones to let everyone know to return to the control station. The heat of the sun felt good as they made their way back along the 200 yard length of the cable.

The electronics, video fees and monitors were house in the control station. Just off to the side was the spooler room. All five miles of the Flexwing's cable was mounted on a spooler. Weighing just 2.75 ounces per foot, the Flexwing's cable was an engineering marvel. Sensors running the length and width of the Flexwing instantly sent data through the cable to adjust the Flexwing's flight pattern.

Saul called Steve who was in charge of monitoring the tension on the spooler.

"The monitor shows bridle cable number twenty-five not engaged. Steve, check it out."

Keeping clear of the cable and bridle lines, Steve quickly jogged out the two-hundred yards to the leading edge of the Flexwing. After a few minutes he radioed back, the crew just barely making out his voice over the howling wind.

"The clip didn't have contact with the sensor, but the bridle's secure."

Saul shot back, "Steve, get back here pronto. Rachel, once everyone is in position, take a head count and let me know when we're clear to launch."

After several tense minutes, Rachel announced, "Good to go, sir."

"Steve, you back in position?"

"Yes sir."

"Okay everyone. This is what we've been working for. You all know what to do. Steve, begin spooling out at 1200 pounds resistance. I'm commencing launch now."

Moments after punching in the pass code, thirty-eight silver pistons began slowly rising from the ground. Saul waited for the Flexwing to gradually fill with wind until the cable became taught enough to allow it to fly. Once flying, based on dozens of preflight tests on scaled down models, the Flexwing would slowly gain altitude, flying against the resistance of the cable by means of a breaking system mounted on the spooler.

Instead, as soon as the pistons rose, the foils instantly inflated, shooting the Flexwing into the sky as if it was shot from a cannon. In seconds, the Flexwing drew up all two hundred meters of cable and began straining against the spindle's breaking system. The stench of acidic steel smoke poured from the spindle's breaks as a loud cracking sound reverberated against the walls.

Like a grenade exploding, hundreds of metal shards sprayed from the spooler.

Steve cried out, his hand flying up to the side of his neck to staunch the blood streaming down his fingers.

Stunned, Saul watched in amazement as the spooler spun violently out of control. In a flash he realized the Flexwing's thrust had been too great, causing the spooler breaks to overheat and explode.

Realizing the Flexwing was now flying out of control, Saul barked out over the walkie-talkie, "Everyone get out of the spooler room! Get the hell out of there now!"

Before Saul could get the words out, people were already running from the spooler room. Staggering, trying with all his might to remain standing, Steve held the side of his neck and made for the door. Seeing Steve stumble, Rachel ran to him and with a supportive arm around his waist, helped him get outside.

Laying Steve down in the grass, Rachel placed her hand over his, applying pressure to the neck wound in a meager attempt to stop the gushing blood. She said a prayer to herself and looking into Steve's deadly pale face, she whispered, "You're going to be alright, Steve. You're going to be alright."

As Steve nearly lost consciousness, Rebecca looked up frantically and screamed, "Call an ambulance!"

Saul knew that the Flexwing would exhaust its five-mile cable soon. When that happened, the concrete block anchoring the spool would give and more people would be hurt. He ran to the parking lot, shouting, "Stay upwind of the spooler room!"

Frantic, Saul ran to his car, got inside and gunned it, careening out to the spooler room where Rachel was nursing Steve. Shaking from the adrenaline coursing through his veins, Saul summoned super-human strength and hoisted Steve off the ground and thrust him into the back of his car.

Seconds ticked by as Saul sped down the dirt road that lead to the highway. Checking the rear view mirror Saul watched Rachel do her best to keep Steve conscious as he dialed 911.

"This is Saul Beckman of Jetstream Energy. There's been an accident. Steve McCormick, male, age thirty-two, is profusely bleeding from the neck; could be an artery. I'm speeding down Route 95 heading for the Marietta clinic. Alert the staff and send a police escort."

The dispatcher asked, "What is the nature of the accident?"

Saul went a deep shade of red and shouted, "The nature of the accident doesn't matter! We have a dying man here! Notify a patrol car and the clinic now. If you have more questions, call me back after you get help. Do it now!"

Saul heard the words, "Yes Sir," before the line went dead.

From of the corner of his eye, Saul saw the Flexwing racing across the field to his left. It looked like a out of control Zeppelin. Knowing the cable was about to run out, Saul felt his throat contract as he envisioned the forty-four hundred pound spindle being ripped from its base.

With shaking hands, Saul called Robert Barns, the engineer who programmed the Flexwing's auto pilot.

"Robert, is everyone clear of the spindle?"

Robert shouted back, "The Flexwing's out of control…no resistance… there's no way to make her turn or bank!"

Saul shouted back, "Robert, focus. Is everyone clear of the spindle?!"

Robert shot back, "Hell if I know! There's just me and Banks here at the control station."

Before Saul could say another word he heard what sounded like a gun shot and saw the Flexwing launch straight up like it was powered by jet fuel.

Seconds ticked by before Saul shouted into his phone, "Is the spindle holding?"

Robert shouted back, "You're not going to believe this, but the concrete base has a huge crack running down the middle, the two front spindle supports are bent in, but its holding! My god, the Flexwing's already at 12,000 feet! We should hit the jet stream in minutes."

A momentary sigh of relief passed over Saul. "All I need is a few more minutes," he thought. "If I can get Steve to the hospital in time…"

Either the police cruisers were slow to respond or they were just too far away, but they never showed. At least the medics were waiting outside the Emergency Room doors. Driving too fast Saul scrapped the front end of his Ford Fiesta against the ramp leading to the Emergency Room parking lot. Catching a glimpse of Steve's ashen face and blood-stained shirt as they pulled him from the backseat, Saul prayed they'd made it in time.

Saul desperately hoped they could patch Steve up just long enough for him to be airlifted to a hospital in Seattle. After many agonizing minutes rolled by, a stout elderly nurse walked into the waiting room and addressed Saul and Rachel.

"You must be the ones who brought Mr. McCormick in."

Before Saul could respond, Rachel jumped up and said, "Yes! Is he alright?"

"His vital signs are stabilizing. Fortunately, only a minor artery was severed. We were able to stop the bleeding. He'll need re-constructive surgery. He lost a lot of blood, but he's responding well to the transfusions."

Saul asked, "Is a helicopter on the way?"

"He's no longer critical. I'm not sure that would've been the case if you didn't get here as soon as you did; his blood pressure was critically low."

Saul felt an incredible wave of relief pass through him. Smiling, he turned to Rachel: "Can you stay with him? I need to get back."

Without hesitation, Rachel said, "You go. I'll stay with Steve. Let me know how the flight is progressing."

Saul felt a sudden jubilance and said, "Will do. I'll send someone to relieve you later this afternoon."

With that Saul rushed back to his car, started up the engine and called Robert Barns.

"Robert, has the Flexwing reached the jet stream?"

Robert's voice was so soft it was nearly inaudible: "She reached the jet stream about ten minutes ago. The flight pattern is normal, but our pull resistance is only 2350 pounds."

In disbelief, Saul shouted back, "What? Speak up Robert! What is the pull resistance?"

Louder, Robert exclaimed, "She's only at 2350 pounds of resistance, generating 6520 kilowatts."

A shot of panic went through Saul as he asked, "What's the wind speed?"

"Ninety-Seven miles per hour."

Time stood still. In a flash Saul knew it was over.

In winds over sixty miles per hour, the Flexwing should generate three times that amount of power. The theory that jet stream winds are powerless in their frictionless environment has proven to be true.

Closing his phone, Saul looked up at the sky through his windshield, his quivering lower lip responding to the tears welling up in his eyes. Half-blind, Saul pulled to the side of the deserted country road and buried his face in his hands, his shoulders heaving up and down by the strength of his grief. Saul cried for all the days, months and years he spent chasing what turned out to be a plastic rabbit. Saul cried for all the time he could have spent with his family. Saul cried because he wouldn't be the person to bring large-scale sustainable energy to the world. Most of all, Saul cried because a part of his self just died.

Chapter 5

Six weeks later, Cliff Higgins, the founder of Vorbine, was about to challenge Saul's Flexwing results outside Boise City, Oklahoma.

A flowing palette of green-gray sagebrush spread out as far as the eye could see. A warm wind, strong and steady, drove wispy cirrus clouds across the deep blue sky. Near Boise is the Cimarron Grasslands. Ranked third in the world, America's most fertile wind corridor stretches from Northern Texas and passes through Oklahoma, Kansas and Nebraska, before ending in the Dakotas. In the heart of this wind corridor is the Cimarron Grasslands. To most, the Cimarron Grasslands is a vast void of sky and sagebrush, but to Cliff Higgins, it is a treasure of untapped potential.

Cliff Higgins was a goofy genius. One couldn't help feeling elated in his presence. His tall, wiry frame matched his overgrown, electrified wiry hair. His comical smile was ever-present under his abnormally large tomahawk nose, accentuating his "oh-boy!" attitude toward life.

People loved being around Cliff as much as Cliff loved being around people. His limitless enthusiasm for whatever he set his sights on was contagious. Embracing his goofiness, Cliff prided himself on his collection of wacky t-shirts and mismatched clothes. His goofiness put a soft edge on his stunning brilliance. Born with the rare ability to instantly recall practically any information presented to him, be it visual, written or audio, Cliff's mental capabilities were in a class of their own.

Everything about Cliff was unconventional. Never having graduated from college, he was the leading authority on sustainable energy technology. Turning down full-ride scholarships, Cliff choose to study independently under the world's leading professors. Like a bee collecting honey, Cliff collected knowledge at the Institute of Clean Technology in Mississippi, the Center for Energy in Pittsburgh, Renewable Energy System Technology in Loughborough, Sustainable Energy Technologies in Southampton and Princeton's Environmental Institute. Once Cliff tapped the knowledge of one institute, he was off to another.

Cliff was always more like an associate professor than a student. Caring nothing for credits, most institutions didn't even have Cliff registered as a student, let alone as a professor's aid. As Cliff's acumen grew, professors began to seek him out, rather than the other way around. After years of study, the day finally came when Cliff discovered how to create a vortex using a spinning propeller.

Despite the fact that thousands of people were trying to increase the energy output of propeller driven wind power, the answer Cliff found was surprisingly simple. He discovered that, by placing a concave ring in front of a wind turbine, an artificially low pressure zone was created directly behind the turbine. The vortex created by the concave ring transformed typical corridor winds blowing 15 to 20 miles an hour to winds blowing 35 to 40 miles per hour. Cliff called his concave rings 'trumpets' because of their shape.

Once Cliff discovered how to double wind speed using trumpets, he was able to re-engineer modern wind turbine design by replacing standard propeller blades with sails.

For hundreds of years windmill propeller design was based on wind speed. Design the blades too small and the windmill does not produce enough energy. Design the blades too large and you must shut down the windmill to prevent the blades from being shattered in high winds.

Cliff would scoff at modern mega-wind turbines. Their huge blades had to be turned out of the wind when wind speeds exceed twenty miles per hour and could produce hardly any energy when the wind dropped below ten miles per hour.

To overcome this fundamental problem of matching propeller blades to varying wind speed, Cliff engineered three-dimensional flexible propeller blades that are able to expand and contract. Using modern sail technology, Cliff's windmill propeller blades adjust to wind speed for maximum efficiency. Conforming to the ever changing weather, Cliff's flexible propeller blades were able to expand during light winds and contract during high speed winds.

While pursuing his education in Loughborough, Cliff had engineered the world's first low-cost transparent photovoltaic film. Utilizing transparent resin infused with photovoltaic cells, and incorporating resonant inductive coupling, the energy produced by the photovoltaic panels was wirelessly transferred to a Van de Graff generator, thereby transforming any window into an energy-generating solar panel. By simply applying the photovoltaic film over existing windows, skyscrapers around the globe could produce upwards of fifty percent of their own power.

Cliff adapted his photovoltaic film breakthrough to the flexible propeller blades and trumpets of his vortex wind turbine, increasing its overall energy output. Cliff called his invention a Vorbine.

Unlike Saul Beckman, Simion Ruzart had his eyes on Cliff Higgins for some time. When he realized Cliff's potential, Simion decisively offered Cliff seed money to build and launch a Vorbine prototype. Knowing Cliff insisted on publishing all of his company's discoveries on the web took some getting used to, but Simion finally accepted turning over the keys.

Blueprints, materials, suppliers, fabrication methods, and every aspect of how to manufacture a Vorbine was available for download.

Standardization was Cliff's motto. He argued that the US would be neck and neck with France's nuclear program if they simply followed their example of standardizing nuclear factory components instead of reinventing the wheel every time a new plant was built. As he did with his education, Cliff said to hell with convention and took the fastest route possible to achieve his goals by posting his results on the net.

As far as Cliff was concerned, the more people building efficient wind turbines, the better.

In typical Cliff fashion, when Simion told Cliff about Thomas Quinn and huinomics, Cliff was in his car headed to Wichita before Simion hung up the phone. Like long lost brothers, Cliff and Thomas immediately hit it off. Over the next three days, Cliff immersed himself in the world of huinomics.

Though he grasped the general concept instantly, puzzling out the global socio political ramifications of huinomics was a challenge even for a mind like Cliff's. Once he did, the world became a different place for Cliff. Chaos from clashing political regimes and economic systems dissipated. The planets aligned. For the first time in his life, Cliff truly believed that prosperity and peace for all of mankind was not only attainable, it was imminent.

Cliff and Thomas parted with high expectations. During the months that followed, they stayed in close contact until the day they were reunited, when Thomas and Jackie drove the 265 miles to Elkhart to witness the first full-scale test of Cliff's Vorbine.

Bouncing down the freshly-cut dirt road, Thomas looked with excitement at Jackie as they made out a Vorbine's solar trumpet arch reflecting the sun far off on the horizon.

Squinting, Jackie exclaimed, "I see it off in the distance…it's beautiful."

Concurring Thomas said, "It's beautiful in more ways than one. Saul joined the effort, so Vorbine now has two generators. The main generator is a conventional spindle-generator deriving its power from the Vorbine's propellers, while the second generator is Saul's regenerative break generator. Instead of anchoring the Vorbine to a cement base, Saul came up with the idea of mounting the Vorbine on a monorail track. When wind exerts pressure against the Vorbine, it's breaks prevent it from moving along the monorail. The pressure exerted is then transfered to the regenerative break generator. Even Vorbine's frame generates energy. Being a perfect example of stacking theory, a Vorbine is a symbiotic energy powerhouse, capturing wind, solar, and regenerative energy."

"Saul joined Vorbine?"

"Officially, Saul is just a consultant. Unofficially, Saul is an integral part of Vorbine's design team. Flexwings are still being used; a prototype is pulling a container ship across the north Atlantic as we speak. All the same, the test results on Vorbine's energy production are off the charts. Since Saul incorporated a second thrust generator into the matrix, it is unlikely that a Flexwing can ever match the power of a Vorbine, especially considering that jet stream winds have virtually the same power as ground based winds. Still, unless a major calamity occurs today, it is unlikely that Flexwings will be utilized for anything but small-scale energy production."

"So is Jetstream Energy finished?"

"Saul changed the name to Flexwing Energy. There are still applications for Flexwing technology. Saul's container ship Flexwing application is of great importance, especially when you consider that a single oil tanker can burn up to sixteen tons of crude diesel fuel per hour. We desperately need to reduce carbon emissions from container ships."

Unable to get her head wrapped around that amount of oil, Jackie stammered, "What? Did you say sixteen tons per hour?"

"Massive container ships burn so much fuel that they measure consumption by tonnage burned per hour. The largest container ships throw out the same amount of toxic carbon emissions as fifty million automobiles."

Looking like she just smelled something foul, Jackie said, "That is just plain wrong."

"It is wrong on so many levels. Irresponsible oil consumption is rampant. But at least Flexwings are helping to stem the tide."

As they drove closer, the Vorbine began to look more and more like the London Eye. Towering 426 feet into the air, the Vorbine was the largest object on the horizon. It took on the shape of a gigantic twenty-one pedaled flower encircled by a huge silver trumpet horn. The pedals bowed and twisted as if they were shaped by the wind.

After trashing more prototypes than he would like to admit, Cliff found if far better to borrow from nature's designs that evolved over eons than try to create something from scratch. The elegant design of the maple leaf seed proved to be the ideal shape for the propeller blades. Cliff applied the Golden Mean to design the frame and the actual number of propeller blades.

Surrounding the lone Vorbine, vast stretches of prairie grass flowed like a symphony played by the rhythm of the wind. As they drove closer, Jackie said, "It looks like it is alive."

To Jackie it looked like an alien cybernetic aquatic organism. She imagined the outer silver trumpet was a protective shell for some kind of bizarre polyp, that used spinning floral petals to capture tiny phytoplankton.

Thomas pulled his old pickup truck into the makeshift parking lot. The red-brown ground looked as if had been dry for a long time. On the platform in front of the Vorbine Thomas saw Cliff wildly waving his arm. Thinking at first something was terribly wrong, Thomas thought to run and help, but then realized it was only Cliff's enthusiasm.

Thomas and Jackie walked up the recently cast cement steps leading up to the platform. "You were right," said Thomas. "I can't believe it took only eight people six days to assemble the frame"

Cliff, full of energy, jubilantly cried out, "You ain't seen nothing yet! Wait till she spins! It'll blow your mind. We're just fine-tuning the tension on her propellers, then she'll be good to go."

The circular die-cast aluminum frame had the diameter of a telephone pole. Almost entirely devoid of weld joints, the frame fit together by inserting and turning two interlocking pieces. The base of the frame sat on a round swivel mounted to what looked like a freeway pillar. The swivel's ball bearings enabled the Vorbine to effortlessly turn into the direction of the wind. Six massive supporting braces ran from base of the pillar to a monorail.

Cliff's fluid Vorbine design stood in stark contrast to conventional ridged mega-turbines. Openly criticizing conventional turbines, Cliff called them 'archaic pinwheel obelisks,' requiring as much energy to build as they were able to produce.

Today Cliff planned to finally prove to his clean energy colleagues that his Vorbine design can produce more energy than Ventus' massive X-428. The X-428 towers 660 feet off the ground with propeller blades spanning 418 feet. The Ventus' scale is so massive that installing the propeller blades required building the world's tallest crane to put them in place. Despite Cliff's criticism, a single X-428 can churn out 7.8 megawatts of power, enough energy to fuel 1800 American homes or 5000 European homes.

Seeing Thomas and Jackie, Simion walked over to join their conversation.

"Cliff, how long can the generators run before the current flowing into the ground backs up?"

"We have a grid of re-bar extending ten feet underground that should be able to ground the current for at least 30 minuets before the we need to shut it down. It looks like we are good to go; do you want to throw the switch?"

Simion tilted his head to look Cliff squarely in the eye and said, "She's your baby, Cliff. You do the honors."

Cliff and the rest of the crew gathered twenty-five yards in front of the Vorbine. In the event that anything should go wrong, Cliff wanted to make sure everyone would be safe from flying debris. Cliff entered a pass code into his smart phone to release the breaks on the spindle shaft and the Vorbine slowly began to turn. At first the 426 foot tall structure turned about the same speed as a Ferris Wheel; but with ever passing revolution the Vorbine increased in speed. Soon the massive blades blurred into a solid ring like some huge fan. Over the low pitched deep resonating sound, Cliff held up his smart phone and shouted, "Ten point six megawatts! We did it! Ten point six megawatts!"

In that moment, Simion once again pledged deep within himself to make carbon-free energy a reality worldwide. Looking out over the horizon, Simion envisioned thousands of Vorbines pumping out clean abundant energy. With more resolve than he'd ever felt before, Simion touched Cliff's arm and solemnly said, "Now we begin."

Chapter 6

Twenty-two days later, Simion pulled up to the Boise City Courthouse. The perfect cool blue sky contrasted sharply against the three-story red brick courthouse. It tried to look proud with it's four Romanesque columns holding a large cement plaque that read: CIMMORON COUNTY COURT HOUSE. The dry yellow crab grass surrounding the courthouse made it look even older and more unkept than it actually was.

Unlike the hip city of Boise Idaho, Boise Oklahoma had more than its share of hard knocks. In 1908, a brochure showing tree lined streets suckered three thousand people into buying home lots, only to discover that the beautiful photos in the brochures were taken in Connecticut and the tree lined streets turned out to be dirt roads flanked by weeds.

As time moved on the city suffered even more. It was located right in the heart of the 'dirty thirties' dust bowl. To add injury to insult, Boise was the only continental city bombed during World War II. The training pilot in the B-27 must have had one too many drinks before taking off that night. Their mission was to bomb a small square illuminated by four lights. The B-27's men mistook the court yard lit up in front of Boise's city hall as the bomb site, and for thirty minutes let their bombs drop. Thanks to the mayor turning off the lights, along with the fact that the bombs were mostly filled with sand, no one was injured.

After decades of disasters, Boise's fate was about to change. Her surrounding wind corridors, once the bane of her existence, were about to become her salvation. Surrounded by the Cimarron National Grass Lands to the north, the Comanche National Grass Lands to the west, and the Rita Blanca National Grasslands to the south, Boise is at the center of two thousand square miles of arid grasslands. The unobstructed landscape coupled with consistently high-speed thermal winds, made Boise an ideal location for Vorbine's central power station and manufacturing plant.

Parking directly in front of the court house, Simion felt a renewed spring in his step as he briskly walked to the front door. As if living a second life, Simion rejoiced in not being flanked by security guards. Feeling more alive than he had in years, Simion pulled the swinging aluminum glass door open.

Waiting for Simion in the dimly lit foyer was the entire City Council, with the city's Mayor standing front and center looking as proud as he could be. The Mayor appeared to be hatched from the courthouse. He had a push-broom mustache and leathery, red-brown sun worn cheeks.

The pearl buttons of his plaid cowboy shirt strained against his rotund midsection, while his overly tight crisp blue jeans looked as if they would split open if not for the bronco belt buckle holding them up.

Any Mayor would get a twinkle in their eye if a man like Simion Ruzart walked through their doors. Considering that Boise, like so many other cities, had nineteen percent of its meager population of 2471 residents living below the poverty level, it's no surprise that Simion's presence drew such excitement.

After introductions, the group marched up old linoleum steps to a conference room. Amid the hum of an overtaxed air conditioner, the group settled on army green steel chairs along side two plastic collapsible tables set end to end. The room smelled of old dusty oak and the floor was cracked and worn. The Mayor's neck pulsed as he tried to calm his racing heart to announce his memorized greeting.

"We are overjoyed to welcome you to our humble community. We will do our best to provide your new business venture our full support."

With all eyes glued to him, Simion said, "With your cooperation, we have great plans for the city of Boise. As put forth in the proposal, we are seeking a location to build a large-scale manufacturing facility for a new wind energy company called Vorbine."

The Mayor and Council looked like eager game show contestants as Simion continued.

"Unlike your typical manufacturing plant that relies on the city's existing infrastructure, the facility we intend to build will be self-contained.

"The Vorbine facility will be like no other. Traditional manufacturing entities lie on the outskirts of cities; their employees must commute to work. At Vorbine, the manufacturing facility is the city. All the elements of a city, including housing, education, health care, entertainment and restaurants are contained within the grounds of the manufacturing plant. The internal components that make a city run, including water, electricity, sewage treatment, and security, will be provided by Vorbine.

"Boise Oklahoma will become world famous for being the epicenter of a new generation of clean, carbon-less wind-generated energy."

Feeling as though the Mayor was about to cheer, Simion continued.

"Vorbine will have approximately 3000 employees. The counties of Stratford, Dalhart, Clayton, and Elkhart consist of 8800 square miles of grasslands resulting in one of the world's most fertile wind corridors.

"The initial 3000 employees will come from the communities located within these 8800 square miles. For the first thirty days, Vorbine will fill positions with members of these surrounding communities.

"In return, Boise and the surrounding member communities will permit Vorbine unrestricted access to erect wind turbines on land owned or leased by Vorbine.

"Over this vast area, Vorbine intends to erect 21,000 wind turbines. The amount of energy produced in this wind corridor will supply enough power to replace 297 coal burning factories, amounting to roughly 50% of the total coal-produced energy in the world, thereby reducing green house emissions by 12% worldwide.

"Vorbine is establishing contingent agreements with private landholders who will provide Vorbine with 125 year leases to erect Vorbines on one-acre plots. The surrounding counties have changed their ordinances to allow the construction of Vorbine wind turbines. Do I have the support of Boise?"

The Mayor extended his neck and with wide eyes gave an enthusiastic, "Yes!"

Being more on the skeptical side, Maybelline, the Vice Chairman of the City Council, ventured to ask, "Twenty-one thousand wind turbines. Isn't that an awful large amount? Won't that affect our view?"

The Mayor knotted his brows and blurted out, "What view?" Becoming conscious of the curtness of his statement, the Mayor smiled broadly and said, "I'm not going to miss looking at anyone's cows. These wind turbines can't look that bad."

"Maybelline has a good point. 21,000 wind turbines, each the size of a four story building, might be considered an eyesore if we built them right next to each other. But each individual turbine takes less than one-half acre, so spread across 8800 square miles they represent less than one one-hundredth of a percent of the total land area."

Looking satisfied, the Mayor asked, "Your report also mentioned that in addition to the permanent employees, you will also be providing temporary construction jobs?"

"That is correct. Keep in mind, though, Vorbine is not a non-profit corporation. It needs to make money just like any other electric company, so although we will be giving residents the first shot at available jobs, employees will be hired based on their abilities. As this will be a manufacturing facility, employees will need to pass a physical and a drug screen."

A few other questions were bantered back and forth for appearances before pen was put to paper. Along with unlimited rights to erect Vorbines, the city also agreed to have the land, water and mineral rights for twenty-five square miles to be held in escrow by Vorbine. The counsel also signed off on a deferred taxation rate, delineated over ten years, and access to all unpaved county roads.

In the end, Simion got everything he needed to launch Vorbine, and the city got everything they ever dreamed of.

Working out of an oversized office trailer three miles up a dirt road just off East 180, Simion, Cliff, Thomas, and a handful of others were gathered around a table with Lars Kendrick, the famous Dutch architect. Lars's accent made every word he spoke sound like it was yanked from of his mouth. Speaking above the din of the swamp cooler, Lars said, "In this climate, heat is our enemy for most of the year. The location is very hot and dry. It takes a lot of energy to pump water out of the aquifer, so we must treat water as a precious resource.

"The landscape has some rolling hills off in the distance and a few trees.

Our plan is to create a community that adapts to the environment. The five main housing complexes will be modeled on the surrounding hillsides. Each dwelling unit will have its own outdoor terrace that will accumulate water from rain runoff to supply their hanging gardens. The vegetation will provide additional cooling while giving the building the appearance of growing up from the ground, in harmony with the landscape.

"Unlike water, space is widely available here, so we are not constrained by the confines of an urban center. The five housing units will be arranged with two buildings facing the north, two facing the south and one facing the east. The eastern structure will be separated from the others by one hundred yards, while the north and south buildings will be separated by two hundred yards. In their center there will be a park with a flowing river, providing beauty as well as irrigation for the park area. To the east we have located the school, sports facilities, restaurants, entertainment center and clinic.

"You will see there are no roads for automobiles. This will be the first modern city that has no roads for combustion engines. Occupants of the city will travel by foot or by communal bikes. There will be electric vehicles to transport people to and from the factories, farms and ranches, though people can opt to walk or bike to the factory, as it is just a little more than a mile from the residential facilities.

"The roofs of the three factories will be rounded to resemble the landscape. Made from flexible photovoltaic film-coated fiberglass canvas, the roof will provide indirect sunlight sufficient for most working conditions while generating electricity for additional lighting needs.

"While being sustainable, our construction costs will be significantly less than conventional buildings. The primary building material will be Reblock. Reblock is six times stronger than traditional concrete and made entirely from recycled products. Glass, scrap metal, sewage sludge and other materials are compressed using recycled plastic as a binding agent. This mixture is then mold-cast and heat-cured. Blocks interlock on both their vertical and horizontal axis, with predetermined stress-load calculations for various construction applications.

"Like putting together a giant puzzle, each block has its own distinct number classification to guide workers during assembly. Foundation blocks are cast from larger size molds. As the building increases in height the size of the block decreases. By manufacturing blocks in relation to the size and stress requirements of the building, no other materials are needed in assembly. Unlike conventional buildings, no cement mortar or re-enforcing steel rods are needed. Once the building is constructed, a poly-carbonate coating is sprayed on the interior surface, providing an environmental seal against allergens and dust.

"Reblock not only reduces the amount of time and money spent on construction, it also conserves natural resources. Worldwide, the cement used for construction constitutes about seven percent of all global CO_2 emissions. Simion has purchased a landfill outside Norman so we will be mining and producing our own Reblock for construction."

Cliff could hardly contain himself. Wanting to ask a hundred questions, he finally blurted out, "How many homes per dwelling unit? How big are they?"

"There will be a total of 3000 homes. Each dwelling unit will have 600 homes, each with two bedrooms, one bathroom and one activity room, totaling 900 square feet. Each will have a terrace and garden. Aside from a small fridge and microwave, the homes will not be equipped for cooking.

"Although they're small by American standards, all of the buildings and gardens are community-based; they're not meant to be self-sufficient like typical American homes. So while 900 square feet seems small, the community access to the shared space is over 500,000 square feet."

"Tell us more about the sustainable aspects of your design," Simion said.

"In addition to using recycled building materials and plants to help cool the residential buildings, we have developed a rather simple but effective way to recycle waste water. Processing human waste has been challenging because the waste water is full of soap and detergents that kill the natural bacteria in our bodies that aid in converting human waste into usable fertilizer. So toilet plumbing is separate from sinks and showers. Water from sinks and showers will be fed through the river running through the center of the park, where organic biomass will break down contaminates in the water. The water is then drained down to a catchment area where it is filtered for use in the homes or for farming.

"Human waste will be diverted to leaching fields where it is quickly composted. To speed up composting time, toilets are equipped with self-contained washing and drying units, like toilets found in Japan, to avoid the use of toilet paper."

Cliff butted in: "No toilet paper? I can't imagine your average Joe giving that up!"

"I believe that, given the opportunity, people will ultimately prefer this method, as they do in Japan and much of South East Asia. It is more hygienic."

Thomas interjected: "While the layout you have presented is impressive, I am concerned that you have plans for a farm and a ranch. We want to achieve maximum positive exposure for how a hui works with the least amount of criticism. You don't want people to think that a hui is a self-supporting commune."

Lars smiled and said, "It is my English that has the problem, not the design. What is the word you use to describe a place to keep horses and other animals to ride?"

Cliff quickly answered, "Equestrian Center."

"Yes, that is it, a place to keep horses and other animals for amusement. I should call the farm a vegetable garden and the ranch, an equestrian center. Those who enjoy riding horses and growing their own food have the opportunity to do so. Like mountain biking, motocross, a fifty meter swimming pool, an enclosed gym, athletic fields and tennis courts, the equestrian center and garden are available for leisure time activities."

Clearly pleased, Simion said, "Without going over the top, we want Vorbine to be a showcase for all other huis to follow."

"What is the time frame?" Thomas asked.

"Roads and utilities will take six weeks to install. The buildings will take another sixteen weeks. So, in less than six months, Vorbine will open its doors," Simion said enthusiastically.

Cliff, ever the mathematician, stated: "In just six months you will build three million square feet of living space and one point eight million square feet of factory space! That will be an amazing achievement."

In a somber tone, Simion said, "I will need all of your help to get this project off the ground. The trailers outside will be our homes until the first building is completed. There's a lot of hard work and sacrifice ahead of us, but with our coordinated effort, we will accomplish our task."

Three days later a brigade of heavy equipment descended on Boise. Five 65,000 gallon Caterpillar Spray King water tankers along with dozens of wheel dozers, hydraulic excavators, tractor scrapers and graders went to work at Vorbine.

Boise never had it so good. Gas stations ran out of gas, restaurants overflowed and the town's grocery stores could not keep its shelves stocked.

The thirty room motel hardly satisfied the hundreds of workers that clamored for a room and a bed. Townspeople rented out their spare rooms, driveways and lawns. The city converted its only park into a makeshift campground. Roadside food stands started to spring up. The mayor of Boise was ecstatic.

Behind the scenes, Thomas worked with Simion's head public relation man, Peter Sadinski. A large chunk of Simion's success rested on the Peter's unique ability to make people believe what he wanted them to believe.

Peter was an impatient, rather smug man, used to having people at his beck and call. He loathed coming to Boise and working inside a trailer. If the decision had been his to make, Peter would have paid $30,000 a night for Thomas to stay at the Royal Plaza Suite rather than slumming it in Boise. Even living in a rented $400,000 mobile home with his own personal chief, Peter made it clear to all around him that he was not happy staying at Vorbine. Yet, despite all the snobbish whining, Peter would willingly endure much worse if Simion asked it of him. They had been through a lot together, and Peter knew Simion's business instincts were invaluable.

Although the setting called for casual dress, there was nothing casual about Peter Sadinski. Wearing a hand-tailored brocade dress shirt from Fielding & Nicholson and sporting a Patek Philippe strapped to his wrist, Peter reeked of wealth. Sitting across from Thomas in the makeshift conference room, Peter looked Thomas squarely in the eye and with tight lips softly spoke: "I don't know if I much like your new hui economics. I am quite happy with my social status, and I, for one, do not like the idea of it being swept away."

Thomas calmly, smiled back at Peter and said, "Even though you realize that our economy has brought our planet to the brink of self-destruction, you can somehow, in all your arrogance, make yourself believe you deserve a thousand times more than anyone else."

Peter's eyes twinkled and the corners of his mouth rose just enough to affirm that he was clearly suppressing a full-blown smile. Peter thought to himself, "Touché, well played. I might find my time useful with this one after all." In no way revealing his thoughts, Peter said, "Just because I don't like it doesn't mean I do not support your cause. I have enough cash stashed away to last my descendants three or four generations. But based on your fifty year countdown, it will be rather meaningless if they are all dead. After Simion confirmed your economic theories with Phillip Brownstein, he called me. Do you know why he chose to call me?"

"Because you owe Simion."

Sucking in his breath Peter snapped, "Now who is being arrogant?" Waiting for his words to sink in, Peter continued in a softer tone, "Simion called me because, quite simply, I am the best in my field. Yes, I made a fortune working with Simion, but I could have made a fortune working for GM or any number of other companies. Simion called me because I am the best public relations man out there.

"Believe it or not, people like me have been shaping our world for the past hundred years. Beginning with Sigmund Freud's nephew, Edward Bernays, all major world events have been shaped by public relations."

"So you believe the general public is being controlled solely by the persuasion of public relations people such as yourself?"

"I would not go so far as to say solely on public relations, but in large part, yes. Edward Bernays, guided by his uncle Sigmund Freud, laid the psychological foundation for modern public relations. Did you know his first job was with the US government to sway public opinion against Hitler? Back then, the art of persuading the masses was called propaganda. The idea of controlling people's minds has such a stink about it that Edward Bernays started calling propaganda techniques 'public relations.'"

Shifting uncomfortably, Thomas said, "Propaganda must have substance to ignite people's spirits. It takes time for propaganda techniques to take effect."

Using a lecturing voice, Peter said, "Is that so? In a single afternoon Edward Bernays' propaganda techniques changed the world His techniques were so good the tobacco industry hired him. You see, back at the turn of the last century, women did not smoke. For hundreds of years, it was unthinkable for a woman to smoke. But in just one day, in 1918, Edward Bernays changed public opinion by making it socially acceptable for women to smoke.

"You may recall that women demanded all kinds of rights around this time, including the right to vote. To gain that right, they needed to show that they were free- thinking, independent individuals. Edward Bernays gave them that chance when he persuaded a group of debutantes, who called themselves the Torches of Freedom, to smoke cigarettes during New York's Easter Sunday Parade. It caused such a sensation that papers all around the globe carried the story. By thoughtfully staging this single event, Edward Bernays instilled the idea in the minds of women around the world that if they wanted to be free and independent, they needed to smoke cigarettes.

"That, my friend, is the power of public relations. Call it propaganda, public relations or whatever you like, but people like me control public opinion."

"So Bernays is in part responsible for sending countless women to an early grave. But I see your point. So how do we use public relations to introduce huinomics?"

"Although the world is infinitely more complex than it was a hundred years ago, politicians today control the masses by satisfying people's inner selfish desires. Using these same techniques, corporations persuade people to buy things they don't need by linking mass-produced goods to their unconscious desires."

"Why can't we simply tell people straight up about the benefits of huinomics?"

"People behave in ways that they believe will benefit themselves; it is built into our species. Industrialization allowed us to move from a symbiotic tribal society, where collaboration was necessary, to one transfixed on the self.

"Jumping ahead, let me ask you this: have you ever seen a car commercial that actually focuses on the attributes of the car, its engine, breaks or any other practical aspect of the vehicle? No. What you see is someone satisfying some vague inner desire by driving the car. Car companies sell cars because people think they will feel better about themselves if they buy that particular car."

"But I don't want to deceive people. People will live better lives with huinomics. Moreover, if we want to progress, huinomics must exist."

"Let me ask you this. The soldiers coming back from Afghanistan have the highest levels of posttraumatic stress disorder and suicide in the nation's history. And yet, despite the Afghani War being America's longest, most traumatic war, recruits haven't been a problem. How is that possible? How can the government convince people that something so obviously detrimental to their wellbeing as being a good thing?"

Without waiting for a response from Thomas, Peter continued, "The only way you can convince people to sacrifice themselves is if you understand their unconscious and manipulate their emotions.

"Sure, we can list a thousand reasons why huinomics is the best thing for America, and even purport that it will save the world from certain destruction, but that would not be as powerful as planting the unconscious message in peoples' minds that huinomics will make them happier. To persuade the general public that huinomics will make their life better, we must convince the individual that their personal desires will be met: you persuade the general public one individual at a time.

"You see, there is no such thing as the Average Joe in this world. In other words, the Average Joe turns out to be Joseph, who has his own ideas and desires. Once we win over Joseph, he not only believes in the hui movement, he becomes an active participant, recruiting other believers."

"Just how do we do that?"

"We will challenge people to question themselves. Why am I so over-stressed, overweight and unhappy? Why don't my relationships last? Why do I hate my job? Why don't I ever have enough money? Why is my future so bleak?

"We will win over the hearts of Americans when they believe, as individuals, that huinomics will cure these ills."

"So you will have Americans questioning their quality of life and then hold the Quasar event as the answer?"

"In simple terms, yes. It sets the stage. You see, people are unconsciously drawn to believe that there is something out there that they must have in order to find happiness. This something is a million different things to a million different people. This 'guiding light' directing people's behavior might be a home, a car, traveling, getting into a relationship, or falling out of a relationship. Our ultimate goal is to become that guiding light that people believe they must have in order to find happiness.

"But Huinomics will bring happiness and contentment."

"Yes, Thomas, I believe it will or I wouldn't be sitting in front of you today. But for that to happen, I need to convince three hundred and fifty million American individuals that huinomics will make their lives better. I need to accomplish this before the government and big business convince them otherwise. It doesn't matter if huinomics is the only answer to save our species, if those in power convince the general public it is evil.

"We cannot underestimate our adversary. Government public relations specialists are unsurpassed in persuading people to act in irrational ways. Using freedom as their secret weapon, they have convinced countless men to lose their lives just to preserve this abstract concept. It is not an easy task to convince an individual that a small backward nation a million miles away is threatening your freedom."

"How ironic, when you consider that a man's measure of freedom is proportionate to the amount of leisure time he has."

Getting up to leave Peter said, "Now you are thinking like a public relations man."

Chapter 7

Senator Bates bellowed across his mahogany desk: "Why is it every time I must tell you what to do? As my campaign manager, it is up to you to keep on top of these things. I want to know: what's the purpose of this big Quasar event scheduled to happen September 1st? I don't want to hear about it tomorrow or the day after next, I want to know about it today!"

Like a flipped circuit breaker, Senator Bates defaulted to disparagement under the slightest pressure. Whenever he got a head full of steam, which was more often than not, he barked out condescending orders like some crazed college basketball coach. It was his auto-response mechanism for dealing with most situations. He told himself he needed to kick some butt to get things done. He believed his approach was a reflection of his strength, but to everyone else, he was just an asshole.

Hailing from Georgia, Bates rose to power like an overinflated Zeppelin. Swinging the conservative bat, there was no question where Bates stood on gay marriage and freedom of choice. Unleashing his rage on underlings, Bates grew red in the face as he pounded his huge fist against the podium, proclaiming himself the protector of American Values, all the while keeping a close eye on public opinion polls to steer his rhetoric. Bates was more of a polished entertainer dancing to public opinion than a politician sworn to serve the people.

Bates's right hand man, Max Harvey, was totally unscathed by his insults. Knowing how to play the game, he snapped back, "I've been on top of the Quasar announcement since the commercials started playing last night. I called all my media contacts; no one has a clue what's going to take place September 1st."

Bates shook out his pudgy left hand as if he got something stuck to it and bellowed, "Is that it? We hear Xavier Lamont, along with a pack of other stars, telling the American public that their life is in the crapper and you mean to tell me no one knows anything about this event?"

Before Bates could catch his breath and expel another extended rant, Max stated, "We know it's not political; at least it's not aligned with any American politician. Everyone on the Hill is looking for answers and finding nothing."

Bates shook his head and said, "Do you really think if a politician knew who the hell was behind this Quasar September 1st event they would want to share it with you?"

By this point, Max had enough. He stood his ground, not saying a word. Like a well rehearsed skit, Bates knew if he continued his tirade Max would leave his office and would be non-communicative for the rest of the day. This moment was too important to squander on the petty satisfaction Bates got from bullying Max, so Bates cut his ranting short and said, "This is what I want you to do: get a hold of Alerkson and have him tell you what's going on. It's about time he antes up."

In large part, Stephen Alerkson owed his position as Vice Deputy of Homeland Security to Bates. Without Bates's support, Alerkson would still be just another unknown somebody at the CIA.

After several tries, Max got Alerkson on the phone.

"Stephen, there are some calls you shouldn't keep waiting."

"I know, Max, but it was impossible to take your call until now. The President is involved. Three quarters of the agency is trying to find out what's going to happen on September 1st. We've spent the past twelve hours scanning billions of emails and came up with squat."

Stephen smirked and thought to himself, "So much for keeping America safe from terrorists," and said, "Stephen, you're holding out on me. I know you have to answer to the President, but getting a jump on this event could assure Bates's re-election." Stephen paused, waiting for a response that didn't come. "Listen. If that doesn't happen we can both begin to look for new work."

Always instep with Washington politics, Stephen replied, "I'm with you on this. Unless I get a direct order to the contrary from the President, you'll be the first person I call the moment I hear anything related to Quasar."

Thomas looked up as Simion entered his office pod. Smiling, Thomas greeted Simion as he sat down heavily. Anticipating a follow up discussion on schedules, Thomas said, "How's the shop floor foundation coming along?"

"You know how it is; we put out one fire and another one starts. If it's not one thing it's another. Now the looms are arriving before the south building's roof is up. But that's not what I'm here for."

Taking a hard look at Thomas, Simion continued, "Thomas, I know you realize how important it is to have your huinomics book ready before Quasar. But I am concerned that you have too many distractions here at Vorbine to get it finished on time. Your presence has been a great asset, but now you have bigger fish to fry."

Sighing, Thomas said, "If anything Johnson is slowing down the project."

"No one wants to change your work. But we need it to be accessible to the lay person. Johnson's idea to footnote the math behind the theories is a great example of your collaboration. Anyway, we're getting sidetracked. The reason I came here is to tell you I think you'll get more accomplished if you and Jackie work at my ranch outside of Taos."

Thomas quickly warmed to the idea of getting away with Jackie. Back at the farm, Jackie had complete control over her world and relished sharing its simple responsibilities with Thomas. Thomas knew Jackie felt like she was being swept under the rug at Vorbine. Realizing that a change of pace would give Jackie the chance to be front and center again, Thomas said, "I see where you're coming from. We'll go. But can I get my desk back when I return?"

Laughing, Simion said, "No question, you can have your desk back. But if you like the place in Taos, you can stay as long as you like."

"You'd better be careful. I might fall in love with the place."

Battling seemingly impossible hurdles, Simion franticly worked crews around the clock to finish Vorbine before Quasar's September first deadline. All the while, Peter Sadinski kept creating more and more hype about Quasar. Quasar had become an viral phenomenon. Everyone knew about Quasar, but no one could really say what it was about. No thanks to Peter. One day Peter would be running advertisements about economic inequality in America, and the next, he was going on about global warming.

Front and center of all the hype was Xavier Lamont. Being an actor of world-wide fame, people identified with Xavier's easy and honest nature. People trusted Xavier Lamont. They believe in him before they even knew what they were believing in. Xavier would always end his commercials with the same message: "There is a better way; watch Quasar on September first."

When September first finally arrived millions of people tuned in to watch Xavier Lamont. Filmed on location in Vorbine, Xavier informed the world of hui economics.

After Xavier's Quasar speech was finished the news frenzy that followed eclipsed all other media. Every major network halted their regular viewing to broadcast special live news reports. News analysts, commentators, and leading politicians filled the airwaves. Among the vultures taking part in the feeding frenzy, none were more aggressive than Senator Bates. His interview with anchor woman Susan Chun aired from his Washington DC office.

"Senator Bates what is your reaction to Quasar and this new hui economics?"

Senator Bates's face grew stern as he answered, "Susan, what we witnessed last night was nothing less than an attack on the American way of life and the values we hold so dear. This huinomics goes against the fundamental principles of this great country of ours."

"Senator Bates, as Xavier Lamont pointed out, huinomics is about improving the lives of Americans, not politics."

"We must inform the American public that huinomics is a wolf in sheep's clothing. It will deprive you of your God given right to own and purchase property. Taking away your ability to buy products is the same as taking away your liberty and freedom."

"That's a different take on the message that was presented to us tonight. Huinomics is supposed to provide us with more freedom, by being free of debt and having the time to pursue our desires and goals."

"What we heard tonight was a lot of fluff to convince people that they will be better off without owning anything. Any rational person knows that if you don't own anything you are helpless. What these founders of huinomics really intend is to have everyone work for free."

"So what you're saying is that the purpose of huinomics is not to raise the standard of living for humanity while saving the planet from global warming, but simply to rid people of their possessions?"

"I can't say what Thomas Quinn is getting out of this so called new economy. But I can tell you it sounds a lot like a new form of communism to me."

"There was no mention of political motivation. Just who do you believe is behind this new form of communism?"

"Time will reveal the true motivation behind this outlandish scheme. In the meanwhile, we have a group of people trying to convince us to work for free. I am sure that most will see through to their true purpose."

Cocking his head with conviction, Bates continued, "We must forewarn the American public not to jump on this band wagon and travel down this dark path. Huinomics is destined to fail because it is man's nature to own possessions."

"Thank you for joining us tonight, Senator Bates. We'll just have to wait and see how many people are willing to go down this dark path that you speak of, as Vorbine's web site just indicated that they are looking to fill 2300 job openings."

Max Harvey was surprised to see Senator Bates come marching into the office at 7:00 AM. One of the few perks of working for Bates was that he spent as much time away from the office as he did at the office. Without bothering to knock, Bates barged into Max's office and held out the Washington Post with his picture on the cover and exclaimed, "It's just like I planned. I am at the head of the pack. Every politician is maneuvering to get this kind of exposure. There's no limit to where this kind of publicity can take me."

Today Max chose not to feed Bates's over-inflated ego and said, "We may be on the wrong side of the tracks with this one. In the past twelve hours, the Vorbine web site has breached two hundred million hits. Huinomics has turned into an overnight sensation. Vorbine has received eighteen million applicants. Everybody is crazy about Vorbine."

Bates lifted up his arm and cocked his hand in his patented speech delivery pose, and blurted out, "Huinomics is an abomination. It threatens our way of life and must be destroyed at all cost." Seeing that his rhetoric was lost on Max, Bates laid his pudgy hands on his desk and leaned over: "It will be my personal quest to see that huinomics fail. Do you know they're now telling folks how many children they can have? Huinomics is worse than communism. It must be eradicated before it spreads."

Clearly repulsed, Max rolled back from his desk saying, "Vorbine's limited financial support for more than one child per adult will play well to your Christian Coalition constituents."

Hoisting himself up, Bates said, "Damn right it will. This Thomas Quinn is going down. No man has the right to say how many children another man can have. Wait and see, by the time I'm through with Quinn, huinomics will be finished."

"Before you hit the media with that kind of rhetoric, we need to scrutinize your position. The last thing we want is for you to get your foot caught in a bear trap."

"I want to see Thomas Quinn buried so bad I can taste it. You texted that Alerkson has made progress, what is it?"

Max explained how Stephen Alerkson's night crawlers may have found a way to permanently destroy Thomas Quinn.

Backed by the might of Homeland Security, Stephen's night crawlers prowled every location and contact Thomas Quinn ever had. No stone was left unturned. Intel was gathered on overseas relatives Thomas never knew existed. Every contact came up blank. Not one individual could come up with dirt on Thomas. The only kink in his armor was Rebecca Swanson.

Thomas took Rebecca Swanson to the senior prom. Actually, out of sheer desperation, Rebecca asked Thomas to go to the prom with her. Like Thomas, Rebecca was on the fringes of their high school's social core.

Rebecca dressed and acted like a Goth. Her shoulder length jet black hair stood out against her opaque white skin. She rimmed her eyes with thick black eyeliner and wore skin-tight black clothes to emphasize her pencil-thin frame. When shuffling down the hallways in her heavy punk boots, her eyes transfixed on the ground, Rebecca looked perpetually stoned. Even on the stoop below the gym steps, where students could sneak a smoke without being hassled by teachers, students kept clear of Rebecca Swanson.

People kept their distance from Rebecca, until one day, out of the blue, she asked Thomas to go to the senior prom with her. Thomas and Rebecca threw in forty bucks to help pay for a limo and went to the prom with a bunch of other seniors they hardly knew. They looked like the most unlikely couple. Thomas rented a sky blue tux and Rebecca wore a tight black dress .

As the other couples were having a grand time, Rebecca sat staring out at the dancers while taking hits off a flask of vodka. Thomas tried to pass the time as best he could but he couldn't help wishing that the night would end soon. By the time the limo arrived, Rebecca couldn't walk straight. Living on the outskirts of town, Rebecca was the last girl to get dropped off. She was so smashed by then she could barely make it to her front door.

Eighteen years later, Rebecca spent the majority of her time being in the same state of mind as she had been that prom night so long ago. In and out of city-run drug and alcohol rehab centers, moving from odd-job to odd-job, Rebecca made a mess of her life.

After interviewing no less than twenty-one fellow students, one of Stephen's men finally found two students who remembered Thomas Quinn taking Rebecca Swanson to the senior prom. After another week of digging, one of his night crawlers located the limo driver who never left that small New Mexico town, working as a lonely strip-mall night guard.

With that, Stephen Alerkson had all he needed to concoct a plan to destroy Thomas Quinn. Like a bloodhound on the scent, Senator Bates spent the next two days casting his political net to amass resources to squash Thomas Quinn. Ever fearful of scandal, Bates kept his distance by assigning Max as Stephen Alerkson's contact person. After ensuring nothing could be traced back to him, Bates gave Max the green light to notify Alerkson to send in his men.

The following day, James Blake arrived in Quartzsite Arizona. Living in a small trailer on a barren plot of land, Rebecca punched a cash register all night at a 24 hour truck stop servicing a small but steady stream of drivers traveling the LA- Phoenix corridor. Most of the tired drivers crossing Rebecca's path had only one thing on their mind: to get the hell out of Quartzsite as quickly as possible.

Quartzsite was a haven for people like Rebecca. Most of the town's residents were drunks or headed that way. Quartzsite was never a normal community. At one time, in its hay day, hundreds of motorhomes migrated to Quartzsite to occupy vast trailer parks where retired rock hounds ravaged the desert searching for amethyst and turquoise. Now with its riches gone, only a handful of retired rock hounds bother with Quartzsite, leaving it a hollow petrol oasis in the middle of the desert.

Working the graveyard shift suited Rebecca just fine. Armed with a huge coffee thermos, Rebecca sipped gin and tonic during her eight hour shift. Slowly getting juiced over the course of the night was Rebecca's way of life. If it wasn't for the bright lights and the ever present cameras recording her every move, she might find the work to be a degree above deplorable.

Just before her shift change, Rebecca spotted the undercover cop through her glazed over eyes as soon as he walked in. He was trouble. Most customers were in a hurry to get the hell out as soon as possible. But this guy lingered around the aisles of edible trash way too long. He was too cool to be suspected as a thief.

Yes, this one had a different purpose other than to tank and piss.

Just as the sun was rising, he approached Rebecca in the parking lot as she was taking out her car keys. After a night of sipping gin, Rebecca was in her zone, that state where she was finally feeling decent, where her mind was cranked up enough to feel empowered, but not too wacked to where she couldn't think coherently.

Shielding her revealing eyes with dark sun glasses Rebecca suggestively turned to him and said in her sexy voice, "What can I do for you, officer?"

Blake couldn't stop a slight smile from pushing at the corner of his mouth.

"You're quick. But I'm not a cop, and I'm not here to hurt you. In fact, today is your lucky day. Have you ever heard of people inheriting a bunch of money from some long lost relative they never knew? Today is your day, your million dollar day."

"And I suppose you are my fucking ferry godmother. Right?"

Again with renewed respect Blake said, "Fair enough. No bullshit. When you were seventeen you went to the prom with Thomas Quinn. You have lived in Quartzsite for four years. You live in a trailer on 12th Street and you drink a pint of gin every night. Have I got your attention now?"

Hearing the sound of Thomas Quinn's name Rebecca froze. Along with everyone else, Rebecca watched the Quasar speech. For days after the speech, like imagining a sweet song that's never been sung, Rebecca's mind played out intricate fantasies of what her life would have been like if somehow they had found love together so many years ago.

Rebecca just stood there with her mouth half opened giving way to her recurring fantasy.

Thinking that Rebecca was zoning out like a drunk, Blake said overly loud, "Hay! You don't look so good. Why don't I take you to your trailer."

Like a cat doused in cold water, the fantasy vanished and reality sunk in. Of course. Now that Thomas was famous, having a pro look her up seemed almost natural. Hard as her coin chipped nails, Rebecca put on her sexy voice saying, "Oh, you want to take me back to my trailer do you?"

Out gunned Blake said, "The camera on the corner is unlikely to be able to read our lips at this distance, but just to be sure lets talk in my car."

"Standing out here is just fine with me, Mister…?"

"Sorry. James Blake." Squinting into the rising sun, Blake got straight to the point.

"You are to bring Thomas Quinn to trial for raping you on prom night. Bert Vargas, the limo driver, will corroborate your story and we have DNA evidence against Quinn linking him to the crime. There is no way he will be found innocent. For your effort you will receive $100,000 each year over a ten year period, starting twelve months after the success of the trial."

Rebecca, slit-eyed with gin, closed her eyes entirely against the brightness of the sun and spoke in a cold, sweet voice.

"Who are you, and how do I know you will not fuck me."

"You will never know who I am. Who I am is not important. The only thing that is important to you is money. Before going to trial, you will have a trust fund according to the terms of our agreement, drawn on a Swiss bank account."

A seductive smile played on Rebecca's lips. In a flash Rebecca came to the stone cold realization that the only reward she was going to get for having known Thomas Quinn was standing right in front of her.

"Mister I may be trailer trash, but I know when I'm getting fucked. When you are serious about taking down the world's most famous person you can come by my trailer. Just make sure you bring five million with you. Five to begin with, and five if he gets busted."

Chapter 8

Getting off a plane was something Thomas Quinn did not envision himself doing. Opting to travel by more environmentally sound methods, the last time Thomas took a flight was many years ago. But tragedy had struck outside the corporate gates of P&G in Cincinnati Ohio. Setting his moral preferences aside Thomas and Jackie, along with their body guards grabbed the first flight out.

P&G's corporate head quarters was the focal point of protest spread across the nation. The purpose of the protests, aptly named 'Corporate Acquisition Rallies' by Peter, were to inform the general public to boycott P&G products. Not that P&G was a bad company. On the contrary, Thomas choose P&G because its early corporate policy placed the working man first. All the same, the purpose of the boycott was to do one thing; force P&G into converting into a hui corporation.

Knowing full well that any public corporation would not voluntarily convert into a hui corporation, Thomas knew he could force a corporation to covert if he applied enough pressure. Thomas gave P&G's stockholders an ultimatum; either accept a three-year pay-back of the value of their stock at current prices, or watch their investment eventually shrink to zero as the nation boycotted its products.

Not surprisingly P&G's board basically told Thomas and the hui movement to go screw themselves. In retaliation boycott protest sprang up at rallies across the nation. It was as if every underemployed, overworked, and unhappy worker across the nation took to the streets. Their ranting was far beyond the anger brought on by countless years of struggle to keep their heads above water, the protesters believed their demonstration would make a tangible difference in their lives.

Overnight P&G's products stopped flowing from the shelves and the value of P&G's stock plummeted. True to his word, Thomas pledged a stock buy-back at pre-boycott prices if the stockholders voted to convert. Desperate not to loose their investment the stockholders put pressure on the board to enact policy to convert, but P&G's board, lead by the chairman, refused.

Consequently, thousands of protesters had gathered outside of P&G's front gate to direct their protest directly at P&G's board. When the police were called in to break up the protest, an overzealous cop cracked the skull of an unwitting protester. In retaliation, the protesters became violent and quickly overpowered the police. Fearing an out and out riot, the Mayor called in the National Guard.

Responding to the situation, Peter had a Winnebago waiting for them when they got off the plane. A ten thousand watt stadium speaker was mounted to its back ladder and on either side was a huge photo taken of Thomas during a speech, with "OUR TIME" written in bold letters across the bottom. Looking at his enormous face plastered to the Winnebago, Thomas thought, "Good God Peter, what are you getting me into".

One of four motorcycle cops standing nearby spotted Thomas and quickly walked over to him.

"I can see that you are Thomas Quinn, but I still need to see some identification."

The police escort did not make sense to Thomas. After much debate with Simion, Thomas had agreed to two body guards. Now, was he expected to travel around with police?

In dismay Thomas asked the officer, "Why all the security? Why I am being escorted?"

"You don't know what you're facing. We may not even be able to reach P&G. Mobs have blocked the roads up to half a mile in all directions from P&G's main gate. The streets are full of overturned burning cars."

Realizing how serious the protest had gotten, Thomas said, "Get me as close as you can, officer." Turning to Jackie, Thomas said, "I need you to wait here."

"Like hell," responded Jackie, turning to board the Winnebago. "Let's go."

As the Winnebago approached the main street leading to P&G, it became obvious the protesters were out of control. The Winnebago crept past overturned burning vehicles until inching to a stop behind the main crowd. Seeing Thomas's photo on the sides of the Winnebago, a wave of protesters began to close in around it. Fearing for their safety, the motorcycle cops fell back as the crowd swarmed the Winnebago and began to beat on it. Mack, one of Thomas's body guards, shouted out to the driver, "Back up, get us the hell out of here."

But Thomas shouted, "No! Stay where you are. We're not leaving."

Hundreds of protesters were pounding on the sides of the Winnebago as it started to rock back and forth. "Thomas, we've got to go. This mob is out of control. We're going to be crushed," Jackie said with fear trembling in her voice.

Completely ignoring Jackie and looking as if he was going to strike someone, Thomas shouted to Mack, "Help me get on top."

Knowing further protests were futile, Mack helped Thomas open the door to the back and Thomas grabbed the ladder to climb on top of the Winnebago. In the frenzy, Mack had to beat off several protesters trying to grab onto Thomas's legs as he climbed.

To help his balance on top of the shaking Winnebago Thomas stood like a sumo wrestler. He shouted into the remote microphone, "Is this the end?"

To Thomas's surprise, his voice blasted out of the stadium speaker so loud that protesters near the back of the Winnebago fell back with their hands over their ears. Hearing Thomas's voice, protesters off in the distance quickly began to descend on the pulsating crowd swarming the Winnebago.

Again, but even louder than before, Thomas yelled out, "Is this the end?"

Like a heat wave over desert black top, Thomas felt as if he could see hate emanate from the crowd.

"What you choose to do right now will decide if today will be the last day of the hui movement."

The crowd continued to rage as Thomas shouted, "If you don't stop this madness the hui movement will end today! The national guard is on its way. They will attack us with water canons and tear gas. Many of us will be injured and we will respond with more violence. The circle of hate will grow and grow until the hui movement will be smothered by its own hate."

Like a dessert rain, Thomas felt his words begin to cool the crowd.

"Huinomics will not spawn from the end of a gun barrel. For thousands of years we choose to revolt in violence. We have passed that point in human history; we have evolved. We know violence only brings more violence and with it greater and greater oppression. This is not our path. This is not our power. Our power is our collective will to change how we live and work."

"We are one. We have no enemies. The policeman who struck our brother today is our cousin. The national guard on its way are our friends. They are us. The only enemy we have lies inside of us."

The thousands standing around the Winnebago were nearly silent.

"We have made great progress, but earlier today we failed. It is time for you and I to stand up once again. Today we will correct our mistakes. We will clean the streets. We will replace the destroyed cars. We will repair P&G's gates. And we will peacefully wait until the day P&G chooses to convert. Join me in cleaning up our mess."

Ignoring the pleas of his body guards, Thomas climbed off the Winnebago and disappeared into the cheering crowd.

News coverage of the P&G riot and what soon became known as the 'Our Time' speech reverberated across the nation. Despite Senator Bates's ongoing verbal attacks proclaiming Thomas Quinn as a new breed of liberal communist, driven to destroy the American way of life, it was becoming more and more clear that the hui movement was gaining ground.

Chapter 9

Only after negotiating to get the cash deposited into a trust that matured upon the completion of the trial, Rebecca Swanson finally settled for five million. She dreamed of using the money to go off to India to replace her terminally damaged liver. She figured she could buy some poor soul's liver for around half a million. Rebecca dreamed of being rich and healthy, but deep down she knew it would take a lot more than a new liver to be happy.

An unsolicited donation of five million dollars for Rebecca Swanson, and another two million for the limo driver, materialized out of thin air. The Wall Street white shoe law firm of Baker, Smith and Hines, which rakes in millions representing Fortune 500 companies, covertly handled setting up Rebecca's trust with a Swiss bank, along with discretely preparing Rebecca for the trial.

Baker, Smith and Hines hired an independent agent to move Rebecca to a rental home on the outskirts of Phoenix. As part of the lengthy process to get Rebecca ready for the trial, two round-the-clock independent drug rehab specialist began the difficult task of curing her addiction.

As soon as Rebecca stopped drinking she swore to herself that the five million in the Swiss trust account wasn't worth it. Even on acamprosate, delirious tremors racked her body and mind.

The hallucinations were worse at night. Lying in bed under a white sheet, Rebecca waited for each successive attack. In the stillness of the night, the hollow plastic scraping noise emanating from the electrical outlet became intolerable. Rebecca tried to force herself to believe the sound was imaginary. She held her breath, her heart pounding in her throat, quietly listening for it to go away, only to hear the horrid scraping sound grow louder and louder. With wide, panic stricken eyes, Rebecca tried to sit up and escape but her muscles would not respond. Paralyzed with fear, Rebecca groaned and sobbed, "No....no...nooo", as the face plate to an electrical outlet cracked open and a snake-like reptile slithered out.

The serpent's bioluminescent glow pulsed from emerald green to iridescent amber as it slithered across the floor, heading right for her. Growing in size with each passing moment, it slithered up onto the bed. Rebecca could see its ruby eyes burning down on her as it coiled its body, swaying as it rose to strike. Too horrified to utter a sound, Rebecca convulsed in shear panic as the serpent opened its mouth and struck, plunging its fangs deep into her skin. Ripping out her flesh, the serpent recoiled, only to rise and strike again and again. With blood flowing from patches on her face, neck and chest, the serpent finally slithered away while Rebecca sobbed, too weak to scream out.

After each hallucination Rebecca swore she would sell her soul to the devil if only he would make them stop. Naked under sweat stained sheets, Rebecca trembled. Her body had withered to the point where her ribs were clearly visible under her emaciated breasts. Her graying opaque skin emphasized the tiny blue veins rimming her charcoal eyes.

Rebecca looked more like death than any Goth getup she donned in high school.

The back of her throat was swollen and caked with a thick yellowish brown layer of mucus. She would contort her body in coughing spasms in effort to dislodge a glob of the vial substance onto a tissue. Rebecca felt as nasty and disgusting as the mucus she hacked out.

Toward dawn, Rebecca's mind filled with the image of glass bottles; beautiful blue and green bottles. For hours Rebecca would meditate about gin. Visions of gin bottles with their clear intoxicating liquid were so pleasing. Even the sound of gin pouring into a glass was like sweet music created by angels, descending from heaven.

Gin was all that mattered to her. If only she could taste that nectar and experience peace once again!

When lucid, the mere thought of stopping drinking for good was banished from her mind. Even after two weeks of constant agony, when the poison was finally out of Rebecca's system, all she could think of was having a drink…a nice, long, cool drink.

Ironically, Baker, Smith and Hines had an impeccable reputation. The New York head office had four hundred lawyers on staff, with another eight hundred spread around the globe. The top guns at Baker, Smith and Hines did not go to work; they lived at work. Most arrived before seven and left around ten, while many were frequently at the office after midnight.

David Mulland was one of Baker, Smith and Hines' rising stars. David had a particularly refined ruthlessness he could beckon at will. His overwhelmingly condescending confidence worked. People unconsciously accepted whatever he said, if only to minimize the amount of time they needed to spend with him, which, quite frankly, was more than agreeable to David. He disdained most people, thinking that, by and large, most people were idiots, too stupid to be of any use to him.

Like all young associates, David had the disagreeable task of taking on pro bono cases on top of his already packed schedule. Baker, Smith and Hines specialized in providing legal counsel for corporate mergers and acquisitions. With revenues exceeding two hundred and thirty-five million, Baker, Smith and Hines was one of the most profitable law firms in the nation.

When David's boss, Michael Simmons, strolled into his office, he instantly knew something big was up.

"Don't get up David. I have some news for you that can't wait. Rebecca Swanson came to us with a pro bono case against Thomas Quinn."

"Thomas Quinn? That is news."

"Rebecca Swanson swears that Thomas Quinn raped her the night of her senior prom."

David's brows furrowed.

"Senior prom? That must be more than fifteen years ago. The case will be thrown out. The statute of limitations is six years."

Michael Simmons' smile spread. "She kept her senior prom dress. We sent it to CTR Labs, who verified that the dress was soiled with semen. The extracted DNA sample proved to be positive. As you know, the statute of limitations for DNA evidence is 25 years."

Instinctively, David sensed a frame. "How reliable is this Rebecca Swanson?"

"She's an absolute wreck, a lifelong trailer-trash drunkard, a real challenge. I consulted the men upstairs. They want you to try the case."

Like a shark smelling blood in the water, David knew that this case would make or break his career. If he refused, the thousands of hours he spent climbing the rungs at Baker, Smith and Hines would have been in vain. The senior partners would secretly blacklist him as being uncooperative and his career would stop dead in its tracks.

On the other hand, if he cooperated, who knows how far he could go?

With only the slightest hesitation, David said, "This will be biggest publicity case since the OJ Simpson trial, probably bigger. Wouldn't a case of this magnitude warrant the expertise of an Associate Partner?"

Michael's smile grew even larger: "It's the chance of a lifetime. All but two of the partners thought you wouldn't miss such an opportunity to be fast-tracked. And yes, unofficially, you win this case and you can consider yourself to be the youngest partner at Baker, Smith and Hines.

"But keep in mind, David, we can't lose this one. I'm reassigning all your cases. You'll head a team of ten: four staff lawyers and six assistants."

Instinctively, David knew Thomas Quinn didn't do it. That fact was not important to him. To David, law was not about justice; it was a high-stakes poker game with winners and losers. And if there was one thing important to David, it was winning, and winning court cases was something he was very good at.

David wasted no time hiring Harris Thompson to coach Rebecca Swanson in a home near the courthouse in Los Alamos, New Mexico. Like David, Harris Thompson was in a league of his own. He called himself a 'personality coach,' but no title could adequately describe his profession.

Harris Thompson had the uncanny ability to transform people like Rebecca Swanson into respectable, honest, compassionate, hard working citizens. Commanding $40,000 per week, Harris Thompson was paid handsomely for his unique skills.

In college Harris studied acting, and like most students, set aside his dreams and took up an alternate career to pay the bills. Harris choose Rolfing. With the ability of changing a person's posture through Rolfing, coupled with his acting skills, Harris stumbled upon the idea of prepping clients for court appearances.

With Rebecca, he had his work cut out for him. After a lifetime of alcohol abuse, it would take all the magic Harris could muster to transform her. Even as a child, Rebecca did not eat much and took a twisted pride in her emaciated appearance. He started her on a whole food diet of 2600 calories. She vomited up most of the healthy food he fed her until Harris came up with the idea of putting her on a liquid diet.

Drinking was something Rebecca was good at.

Between slurping down vegetable cocktails laced with fat and protein, Harris forced Rebecca to participate in acting lessons. Harris never believed he could change a person's personality, but he knew he could make them act as if they were a different person. Long before David's team began to feed Rebecca defense questions and their appropriate replies, Harris was building an attractive character for Rebecca to play.

After his first few clients, Harris discovered it was easier for them to play a character the opposite of their actual personalities. The character Harris picked for Rebecca was kind, respectful and considerate of others. Although this character was not educated, she was hard working and a credit to her community. She got along well with others and was helpful to those in need. She was a modern Doris Day.

The character Rebecca learned to play stood in stark contrast to her true personality, which was depressed, self-absorbed and callous.

Under Harris's guidance, Rebecca watched April in Paris and Please Don't Eat the Daisies until she learned to mimic Doris Day in every way. If she broke character, she would have to watch another one of Doris' 39 films. Inundated with these syrupy-sweet images of a naive, caring, fun-loving girl, Rebecca finally managed to assume Doris' persona. For the duration of the trial, in the courtroom and out, Rebecca was to stay in character, continually acting as the new Rebecca.

While the makeover work was transpiring, David's team spent countless hours writing a trial script for Rebecca to memorize. The team came up with every probable question the defense lawyer could ask, followed by Rebecca's appropriate response. Day after day the rehearsals continued. Many of Harris's clients had broken under the pressure, but for Rebecca, playacting someone else was refreshing. For the first time in a very long time, Rebecca began to like herself.

In the back of her mind, Rebecca began to toy with the idea of really becoming a new person. She found herself thinking: "God, just get me through this and I will become a new person…a new person with a five million dollar bank account!"

While David's team created a new persona for Rebecca and rehearsed her performance for the trail, David worked on building a list of witnesses.

Finding character witnesses for Rebecca proved much more difficult than David ever imagined.

When Rebecca first told David that she didn't have any high school friends, he didn't believe her. Everyone had at least one friend in high school. Only after going over and over Rebecca's high school yearbook with her did David finally come to the realization that Rebecca truly did not have a friend in high school.

Regardless how polished Rebecca appeared, David needed the jury to believe that Rebecca had at least one person she called a friend in high school.

With no one else to turn to, David called his boss, Michael Simmons.

"We have a problem."

Michael let lose an audible sigh, and in a condescending voice, said, "What is it, David?"

"We need a high school character witness for Rebecca Swanson."

"So?"

"So that's why I'm calling. Rebecca Swanson does not have a single person who can say was her friend during high school."

A long pause ensued before Michael said, "How important is such a friend to your case?"

"The defense will have a multitude of high school character witnesses for Thomas Quinn. The jury will suspect something if Rebecca Swanson doesn't have at least one person who could take the stand as her friend."

"This is going to be costly, David. Why didn't you tell me before?"

"I had no idea! How many people do you know without a single friend in high school?"

Seeing David's point, but not relinquishing his consternation, Michael said, "Give me a list of the girls in Rebecca's senior class. We have some fishing to do."

After conferring with the senior partners, Michael Simmons was given the green light to hire an exclusive detective agency. Known only by an elite handful of Wall Street firms, it cost $100,000 just to knock on their door. The only information anyone had about the detective agency was their off-shore banking account number. When $100,000 was deposited into the account, a 24 hour email address would be provided. If the detective agency took the case, payment in full was needed to proceed.

For the tidy sum of million dollars, the detective agency persuaded Susan Torres to give David Mulland a call because she was concerned about her old friend, Rebecca Swanson.

While Susan Torres was not an ideal character witness, she proved far better than none at all. She was one of eight girls at Rebecca's high school who didn't make it to senior prom. Although being overweight and having acne didn't help her chances, Susan had been virtually invisible during high school because she spent all her time outside of school watching her two younger brothers while her mother worked.

Like her mother, Susan ended up being a single mom. She had a ten year old son. Knowing what it meant to endure, Susan had worked the deli counter at a local chain grocery store for the past eight years, making just enough to keep food on the table and pay for their rundown two bedroom apartment.

One evening while she was watching TV and her son was busy doing his homework, a stranger knocked on the door.

"Miss Torres?"

Upon hearing her name, Susan felt a wave of apprehension. Going over to the door, she stood to the side and cracked it an inch, suspiciously eying the pleasant-looking man standing there.

"Yes, I'm Miss Torres. Who are you?"

With a warm smile, the man took a card from his overcoat pocket and said, "I'm Walter Barns. I work for the law firm Britten & Company, out of El Paso. You have a wealthy relative from Chihuahua who bequeathed you a sizable inheritance. May I come in?"

When met with a smile, Susan could never resist smiling back. Taking his card, she said, "Well, yes, I guess so. I didn't know I had any relatives in Mexico. Are you sure you got the right person?"

"Absolutely. You're Susan Torres, right? I drove all the way from El Paso. Is it okay if I come in? I have your inheritance right here with me, but you'll need to sign for it."

For a moment, Susan considered the possibility that this man might be a sexual deviant, but reflecting on his good looks and clean cut appearance she felt embarrassed by the thought and she let him in. She took a few steps over to the coffee table, turned off the evening news and invited him to sit down, then took a seat some distance from him on the same worn brown corduroy sofa.

Walter placed an expensive looking briefcase on the glass coffee table, snapped it open, and took out an embossed GCAL trade diamond certificate and a black felt jewelry box. Opening the box, he held it out for Susan to see a large diamond ring.

"This is a 2.8 karat diamond with excellent clarity, color and cut." Placing the jewelry box in Susan's hand, Walter continued, "This diamond ring was recently purchased from Alkai Jewelers for $40,055. This ring is yours."

Ever cordial, Walter waited with a smile on his lips, letting the information sink in. Instinctively knowing something wasn't right Susan was nevertheless overcome with happiness. She apprehensively held onto the box holding the diamond.

"It's mine?"

"Yes. The ring is yours, and as any jeweler will tell you, it is absolutely authentic. The GCAL certificate to proves it. But you're probably asking yourself, 'why would a rich relative leave me such a valuable diamond ring?' That question takes some explaining.

"You may remember Rebecca Swanson from High School?"

Susan didn't respond. She just stared at Walter with a worried, untrusting expression.

"Well that is not important. What is important is that Rebecca Swanson is filing a case against Thomas Quinn. Like you, Rebecca Swanson didn't have many friends in high school. When Rebecca goes to trial it is important that she has someone she could name as her friend. We want you to be Rebecca Swanson's high school friend."

Feeling her elation dissipate, Susan set the ring down on the coffee table and said, "So I don't have a rich relative?"

Reassuringly, Walter exclaimed, "I'm sorry I had to say that. It's true, the ring didn't come from a rich relative, but this $40,000 diamond ring is still yours. In return all you need to do is to say you were Rebecca's friend when you are subpoenaed to appear in court."

"Isn't that against the law?"

"We're not asking you to say you were her best friend, only her acquaintance. During your senior year, the two of you talked on the phone once in a while. You went to the movies two or three times, and on two occasions you went to Rebecca's home and listened to her Judas Priest album."

"I don't think I said two words to Rebecca Swanson, ever. I can only remember seeing her in the hall; we didn't even have a class together."

With a warm smile Walter continued, "Do you ever feel life has been unfair to you, that folks have been unkind? Well, life's been unkind to Rebecca Swanson, too. She's been kicked around a lot, starting with Thomas Quinn. He took sexual advantage of Rebecca on prom night. There is undeniable DNA proof. After getting her drunk, Thomas Quinn raped her. Now, when she finally has a chance at justice, she needs a friend, a friend she never had. She needs you, Susan."

Susan thought about all the hardship she'd endured and said, "But I don't want any trouble. Rebecca and I did none of those things together."

"You won't have any trouble whatsoever. There are no phone records from fifteen years ago to prove you never talked on the phone. Nobody could say you were not friends. You were just two loosely acquainted friends that went to the movies together a few times, and only you two were present when you visited her at her home. Nothing's going to go wrong. Besides, Susan needs your help. Can you give it to her?"

Susan passed over the jewelry box to Walter, "I'd like to help Rebecca, really I would, but I need time to think about it. I'll call you."

Picking up the box and pressing it into Susan's hand, Walter said softly, "I understand. And what a fine son you have. Marcus is doing very well in school. Miss Evans is such a good teacher. And you're lucky Mr. Branson allows you to have such a flexible schedule to care for him."

Susan felt like she'd been slapped. With fear permeating her voice she said, "I want you to leave now."

With open hands Walter said calmly, "It's not going to be like this. Everything will be perfectly fine. You'll be doing Rebecca a big favor. She needs you. The ring is yours. You found it under the display refrigerator at work. When Marcus is ready to go to college, you'll sell the ring. He'll go to college. You always wanted him to go to college, right?"

Reeling, Susan said, "You're not going to give me a choice, are you?"

Still smiling, Walter said, "You'll never see me again. You were Rebecca's friend for a few months right before and after Christmas. You saw a few movies and talked on the phone. You talked of boys and how you hated school. You went to Rebecca's home twice. Each time you listened to Judas Priest. You never liked her music. You stopped seeing Rebecca after the second time you went to her home. You were too busy taking care of your two younger brothers, Jose and Christopher. Here is one thousand dollars that will more than cover your travel expenses to be at the trial in Los Alamos. Do I have your word that you will help Rebecca?"

With tears welling up in her eyes, Susan said, "I never want to see you again. I'll do it, but don't come back. Get the hell out of here."

With that, Walter rose to leave and Susan slammed the weathered door behind him.

After weeks of preparation, David and his team were confident that Rebecca was ready for trial. David filed the case electronically with the court of Los Alamos, New Mexico, where Thomas Quinn allegedly date-rapped Rebecca Swanson nineteen years ago.

Moments after filing the case, Baker, Smith and Hines leaked the story to the press. Like a bear to honey, the public ate up the sensational news story as fast as the media could spin it. Like so many others, White House Chief of Staff, Larry Baker, believed that false allegations were levied against Thomas Quinn in order to derail the hui movement. As much as Larry Baker disliked the hui movement, he hated false accusations more, especially if the government was involved. Smelling a skunk, Larry Baker put through a call to Lt. Gen. Anthony Wiley, the Director of National Intelligence. "Mr. Wiley, what is the credibility of the Quinn case?"

Wiley shot back, "I have no knowledge of Thomas Quinn's innocence."

"Mr. Wiley, you know what I am alluding to, but I'll spell it out anyway. What is the US government's involvement regarding Thomas Quinn."

"In the country's best interest we have an ongoing investigation of Thomas Quinn. Homeland Security is assigned the task of investigating Quinn's background to confirm whether or not he is associated with any terrorist groups."

Growing more exasperated, Baker exclaimed, "And just what has your investigation discovered about Thomas Quinn as it relates to him allegedly raping a seventeen year old girl on prom night?"

"Nothing."

Unable to restrain himself, Baker let loose: "Look, Mr. Wiley. You can either speak frankly to me or I can have the President give you a call. You know, the man who gave you to your job? Do I need to remind you that your predecessor was forced out of office due to his unwillingness to communicate?"

Receiving orders from anyone, let alone from a civilian, was something Lieutenant General Anthony Wiley abhorred; when he heard the word 'President,' he scowled like he'd just stepped in dog crap.

"We thoroughly investigated Thomas Quinn. Past teachers, relatives, friends, and just about anyone else who ever came in contact with Thomas Quinn were contacted. Anything less would be negligent. We must protect the people of this nation. A man as popular as Thomas Quinn needs to be thoroughly investigated for any potential terrorist activity."

"I will be blunt with you, Mr. Wiley. Did Homeland security bribe Rebecca Swanson to file a case against Thomas Quinn for a crime he did not commit?"

The line went silent, indication that the Director of National Intelligence was upset and was weighing his next words.

"No, I have no knowledge of Homeland Security influencing Rebecca Swanson. She filed the case against Thomas Quinn on her own accord."

"If indeed your intelligence is correct and Homeland Security did not bribe Rebecca Swanson, you need to investigate who did bribe her. Because I, along with most Americans, do not believe that Rebecca Swanson just woke up one day and said, "Today I am going to send Thomas Quinn, a person I have not seen for eighteen years, to jail."

Smug as ever, Wiley retorted, "Homeland Security does not investigate the validity of domestic rape cases. Our sole purpose is to protect the citizens of this country from national and foreign threats."

"Mr. Wiley, you are the conduit between the President and the United States Intelligence Community. With 230,000 personnel at your disposal, any competent man in your position would able to determine if a government employee, took part in persuading Rebecca Swanson to file a case against Thomas Quinn. The President wants your answer within 48 hours."

Feeling sick to his stomach watching the television, Thomas reached out for the ringing telephone in a stupor. He heard Simion's soothing voice.

"Thomas, how are you holding up?"

"This is bullshit! I had one date with Rebecca Swanson. Our only physical contact was when I helped her back to her front door."

"Enough said. I have full confidence in your innocence. Someone powerful is behind this. It's no simple feat to have your DNA sample wind up in a laboratory like CTR. To pull off something like this takes money."

Peter, who was also on the line, chimed in, "Anyone in their right mind can see right through this low-ball attempt to derail the hui movement. Someone powerful wants to create a monster out of you. We knew something like this could happen. But don't worry. We'll fight this frivolous law suit tooth and nail."

"Thomas, we know you are going through a lot, but we'll get through this together." Simion said reassuringly. "We'll find out who put Rebecca

Swanson up to this."

With real concern in his voice, Thomas stammered, "I feel like the walls are folding in on me. Can't the judge simply throw the case out?"

Simion sighed and said, "Not according to William Emmings, your defense lawyer. Whenever DNA is submitted as evidence the courts have no recourse but to hold a trial. Due to their difficulty to prove, date-rape cases are tried in a courtroom. Since Baker, Smith and Hines filed the case, you can be assured they have enough evidence to convince a judge that the case is worthy of a trial."

Thomas asked, "Can't we disprove their evidence before it has a chance to go trial?"

"We'll do everything we can, including getting statements from everyone you came in contact with on prom night, but somebody, big business, the government, or a combination of both, is behind this. You need to prepare yourself mentally for this case to go to trial."

"How has this affected the movement?"

"Opinion polls show a drop in support," Peter said. "On top of claiming that you are a liberal communist, Bates is now painting you as a sexual deviant. It's so much easier for the general public to hate than to respect. Unconsciously, we project our own inner darkness onto an external villain. We will aggressively in counter his ranting, but there is no denying that a large number of us love to hate a bad guy, and for the time being, you are that bag guy.

"That's the bad news. The good news is that once you are vindicated, public opinion will swing back heavily in your favor. Whoever is backing Rebecca Swanson is playing a dangerous game. Once you are proven innocent, the tide will turn so swiftly in your favor, the government will be in danger of being toppled."

Shocked by the magnitude of what was transpiring, Thomas asked, "What? You mean an actual overthrow of the government?"

"Faith is the mortar that holds a nation together: faith that your government is working in your best interest, faith that you can trust those in power. Once that faith is broken, distrust leads to revolt."

"I just want my life back."

"That is exactly what we want as well," said Simion. "A warrant will be issued for your arrest sometime today, but the chances that a judge will confine you are slim to none. William Emmings will be there to ensure that doesn't happen."

The following morning when the door bell ring at 7 AM, Thomas immediately envisioned a black and white patrol car parked out front with its lights flashing. Stiff from the sleepless night, Thomas willed himself to the front door. With a pounding heart he opened it and saw a handsome middle-aged man wearing a sleek black lamb's wool overcoat and sporting a stunning Quindici neck tie who smiled confidently when he saw Thomas.

"William Emmings."

Thomas felt shocked to find this richly dressed man on his doorstep instead of a couple of stern cops. It was like having cold water splashed on his face.

"Thomas Quinn, pleased to meet you."

Thomas felt so relieved. The sick feeling of being hauled off to jail was at least, for the time being, evaded. Thomas felt lightheaded as he reached out to shake Emmings' hand. Emmings' handshake was so strong it made Thomas flinch. Jolted to consciousness, Thomas was not so sure how much he liked this Emmings.

"Time to get showered and dressed. We're headed to the court to preempt the warrant coming your way," said Emmings as he brushed past Thomas and strolled into the foyer.

Uninvited, Emmings continued walking into the living room and made himself comfortable. Now wide awake, Thomas reconfirmed his first impression of Emmings. Ignoring Emmings, Thomas ran back to the bedroom and jumped up on the large pear-wood French provincial bed where Jackie still lay. Elated by the fact that he was not being hauled off to jail, Thomas laughed, "We are saved! The cavalry has arrived!"

Pecking Jackie on the cheek, he scrambled off the bed and headed for the bathroom, calling mockingly over his shoulder, "We have been summoned to get showered and dressed!"

Appearing in Judge Becket's chamber with Thomas in tow, Emmings persuaded the judge to conduct an informal arraignment that afternoon before a warrant could be served.

Emmings prepped Thomas and Jackie on what to expect at a posh Italian bistro over Caesar salads with smoked salmon, filling them in on the overall strategy. Picking up the tab, Emmings took the lead back to the courthouse where they waited for the proceedings to begin.

When the courtroom was nearly filled, Emmings nudged Thomas to turn around and there she was. For the first time in 19 years, Thomas Quinn set eyes on Rebecca Swanson, walking gracefully alongside David Mulland, who guided her to the prosecution table on the right.

After a lifetime of alcohol abuse, Rebecca's transformation was miraculous. Looking like a CEO, Rebecca wore a Boucle Ruffle beige suit, back-seam nylons and two inch heels. Her previously glassy-eyed, downward gaze and unsteady gait had been replaced with an easy going demeanor and a confident stride.

With chin up and eyes forward, Rebecca took no notice of Thomas as she settled into the chair held out for her by Mulland.

Judge Becket entered the chambers; everyone stood with an unceremonious scraping of chairs and sat immediately back down. Scanning the crowd, the judge started the proceedings.

"It is blatantly obvious to all that what's on trial here goes far beyond what allegedly occurred 19 years ago. I cannot emphasize enough that the prosecution must have complete confidence as to the validity of their case."

David Mulland stood and said, "We do, Your Honor."

Looking beyond the reading glasses on the tip of his nose, Judge Becket barked,

"I did not intend to elicit a reply from the prosecution." Calming some, he continued, "I am, however, hereby informing the prosecution that should this case be proven frivolous, the offenders will be punished to the fullest extent of the law. The preliminary hearing will take place seven days from today. Bail is set at $10."

David Mulland bolted up like he were yanked to his feet by a giant magnet and said, "The prosecution requests that bail be set higher. Ten dollars hardly sends the right message for a crime as grievous as rape."

Judge Becket stonily replied, "Your request has been duly noted and refused. Thomas Quinn can hardly be considered a flight risk. Besides being one of the most recognizable faces on the planet, there is no place for him to hide." Hitting his well worn mallet against its base, Becket ended any further objections and said, "This court is adjourned."

The reporters waiting outside the court house badgered Thomas with questions. Not directly addressing any of them, Thomas made a brief statement with heartfelt conviction.

"Today I was accused of a crime I did not commit. This trial is an attempt to discredit me in order to slow down the hui movement. Let me tell you right now: false allegations will not hinder our movement. Huinomics is destined to be an integral part of our lives. We will prevail."

Turning from the ensuing barrage of questions, Thomas and Jackie made their way to Emmings' limo waiting outside. On the drive back, Emmings did his best to convince them that their chances were good, but his words did little to quell their ever-growing fear that Thomas might end up in prison.

Still licking his wounds the following morning, Thomas was surprised to see Jackie run to his office clutching a cell phone. "Martin Kimball is on the line. He wants you to visit him."

Failing to connect the name Martin Kimball with Kimball Industries, the second largest privately owned business in America, Thomas looked up, squinting his eyes, and said, "Who?"

"Martin Kimball, of Kimball Industries? You know, one of the largest companies in America? That Martin Kimball."

The lights blinked on for Thomas as he accepted the phone.

"Thomas Quinn."

A deep scratchy voice came over the line: "Looks like you're in a bit of a pickle."

Thomas forced a smile and said, "Who knows what stories they will concoct next."

"You know you are important when you begin to have enemies. Listen, how would you like to have lunch with me tomorrow? I can have my Gulfwing waiting for you in the morning."

Thomas thought how ironic it was, being flown around in private jets when less than a year ago he refused to own a cell phone. Knowing that opportunities like this don't come along every day, Thomas replied, "I would be happy to, Mr. Kimball."

"Please call me Martin, and bring that pretty wife of yours."

Xavier Lamont's speech did not fall on deaf ears; at least not on totally deaf ears. Martin Kimball was only half deaf. Being 78 years old, his doctors told him that his hearing loss was due to old age. Martin knew better. After years of hearing what he did not like to listen to Martin simply choose not to hear. Secretly Martin knew his hearing loss was an inner choice brought on by disgust. Decades of hearing blood sucking whiners begging for cash sickened Martin to such an extent that he physically distorted his body not to hear their cries.

All his life Martin fought to be free. As a young boy Martin's father took in his older brother's family into their small cramped brown stone apartment in southwest Chicago. He never lost the image of his uncle: a broken man who day after day sat on the apartment front steps holding a burning cigarette between two fingers tarred brownish-yellow like his teeth.

As a young boy Martin avoided his uncle. Everything about him was repulsive, from his broken lifeless eyes to his sickly scowling face.

At the age of ten Martin experienced an unforgettable feeling of euphoria when he earned his first dollar from selling newspapers on a corner. After a month Martin saved what seemed to be a fortune for a young boy who had so little. Martin's new found wealth possessed him. He was constantly thinking of all the things he could buy. After relentless pondering the one item that Martin wanted above all others was a watch.

Although not as costly as Martin's father's watch that he strapped on each morning before heading out to the furniture factory, it was his watch that he purchased with his own money. Martin admired its bright silver casing and black leather strap.

After a year passed you could barely see the hands on Martin's watch. With the multitude of scratches it was hard to believe that the watch was only a year old. Although at first Martin did everything in his power to keep the watch looking new Martin grew to like the scratches. To him the scratches were a testament to how hard he worked. Waking up at three-thirty Martin delivered one hundred and seventy eight papers every morning. Any other free time after school Martin spent working at construction sites. At thirteen Martin worked as hard as any man at a job site.

By the time Martin was fifteen, Martin focused all of his effort in construction. Like stacking row upon row of bricks to build a wall, Martin stacked away money. As Martin's bank account grew, so did his lust for the freedom it promised. At eighteen Martin had his own crew, and by twenty Martin found himself in southern California riding the 1950's building bonanza. For more than a decade Martin bulldozed orange orchards in small townships across the valleys, making him one of the wealthiest men in California.

Money was all that mattered to Martin. Using his already vast fortune, he purchased one of the nation's largest paper mills. Steadfast to his mandate of always having complete control, Martin never considered having one of his companies go public.

Not long after acquiring the paper mill, he bought two large copper mines in southern Arizona. A steel mill, a synthetic fiber mill and a carpet mill rounded out his acquisitions. Due to his diligence and rare business sense, Martin made them all extremely successful, until Kimball industries employed 68,000 workers with net revenues over ten billion dollars.

Tragically, Martin was spending his twilight years in bitterness. His seven children, along with his eleven grand children, were constantly jockeying to get a piece of his fortune. Opulent leisure and excessive gluttony sent Martin's three wives to an early grave. The allowances he gave his children were never enough. Martin was relentless in ridiculing his offspring. Ever since they were little, he chastised them: "If I had half the opportunities you have, I would have built an empire one thousand times bigger than the one I have now."

Whenever one of them found an opportunity to approach him with smothering words of kindness, he treated them like they were intentionally trying to infect him with bubonic plague. He no more wanted to pass on his fortune to his greedy, lazy offspring than he wanted to chop off his hand.

Martin disdained people who were not willing to work hard to get ahead. He believed work was the saving grace that instilled pride and purpose in humanity. Martin believed that without labor that resulted in something that could be quantitatively measured, one's life had no purpose.

Martin backed this idealism by only doing business with American firms. Martin ranted openly, "I'll be dammed if I'll support any other economy over ours. There's nothing free about Free Trade. Free Trade doesn't exist in a world where communist governments own the factories and sell their products below market value to starve out the competition and then jack up their prices once they established a monopoly."

Martin's bile toward free trade centered on China's domination of the steel industry. Diabolically, China's government-owned steel mills operated for decades at a loss to squeeze out the competition by selling steel below market prices. The only way Martin's steel mills survived was to support them with revenues from his other industries. Starving out the bulk of American steel mills, China went on to purchase America's major iron ore mines, effectively colonizing the American steel industry.

Martin believed America turned its back on the working man. In his younger years it was difficult to find a product that was not made in America. Blaming the systematic dismantling of tariffs, the US market was flooded with a multitude of cheap imports sold by a handful big box retailers.

Martin saw huinomics as a way to get back to the days when men and women could take pride in honest work. Huinomics represented a way in which Kimball Industries could reclaim the steel industry. Most of all Martin wanted to see America become the industrialized nation it once was.

Taking in the view of the Golden Gate Bridge to the left of two massive glass entry doors, Thomas couldn't help thinking how incongruent this mansion was to the principles of huinomics.

Answering the door himself, Martin said with warmth: "I'm so happy to see that you brought that lovely wife of yours!" Addressing Jackie, he said fondly, "You must share with me all your secrets. I want to know what makes your husband tick."

Martin guided them into the study overlooking the bay. Martin addressed Thomas as if he was interviewing a prize fighter, "You know that I've been in communication with Simion Ruzart, Phillip Brownstein and Cliff Higgins, all of whom have given you high marks. But before I consider hitching my wagon to yours, I need to know you are, Thomas Quinn."

Taken aback by both the bluntness and sincerity of Martin's words, Thomas couldn't help but follow his lead with honesty: "Recently I have been doing so many interviews, I don't know if even I know who I am anymore."

A smile came over Martin's wizened face.

"Fair enough. I want to let you know that whatever we discuss today is between you and I, so don't bullshit me. You've got nothing to gain. I can smell a stinking pile of shit a mile away. Don't try to influence me. Just give it to me straight: do you honestly believe that man can survive without money?"

"Money is based on an abstract concept of trust, yet we use it to obtain tangible products. Over millennia, the value of every currency has fluctuated, based on trust, and trust is a very fragile thing. A far more concrete way of placing a value to an object is to price it as a length of time. Time has a finite value. After all, the time needed to produce a good or service is far more representative of money than trust is."

"But one man's time is significantly more valuable than another's. You can't tell me that my time is worth the same as the men who clean my factory floors."

"There are deep-rooted archetypes in our unconscious minds ascribing the hierarchy among people. We intrinsically believe kings, queens, dukes and duchess deserve more wealth than commoners based simply on their birth status. Your janitors accept that you get more money for your time just as peasants accepted they deserved less than a duke.

"In reality, the time your janitor has is just as valuable as yours. The true delineating factor between the two is the level of satisfaction a CEO obtains in being the controlling force over a company compared to a janitor who cleans the floors. You go home at night with the satisfaction that you enabled the company to remain competitive, while the janitor goes home knowing that he helped keep the company clean. These two jobs represent two very different levels of satisfaction, but the time you have to live on this planet is just as valuable as the janitor's."

"My time is worth more than a janitor's!"

"Oh really? If both you and your janitor are lying in a hospital bed looking at death coming your way, both of you will place the same value on time."

"You cannot convince me that there is a difference in the value of the type of work preformed."

"To say that I deserve more money because I am better at something is the same as saying you are better than that person. If you earn a million times more than another person, does that make you a million times better than that person?"

"That all sounds very nice, but in reality my managers will not want to get paid the same amount as my janitors."

"In truth we all want more than anyone else. We all want to be fabulously wealthy with the freedom to buy anything and do anything our hearts desire."

"Now that is something I can relate to. People are basically selfish."

"But in reality, the planet simply does not have enough resources to enable all men to live as kings. But we do have enough for all of us to live comfortably and to enrich our lives. From a practical standpoint, your managers will elect to work in a hui because they will be better off.

"You know, when we first opened Vorbine there was real concern that engineers and other highly educated personnel would not be attracted to the hui lifestyle, but we received nearly as many technical applicants as blue collar applicants. That should tell you something about what people really value. Society is changing."

Martin's hard expression softened, "Vorbine is a great planned experiment. Simion Ruzart built a dream city for the workers of Vorbine; no wonder you got so many people to apply. But what you're asking of my employees is completely different. You are asking a lot with your re-urbanization program."

It was clear Martin had done his homework. Re-urbanization was one of huinomic's later phases.

"Without re-urbanization, huinomics will be confined to a few companies like Vorbine building their own housing from the ground up. Although Vorbine is a model for green construction, the concept of using additional resources to construct new housing goes against the conservation principles of huinomics. The only way huinomics can exist on a large scale is by converting existing housing into hui dwelling units."

"In simplistic terms, you want Kimball industries to buy existing employee homes and convert them into duplexes. We will assume the employee's home loan and pay the employee for any equity in the home over a period of time. Correct so far?"

"Yes."

"Well, as simple as it sounds, I don't think you understand the average employee at Kimball Industries. Most of my employees make less than thirty thousand a year, so it shouldn't surprise you that only about half actually own their homes. That would mean Kimball industries would have to buy existing homes and convert them into duplexes for the employees who rent. Do you realize just how many homes you're talking about?"

"Kimball industries will be the largest owner of single family homes in America. During the first eighteen months, Kimball will need to utilize the bulk of its eight billion dollars in annual net review to buy homes for its employees. After this re-urbanization process, Kimball will be ready to expand its industries."

"That is an extraordinarily large amount of money. Sums that large are usually diverted into new acquisitions. That's how we grow!"

"Martin, converting your corporations into huis will forever change the economic landscape of America. Extraordinary sacrifices have extraordinary results."

"That is the question. The question we ask ourselves today. Is the sacrifice worth it? Of course you do realize that your re-urbanization conflicts with urban zoning laws."

"There is no question that there'll be a great deal of opposition to Kimball converting into a hui corporation, starting with zoning laws. There is also no question that each barrier can be overcome as well."

"You can't convince me that management will want to give up their large homes to live in a duplex."

"I never claimed that huinomics is for everyone. It is likely that your top managers who have paid off 80% or more of their mortgage will not want to participate in the residential buy-back program. But how many of your 68,000 employees are in this position? Statistically, you're looking at 87% of your work force embracing this new housing opportunity. As for the wealthiest 13% remaining, you will have thousands of qualified applicants willing to replace them, just like Vorbine."

Martin pondered the ramifications of what he had heard until Thomas broke the silence.

"If you don't mind my asking, what is your motivation to convert to a hui corporation?"

"For the better part of my life I envisioned a day when I could give my children everything I never had. As a young boy, my bed was a mat on a cold kitchen floor.

"Sometimes, when you think you're doing what's right, it backfires right in your face. My children see me like their drug dealer, and the drug they so desperately crave is money. Instead of helping my family, my generosity has alienated me from my children. This causes me immeasurable pain and suffering.

"Now I wonder, if I give away my fortune to my employees, will I once again inflect immeasurable pain and suffering?"

"There will be huge hurdles to overcome. But, I'm afraid we have only two choices. We can continue on our present course and watch the destruction of our atmosphere along with the final depletion of our natural resources, that will no doubt bring man kind to its knees with the inevitable wars that will take place as the remaining ones among us fight over what is left, or we can evolve working and sharing the earth's resources as a group."

Martin looked deep into Thomas's eyes searching for truth before slowly hoisting himself out to stand by the bay window. For some time he stood there watching. There was more than one sailboat out planning over the whitecaps. Breaking the silence Martin said, "That is the biggest ultimatum I have ever heard. Convert or die." Still looking out onto the bay Martin continued saying, "I have my doubts. I wonder if you or anyone else really knows what will happen with this new group economy of yours. I do know one thing though, a man of my age doesn't have much time. Like Getty I could open up some damn museum…hell, I could open up dozens. But throwing it away is not me."

Turning to face Thomas and Jackie, Martin said, "I may go down in history as the old fool who hitched his wagon to a dreamer, or maybe, just maybe, you are right and I will be remembered in a more favorable light. In either case, at least I will be remembered."

As if he could stand no more, Martin got up and slowly walking away said, "We will be in touch."

Chapter 10

Although being the Vice Deputy of Homeland Security gave Stephen Alerkson command over hundreds of people, he was feeling weak in the knees as he walked down the bright hallway to the Director of National Intelligence's office. Even with years of espionage fieldwork under his belt, Stephen was not quite up to being interrogated by the Director.

Desperately trying to play it cool, Stephan adopted a nervous smile as he announced his arrival to the Director's secretary. In an effort to look dignified, Stephan stuck his tongue under his lower lip that made him look like he was chewing a wad of tobacco. Too self-absorbed to recognize just how ridiculous he looked, the secretary glanced over at two chairs against the wall and said, "I will inform the Director of your arrival. Take a seat."

Obediently taking a seat, Stephan thought the secretary's thin straight black hair, pulled taught against her scalp, complemented her cold demeanor.

After sitting an agonizing eighteen minutes, the secretary looked away from her screen just long enough to say, "The Director will see you now," and resumed her key-pounding. Entering his office, Alerkson addressed the Director using his military title: "Lieutenant General Anthony Wiley, pleased to finally meet you in person."

Wiley could not resist smiling slightly as he looked Alerkson up and down before he said, "As you have no doubt surmised, this is not a social visit." Gesturing to the one of the chairs positioned in front of his desk, he said, "Take a seat."

Turning to his phone, he hit the intercom and said, "Ms. Nelson, see that we are not disturbed."

The secretary, whose figure demanded the attention of most men, appeared briefly to close the double doors. Alerkson, feeling like he'd been trapped in a dark slimy pit, said, "This meeting would be more productive if I was given an idea as to why it is being held."

Wiley took his time before answering. Getting up slowly, he walked around to the front of his desk and rested his massive ass on one corner.

Alerkson was now eye-level with Wiley's crotch.

Leaning back with repulsion, Alerkson ground his teeth so hard he actually tasted something metallic. With his hands folded across his massive chest, Wiley looked down on Alerkson and with a cold voice said, "Look here, Alerkson. Why don't you just cut the crap and tell me how deep you're in with Senator Bates."

Alerkson felt he'd been punched in the kidneys. How could Wiley possibly know about his relationship with Bates? Alerkson's spook instincts kicked in and he said, "I don't know who you got your intel from, but its crap."

Secretly Wiley often thought his poker skills was as much a part of his rise to power as his West Point education. Sensing an opportunity Wiley continued, "Bates led us to you. At first his rhetoric was just like all the rest, but when he really began to attack Thomas Quinn our psycho-analytic team, gave an 80% probability that his renewed confidence reflected he had something on Quinn. We didn't know what, but we knew how to find out."

Placing his hands on the desk to help support his massive ass Wiley continued, "You know politics makes it so easy. Since every person is put into power by a network of other people, all you need to do is trace back who Bates helped get into power. Bates got you in power, in turn, you used your people to get to Rebecca Swanson to cut a deal. You are going to tell me who made the contact with Rebecca Swanson. We know a deal was cut."

Alerkson felt a wave of heat flowing over his body. If he simply stood up and left he was sure to be investigated and perhaps imprisoned. The root of Alerkson's fear did not come from within his department, but from Baker, Smith and Hines. There is a hundred ways a spook could have gotten someone at the firm to talk. Believing that Wiley knew Baker, Smith and Hines, was behind the money transfer Alerkson stammered, "Thomas Quinn is a threat to national security."

Wiley smiled inwardly, knowing that his bluff had worked.

"We all hate the son of a bitch. I'm not condemning you wanting to take Quinn down, but you must let me know who you sent." Leaning over so Alerkson could actually feel his breathe, Wiley said, "You don't want me to get tough with you, now who did you send to set up a deal with Rebecca Swanson."

Alerkson knew the power Wiley mastered. With a phone call he could have his hounds on Alerkson and his immediate subordinates. With that much heat, they would be sure to discover James Blake. If that were to happen, the shier number of people who knew of the set-up would force the pendulum to crash right into himself. Fearful for his own well being Alerkson looked to the side saying, "Gilbert Maxwel may of over stepped the boundary in directing James Blake to persuade Rebecca Swanson, but the money came from Baker, Smith and Hines."

With that Wiley felt the pressure roll of his back. Now that he had a recorded admission, even though it was an illegal recording, he was clear of any blame in the covert affair so he went in for the kill.

"We know the money came from the law firm. But it was James Blake who bribed Rebecca Swanson, wasn't it?"

Wondering who the hell at Baker, Smith and Hines Wiley got to, Alerkson desperately tried to save his own skin. Distancing himself Alerkson continued, "It wasn't supposed to go down like it did. Rebecca Swanson was to be persuaded to go to Baker, Smith and Hines to learn of the payoff. James Blake was not supposed to offer a bribe."

Feeling light as a bird, Wiley shifted his massive ass off the desk, "How many of our people know about this mess?"

"On our side of the fence? Just Gilbert Maxwell and James Blake."

"Where is James Blake now?"

Feeling as if he wanted to go far far away for a very long time Alkerson looked down saying, "He was reassigned to a mission in Kabul." With a distant remorsefulness in his voice he said, "He died serving his country.

Walking away towards the window, Wiley suddenly turned on Alerkson and slammed his massive hands down on his desk. "To advance your career, you took the life of an innocent man and put the country at risk. Do you have any idea what would happen if the public caught wind of this fool's game you're playing?"

"This isn't about me. Risks were weighed. Thomas Quinn must be stopped."

"When peons like you begin to make game-changing decisions, you put the entire country at risk. You are a selfish, self serving moron whose greed has endangered the stability of the country."

With a blank look on his face, Alerkson sat looking past Wiley's bulk into space.

"You better hope to hell this doesn't leak. If it does, an avalanche of shit will bury you."

Feeling as though an airtight lid had just been pulled over the pit he was in, Stephen Alerkson blindly got up and walked to the door.

When the President of the United States defers a call from the Director of National Intelligence to the White House Chief of Staff, the message is obvious: the Director is in trouble.

Picking up the phone, Larry Baker wasted no time: "What have you discovered, Mr. Wiley?"

The Director of National Intelligence didn't like most people, but he truly despised anyone who didn't call him by his full title: Lieutenant General Anthony Wiley. Tight lipped, Wiley exclaimed, "One of our Homeland Security agents, James Blake, may have overstepped his boundary by informing Rebecca Swanson that the hui movement is bad for America."

"What exactly transpired between Blake and Swanson?"

"In the spirit of preserving American values, James Blake informed Rebecca Swanson that huinomics is a destructive force and that could destroy the American economy."

"What else transpired between the two?"

"James Blake overstepped his boundary of involvement. He told Rebecca Swanson that, in support of the American way of life, she should disclose any past transgressions they may have had."

"Like rape, for instance?"

With a conviction that could have fooled a lie detector, Wiley said, "James Blake had no involvement in persuading Rebecca Swanson to file a case against Thomas Quinn." Knowing his best option was to admit the truth only when absolutely necessary, Wiley had no dilemma about lying.

"So, you want me to believe that Rebecca Swanson, a clerk at a truck stop in Quartzite Arizona, decided to contact one of the nation's leading law firms?"

"There are innumerable ways Rebecca Swanson could have decided to contact the law firm of Baker, Smith and Hines, but neither James Blake nor anyone we know persuaded Rebecca Swanson to be represented by Baker, Smith and Hines."

"I hope to God you're telling the truth. If it turns out that you or any of the hundreds of thousands of people making up the US intelligence community is lying about this, we'll have a lot more to worry about than terrorists. If the US government is behind the framing of Thomas Quinn, this country will unravel at the seams. Where is this James Blake?"

"James Blake was killed on assignment in Kabul."

Holding back his anger, Baker simply said, "Evil begets evil, Lieutenant. You better pray facts don't emerge supporting a different version of this matter."

Back in Taos, Thomas busied himself with the grim task of preparing for the trial when he received a call from Simion Ruzart.

"I know you haven't heard yet, so I'll be the first to tell you. P&G announced they are going to convert to a hui corporation under a four year plan."

Thomas was stunned. First Kimball Industries, now P&G. Overwhelmed, Thomas said, "Its beginning. We need to prepare a statement."

"Not so fast. P&G's announcement tanked the stock market. In eight minutes the market lost 1200 points. The circuit breaker kicked in, shutting the markets down. God only knows what will happen when it starts back up."

One hand clasping his wrist behind his back, President Joseph Dial stood looking out of the tall Oval Office window. Countless times he stood at this same spot lost in deep thought. But today was different. This morning, the president felt the weight of the world pressing down on his shoulders. Today will be recorded as the day the stock market lost more money than any other day.

For the first time since assuming office, President Dial felt his control slipping. Breaking Dial's hypnotic state, the voice of the Chairman of the Federal Reserve, Ross Hamilton, barked out from the President's speaker phone.

"President Dial? Hamilton here. We must keep the markets closed over the weekend to stem the pressure of this panic sell-off."

Dial shot back, "So what you are telling me is that the circuit breakers are not working?"

Hamilton's felt his stomach seize up like he was being squeezed by a gorilla. Taking a deep breath he said, "This morning, between 10:28 and 10:36, the market lost 1200 points, triggering the first circuit breaker, which halted trading for one hour. When the market went back on-line an hour later, the market lost 1200 points in less than two minutes, resulting in the second circuit breaker shut down for two hours. The third and final circuit breaker shut down occurred when the market lost another 1200 points in 14 seconds."

Unrestrained by his usual self-control, Dial hissed back, "That's nearly a thirty percent drop. My God. And just what do you attribute this economic catastrophe to? P&G's announcement? What difference could it make if one company converts into a hui? You can't convince me that one company's conversion could create a stock market crash of this magnitude."

"P&G set off an avalanche of panic that our modern markets simply can't withstand."

"So you're writing off the single largest stock loss in history as a black swan event? That story may of worked with the Flash Crash of 2:45, but not this one! This is a game-changer and you know it."

Hamilton grimaced as his stomach gave him yet another reminder that there will be hell to pay. "When 70% of the market is being controlled by computer programs trading in nanoseconds, there is very little we can do other than pull the plug. There's no law against algorithmic trading. For the past five years, three out of four stock transactions were performed by computers. For better or worse, today's stock market is controlled by computers."

"The nation is waiting to find out why their life savings just disappeared. Do you expect me to tell them that it's all because of a computer glitch?"

"It's not so simple. Some years ago, high frequency trading used a matrix of algorithms that bought and sold stock based only on price. Today's algorithms use artificial intelligence to analyze breaking news reports to make buy and sell decisions faster than a human can click a mouse."

With growing frustration, Dial stated, "Stock prices dropped across the board, not just P&G's."

"At this time I can only speculate, but it would appear that the artificial intelligence stock algorithms interpreted the meaning behind P&G's hui conversion and concluded that domination of the market place by huinomics is inevitable, rendering all stocks worthless."

The line seemed to go dead. Thinking maybe the line had actually been cut, after several moments Hamilton asked, "Mr. President?"

In a distant voice the president asked, "What exactly are you saying?"

"With the release of P&G's announcement the artificial intelligence programs came to the conclusion that the competitive advantage of huinomics will cause existing shares of stock issued by all corporations to be of no value in the future and proceeded to sell off everything. The only buys today came from people."

"So, today's crash could have been avoided if these artificial intelligence stock algorithms were not functioning?"

"In a word, yes. The overriding problem, Mr. President, is that no one knows if the artificial intelligence trading programs are correct. Huinomics may be the mechanism that will be the end of our current economy, including stock ownership."

"In less than two hours I need to address the American public to let them know exactly what caused today's sell-off and what we're doing to fix the problem. Do you really expect me to go before the American public and tell them that they lost their life savings because humans no longer have control of the stock market?"

"In the past, people invested in a company because they believed in its ability to generate wealth. Today's stock market is vastly different. Since the crash of 2009, the number of billionaires skyrocketed, largely because a select few powerful investors are using advanced artificial intelligent computer algorithms to buy and sell vast sums of stock in nanoseconds. The average hold time of a stock is not measured in years, or even months, but rather in seconds; twenty-two seconds, to be exact. Successfully predicting if a stock is going to increase or decrease in value is making a few already very rich people obscenely wealthy."

"My God, why did the SEC allow this type of trading to take place? Whatever happened to buying stocks based on sound investing?"

"Everyone sings the praises of the economy when the stock market goes up. You may recall your predecessor was gloating about the highest home ownership percentage in history just before the crash. Well, we have a similar problem now. What we need to do is what should have been done a long time ago: prohibit computer-controlled trading in the stock market."

"That's it? The stock market lost almost three trillion dollars in a matter of minutes because controls are lax?"

"That is only half the equation. We must get to the root of what drove the market down in the first place. Huinomics is the underlying problem. If enough corporations convert into hui corporations, there will not be enough tax revenue to keep the government afloat. This is why legislation must be passed to prohibit the formation of hui corporations."

As if the President was lost for words Hamilton continued, "As you know Senator Bates is gaining ground in prohibiting the formation of hui corporations based on hui employees not paying taxes. Retaliating, Thomas Quinn has required hui corporations to have their employees receive a minimum wage so they can pay federal and state taxes. This 'pay' is for tax purposes only, as the funds are automatically retransferred back to the hui. What hurts us is since minimum wages are set just above the poverty level, there is hardly any taxes levied."

Politically speaking, Dial always knew huinomics would bury him. While polls reported overwhelming support for hui corporations, big business vehemently opposed hui corporations. It's a political Catch 22.

"Mr. Hamilton I do not have the time to canvas advisers to make the best decision. Have you examined ramifications? Do you realize that the bulk of Americans support huinomics? If we begin to blame huinomics for the stock crash, we could be adding fuel to the flames. What happens if this fear spills over into the banks?"

"Fear is our biggest enemy. We must restore market confidence to the millions of Americans who have their retirement money invested in the stock market."

"Do you remember the last time a president tried to convince America to keep faith in the stock market? The words of the president fall on deaf ears when people believe their life savings will be completely gone if they don't sell what little they have left."

"Exactly. We must convince the American public that it is logical to have faith in the market based on our actions, not on our rhetoric. We have allowed the stock market to become a massive feeding ground for the wealthy. The monetary gain of the average American investing in the market is minuscule compared to those who create volatility in the market.

"Enforcing fundamental investment principles on the wealthy stock barons controlling the market will not be easy."

"The question is, will ending algorithmic trading stop the panic?"

"Honestly it is too difficult to predict what will happen. The only thing we do know for sure is that if you honestly inform the American public about the events that took place and out line the steps the government is taking to prevent the recurrence of such events, it will help bring confidence back to the market."

"God, let's hope so. If we don't get some stability in the markets, who knows where this will lead? My speech writers will call you as soon as we are off the phone. I don't want them going beyond what we discussed."

Hanging up, Dial felt incredibly heavy. Shuffling over to the sofa, he allowed himself a moment to put his legs up and close his eyes. He felt his presidential power draining from him as the forces he faced grew ever more uncontrollable. Fully aware that the day's events would most likely result in destroying any re-election hopes he had, Dial pushed aside his fear, anxiety and self pity, and forced his mind to go blank.

In his customary manor, Bates slammed his fist on his silver inlaid mahogany desk and barked at Max Harvey.

"Christ. Did you see that? Even the President of the United States is following my lead to outlaw huinomics. My God, man, if I'd listened to you I'd be at the back of the pack instead of leading it!"

True to form, Max Harvey ignored Bates's badgering and said, "The first horse out of the gate does not always win the race. It takes a lot more than the President asking for legislation to curtail huinomics to stop its power. Your insistence on being the most vocal about abolishing hui corporations has cost you dearly in the polls. "

"I'm gaining support in both houses. Mark my words, before this is over the constitution will be amended to prohibit the formation of hui corporations. Wait and see. When all is said and done, I will be the one standing in the Winner Circle. Now that Thomas Quinn is going down, it is only a matter of time.

"By the way, how are the court proceedings going?"

Max leaned in and said, "I thought we agreed that no such discussions would ever take place."

Self-assured as ever, Bates smiled and, knowing full well it would infuriate Max, said, "You know that little contribution from me and my friends will never be traced back to us. What are you so worried about?"

Physically biting the inside of his lip, Max thought, "I'm not worried about what happens to you, you fat bastard, it's me I'm worried about." Controlling his rage, Max simply stated, "David Mulland has begun the jury selection."

Ignoring the President's speech, the following morning US traders joined the rest of the world, stampeding a sell-off in the Asian markets. Within ten minutes of Tokyo's opening bell, Shanghai and Hong Kong markets were forced to close their doors. Trillions were lost in a matter of minutes. Seeing the writing on the wall, Europe simply refused to open its markets.

Less than three hours after the Shanghai market closed, China's premier, Li Ping, called President Joseph Dial. Speaking through an interpreter, Li Ping exclaimed, "It is with much regret that I am calling you today. As you realize, the Asian markets, and now the European markets, have been forced to close, bringing financial instability once again to the world. We have grave concerns as to the consequences of this widespread economic turmoil."

"We share your concerns, Premier Li Ping, and we are taking the necessary steps to curtail the damage inflicted on global markets."

"We fear that once again your inability to enact economic policy to prevent such catastrophes is self evident. Just as America's refusal to establish prudent banking and financial laws lead to the great recession, today the world is faced with economic calamity due to your country's lack of control."

"While it may be politically viable for you to blame this economic problem on the United States, it is not actually true. Many of the same algorithms that crashed the US market are used in Asia. Governments did not create these market algorithms; people created them. These market algorithms are an integral part of all major global trading, including China's. You can't expect the world to believe that the crash was solely due to American economic policy."

"You're neglecting to state the true cause of the sell off deeply troubles me. We both know huinomics caused the panic sell off."

"Premier Li Ping, once again I must emphasize that this problem is not based on one company's decision about how to pay its employees. America safeguards the freedom of its citizens; our economic policy regarding huinomics is accordingly confined to taxation."

"Freedom is a loosely defined term. Because of your 'freedom,' the freedom of the people of China is being threatened. Just as a father will protect his family, the Chinese government will do whatever is necessary to protect its people."

"What exactly are you saying, Premier Li Ping?"

"These are turbulent times. Should economic conditions worsen, we must take steps to protect the welfare of our citizens." Zhen paused for emphasis before he continued. "If forced, we will use our financial reserves to safeguard our economy."

This time it was Dial's turn to take a deep breath and focus. With over a trillion dollars of US treasury bills in their coffers, China had their finger on the button of an economic atom bomb. In a measured cadence, President Dial responded, "The United States and China have enjoyed a peaceful relationship for more than forty years. It would be unforgivable for one of us to sever this relationship."

"President Dial, we have no intention of severing our mutually beneficial relationship. However, my economists predict that China could be facing unemployment levels of 15% if this remains an uncontrollable situation. I am sure you realize the gravity of having 195 million unemployed workers to feed? We will do whatever possible to aid the US economy; however, I called you today so you will understand our position. If we have no choice, we will use our cash reserves to preserve the stability of our nation."

"Neither of our two great nations wants economic warfare, but if it should come to pass, the resiliency and ingenuity of the American public will prevail."

"President Dial, my call is only informative. China has every intention of continuing our economic cooperation. Accordingly, we will do whatever we can to prevent using our financial reserves to survive this new economic obstacle."

Hanging up the phone, President Dial settled himself in his chair, thinking, "If it's a fight they want, it's a fight they'll get."

Filled with enthusiasm, President Dial leaned forward again and called Ross Hamilton.

"Ross, forgive this impromptu call, but I just spoke with Li Ping. As you predicted, they are once again threatening to sell off treasury bills."

"China's economic threats are just hot air. They realize that our retaliatory sanctions would hurt their economy far worse than any damage they could inflict on ours. China barks loud but never bites."

"That remains to be seen, but China's not my immediate concern. What progress have you made with the heads of the US stock exchange?"

Friday morning, Ross Hamilton gathered the heads of the US stock markets to figure out how to pull the market out of its nose dive. The news wasn't good.

"I'd like to say we have the cooperation of all 26 stock exchanges, but that's not the case. Only two of the 26 CEO's have agreed to stop algorithmic trading. Leading the pack against restricting algorithmic trading is the New York Stock Exchange. Nobody wants to give up the billions they earn in commissions every year."

"So the CEO's would rather see a repeat of Thursday's crash than to agree to anti- algorithm legislation?"

"Yes, but can you blame them? Not only are they making a mint in the short-run, in the long-run, they have no faith that such legislation would pass. The markets were ruined in 2008 but to this day the government has yet to enact legislation to protect our markets."

"I won't allow another Wall Street bail out at the expense of the American public."

Ross couldn't agree more. "Our processors should never have permitted our stock markets to be converted from non-profit organizations to publicly-held corporations."

Dial's expression turned stone cold. "We'll see about that. On Sunday evening when I address the American public I will invoke my presidential powers and close all US sock markets until the SEC can enact litigation to outlaw computer-controlled trading."

"I don't know if that's your best option."

"If I don't act, you know what will happen when the markets open Monday morning."

"The hemorrhaging will continue."

"I won't allow it. Not on my watch. Abolishing algorithmic trading is the one option Americans will support."

"I'll have a team work up probable outcome scenarios. Keeping the markets closed until they are protected will allow time for the average 401K investor to gain some confidence in the market."

"At least time is on our side. When the CEO's of Wall Street find their business grinding to a halt, you'll see how fast the SEC passes legislation."

"What about hui corporations? It will take weeks before congress and the senate will be ready to amend the constitution."

"The volatility in the marketplace is the result of lax governmental regulations. So, despite protests from Wall Street, we must pass binding legislation to protect the markets. But legislation is not enough; we must enforce it, police the market. Any progress with Bloodhound?"

Bloodhound is a algorithmic program the government is developing to sniff-out dark pool trading.

Hundreds of highly sophisticated algorithmic programs are controlling the stock market. The most advanced artificial intelligence algorithms interpret breaking news and predict the probability if a stock will rise or fall. Others deal in arbitrage. Iceberg arbitrage dark trading algorithms disguises large blocks of stocks being sold as being small, while Shark algorithms try to uncloak Iceberg trades. Dark-pool trading exists in a world of nanoseconds, completely void of human intervention. Bloodhound is an algorithm designed to detect Iceberg and Shark algorithms.

"Bloodhound's sonar requires real buys and sells backed by actual currency. To police the market, the government will need to be a market player with a bankroll of several billion."

"A few billion is a small price to pay. Two days ago the market lost upwards to two trillion dollars. Just make sure the SEC's legislation sets stiff penalties, not only for buyer and sellers, but for the stock exchanges themselves. The legislation must to go beyond fines; offenders need to be banned from participating in the market."

"You want to close the doors of the New York Stock Exchange if they continue to broker algorithmic trades?"

"That's right. It's high time we get tough with our financial institutions. Middle America hasn't recovered from the crash of 2008! It's like the cyber Wild West out there! Sacrificing public welfare for short term profits will no longer be tolerated. My administration will no longer allow billionaire anarchists to ride roughshod over the common man."

Ross Hamilton could see that the President was no longer concerned with political ramifications. President after president had allowed more and more relaxed financial laws in exchange for greater and greater campaign contributions. Ross Hamilton knew Dial's decision was a clear indication that he had given up all hope of being re-elected.

Enthused by the prospect of actually accomplishing sustainable market regulation, Ross said, "I'll do everything in my power to enact change at the SEC. I know the chairman will vote in your favor, but several of the commissioners come from the financial sector."

"It's preposterous that the President can't just fire SEC board members, especially when they're from the financial sector. We have foxes tending the chicken coop."

"Delivering your speech invoking presidential powers to close the stock market will go a long way in pressuring the members of the SEC to vote in your favor."

"I'm not willing to take that gamble. It must be done now, and on my authority. You inform SEC's board members that I will not re-open the markets until they pass legislation prohibiting algorithmic trading. Then contact the governors of every state operating a stock exchange to convene emergency congressional sessions to pass anti- algorithmic trading legislation. We don't have months or years to resolve this issue. I want to see legislation passed by the end of the week. My Sunday evening address to the nation will let America know that this time they will just not hear the same old promises. We're taking action."

Chapter 11

Judge Becket summoned thirty-six prospective jurors from a fifty mile radius of Los Alamos. In an attempt to hold an unbiased hearing, he refused to release the prospective juror's pre-qualification questionnaire until 24 hours before jury selection. Realizing that both the prosecution and the defense have ample funds to conduct illicit video surveillance on prospective jurors, Judge Becket tried his best to prevent either side to conduct juror risk analysis. Despite the judge's best efforts, everything changed when Terry Evins walked into the court room.

When William Emmings caught sight of Terry Evins entering the courtroom to sit next to David Mulland he felt as if the floor was falling out from under him. Terry Evans had a telepathic gift for accessing a person's inner thoughts. Far more revealing than assessing body language, dress and physical appearance, Terry had the astonishing ability to know how a potential juror would feel about a case. The highly acclaimed jury consultant for OJ Simpson and Michael Jackson, Terry Evans didn't need to watch hundreds of hours of video surveillance or analyze handwriting samples because Terry Evans could read their minds.

The process of jury selection is pivotal for any court case. Eighty-five percent of all cases are won or lost based on the unique characteristics of the jury. Despite their oaths, jurors decide if the accused is guilty or innocent long before any testimony is heard. Even after eyewitness testimony, jurors rarely alter their initial judgment of guilt or innocence.

As the afternoon wore on, for the first time in his life William Emmings felt a case slipping from his grasp. Whenever David Mulland took his turn to question a juror, he kept one eye on Terry Evans, who would subtlety nodded her head yes or no as if buying a priceless antique at a private auction. William could sense the jurors stacking up against Thomas Quinn.

By 5:00 PM, eight women and four men between the ages of 20 and 67 were selected.

From the beginning, William Emmings and David Mulland anticipated that the judge would sequester the jury, and he did. With such a high profile case, anything less would be irresponsible. What neither man had anticipated was that the judge would bring the case to trial in just seven days.

In the limo on the way back to the hotel, Emmings called Simion Ruzart to fill him in.

"Becket fast-tracked the case. The trial will commence in seven days."

"Unusual. What about the jury?"

"They hired Terry Evans as their jury consultant. She's never lost a case."

"My God, Emmings, I told you to spare no expense! Why isn't she on our team?"

"I called Evans the same day you hired me but her office said she was unavailable. I didn't find out until today that Mulland had already gotten to her."

"Have you told Thomas?"

"I don't know if that's a good idea. It may hurt his confidence when he testifies."

"I'll handle Thomas. You just find a way to make sure he is found innocent."

A real spark of anger ignited inside of Simion. Unlike most men, whose outrage is released violently, Simion had the ability to subjugate his fury, to let it course through his veins and reinvigorate his determination. In a few minutes he was calm when he called Thomas.

"Thomas, I just got off the phone with Emmings. The jury selection did not go well. We just found out today that the prosecution hired a jury consultant that has never lost a case."

"I see. How is Xavier Lamont's commercial coming along?"

"Thomas, I don't think you understand the gravity of the problem. There's a good chance you'll be convicted."

"I've always known something like this would happen. I accepted the risks before I started down this road. I don't mean to minimize the agony of spending even one day in prison, but I'll tell you something very odd. When I was a boy I had a dream that I was in prison and now it's actually happening."

"Thomas, it is imperative that you believe we'll win this case or we don't stand a chance. Dreams have nothing to do with reality."

"I want to believe we'll win more than anything. I've had years to imagine having everything I cherish striped from me. Prison will be like a paralytic nightmare, with nothing but dark thoughts to fill my mind. I will fight with all my might to win this case. But I can accept the prospect of jail. I know I can endure. Now, tell me, how is the commercial coming along?"

"I cannot say I would face a similar ordeal with your frame of mind. But the commercial is finished. We are moving up the viewing to tonight."

"Why tonight?"

"We heard rumors that the Presidential Address Sunday evening will announce plans for sweeping stock market reforms. Peter Sadinski recommends we not engage in direct conflict with the President of the

United States. Moreover, Xavier's speech will possibly tone down the President's rhetoric denouncing huinomics."

Like so many other Americans, President Dial sat in the Oval Office watching Xavier Lamont blame the recent stock market crash on the governments continued practice of catering to wealthy by deregulating the financial markets.

Turning off the television President Dial said accusingly to Larry Baker, "It's hard for me to believe that no one knew about this."

Exasperated Larry exclaimed, "No one knew. Simion Ruzart simply bought air time for a two minute commercial. We had no way of knowing what it was going to be about."

"This was a calculated ploy to upstage my speech tomorrow. Someone from inside our staff must have leaked this. Do you see the position they've put me in?" Raising his voice in frustration, Dial said, "If I speak out against huinomics now, it will appear as if I am trying to deceive the American public."

"Just focus on your presidential order to close the stock market, then Lamont's speech won't hurt your position."

Looking at the embossed presidential seal on the ceiling above, President Dial unconsciously tapped his fingers against his leg and thought for some time before he said, "Maybe we jumped the gun on huinomics. Do you think we're doing the right thing for American by opposing it?"

Sighing, Larry said, "Honestly, I don't know."

Seeing that the President was not satisfied with his answer, Larry added, "On the one hand, the proliferation of huinomics will ultimately reduce taxes, taxes that keep the government afloat. On the other, most economists believe that the lower and middle classes will be significantly better off. Ultimately, it's a question of strength: a weaker government leads to a weaker nation. Without our current rate of taxation, we won't have the money to be strong."

Resting his head on his hands, President Dial wondered just how much more he could take. Suddenly bolting to his feet, he began pacing the room and said, "Xavier Lamont's commercial is just short of being traitorous. We are walking through a mine field. One could go off at any time."

Drifting off for a moment, President Dial's voice became more somber as he said, "We are in danger of losing control of the country. Forcing legislation prohibiting the formation of hui corporations could be the straw that breaks the camel's back. I'm talking about a full-blown revolution."

Letting the gravity of the President's words sink in, Larry said, "You're right. We're facing hundreds of thousands of people pushed to the brink. If this amendment goes through, it may very well be a major turning point for this country."

As if addressing himself, President Dial said, "If the economy doesn't crash altogether, supporting huinomics might help me get re-elected."

"Perhaps, but you can kiss any support from big business goodbye. Over the past 100 years, no president has won an election without the support of big business."

"It could be my opportunity to clean up Washington and finally put a stop to campaign contributions; I could sweep out the lobbyists."

"Or you could get impeached."

"Impeached? On what crime?"

"It could be construed that your support of huinomics is a high crime, as you would be supporting an entity that is intent on harming the nation."

"With the economy in turmoil, my prospects for getting re-elected are bleak with or without my support of huinomics. I want your crew to create a feasibility study on me reversing my support of the House amending the constitution."

"It's worth looking into; especially if it turns out that the government had any involvement in setting up Thomas Quinn."

Shaking his head President Dial revisited the empty feeling he got when he considered not running for re-election. Instantly President Dial knew he would never give up the throne, no matter the cost.

"Do you believe the court will find Thomas Quinn guilty?"

"You know what I think. I believe James Blake was following orders when he brokered a deal with Rebecca Swanson, and he was subsequently assassinated. I believe Thomas Quinn is innocent."

"That's not what I'm asking: will the jury find him guilty?"

"That's too hard for me or anyone else to call. But I'll tell you one thing: we're in for a shit-storm of public unrest if he's found guilty."

Chapter 12

Detric Ehrlich led a quiet, scheduled life. Like a precision clock, Detric woke up at six-thirty every morning, took a shower, shaved, and donned a gray three piece suit. For breakfast, Detric ate one slice of toast, one cup of yogurt with fruit and coffee. At precisely seven-forty, Detric folded up the day's paper, pecked his wife of 28 years on the right side of her cheek and walked to the tram stop.

Detric liked the walk. He liked how his crisp Italian leather shoes felt against the rough pavement and how his overcoat and suit made his slight frame appear larger and more powerful. He felt in command of his world.

As a senior account specialist for the small but highly respected Banca Zabin, Detric's mastery of his craft was beyond reproach. For more than a decade, Detric held the exalted position, as unchallenged and immovable as the bank's cornerstone set in place some two hundred years ago.

Aside from engaging in casual cordial greetings, Detric distanced himself from discussions of any type with coworkers. "The less said, the better," was his motto, so he avoided personal exchanges with people. Incredibly introverted, Detric found conversation arduous and unworthy of his time.

Confrontations were especially loathsome to Detric. Once, out of the corner of his eye while riding the crowded tram to work, Detric saw a disheveled young man pick a pocket. Detric felt a shock of adrenalin course through his veins and immediately looked away, trembling from his cold sweat. A few moments later the tram stopped and the youth quickly got off. Relief spread over Detric as the tram pulled away.

Quick to make light of the event, Detric convinced himself that there was nothing he could have done. "He'll end up in Needle Park feeding his addiction. The desperate fool will get what's coming to him. He'll suffer for his crime; he probably has AIDs already. It's the city's fault that such scum run amuck. The mayor should run every last deviant out of Needle Park."

Such thoughts hammered inside Detric's head until he was once again in balance with the world.

Detric had many unvoiced complaints against the mayor, and for that matter, the way the country was run in general. All the same, he still found Switzerland to be light years beyond America's form of democracy. Detric thought American democracy was cruel to the point of being barbaric.

Anyway, Detric did not have the time or the inclination to be running after addicts. Such problems were the affairs of those trained to handle such matters.

Simplicity and order guided Detric. Like the cold steel cogs of the finely-tuned gears of Banca Zabin's gargantuan safety doors, Detric connected accounts, routed numbers, and analyzed a vast matrix of names. Detric was exceptionally good at remembering numbers associated with names. Detric had the specific task of keeping a watchful eye out for accounts exceeding two million dollars.

Such multi-million dollar clients were drawn to Banca Zabin for its steadfast tradition of protecting its clients' identities. In a land where banking discretion was paramount, Banca Zabin was in a class of its own.

To Detric, a client's personal affairs were meaningless. A client's name was simply one of several details required to gain access to an account.

Detric had never concerned himself with any individual name until he saw Rebecca Swanson's in the news. Instantly, Detric recalled a sum of five million dollars being transferred from a Cayman Island account into a trust account associated with her name.

In that brief moment, Detric's life began to unravel.

Watching the early morning sun highlight the fringe of Jackie's auburn hair, Thomas felt that nothing else in the world mattered. Jackie loved it when Thomas looked at her. Breaking Thomas's hypnotic trance, Jackie said, "William Emmings has a point. Maybe you should go over your case with him."

"Jackie, there are not many things I wouldn't do to improve my chances of winning. But, somehow, practicing lines with William Emmings just isn't one of them.

"But Emmings says that the prosecution will find ways to make you look guilty in the jury's eyes."

"True, but giving rehearsed replies will not stop that from happening. I'm better off just telling the truth. Truth is all I have."

"Isn't there anything else we can do?"

"Aside from convincing Rebecca Swanson to tell the truth, I'm afraid we'll need to trust the jury."

Her beautiful face transformed into a twisted scowl as Jackie said, "I hate her. I wish she would just crawl back into the hole she came from."

"I'd be lying if I told you I fantasized about something bad happening to Rebecca Swanson. Being unjustly accused breeds hatred. But we need to dissolve that kind of hatred or it will consume us, heart and soul."

With her body taut like a clenched fist, Jackie ignored Thomas's reasoning and repeated even louder, "I hate her."

"Hate is the easy road. It's much easier to hate Rebecca Swanson than to understand her. Besides, your feelings aren't hurting her, they're hurting you. Hate can eat you alive. It spreads like cancer until every thought you have is hateful."

"What do you want me to do, just forgive her?"

"You don't need to be a saint. Just replace hate with understanding. Rebecca Swanson has never known anything good. She has lived a life without love. If Rebecca Swanson had someone she loved, she probably would have never falsely accused me."

"Don't say that, you'll win this case."

"I want to believe that with all my heart, but I want us to be prepared for the worse."

Fighting back tears, Jackie said, "Do you really believe they have a DNA sample of your sperm?"

"They had ample opportunities to go through our garbage for a used condom. Peter believes they had the sample before they talked Swanson into selling what little soul she had left."

Jackie's eyes welled up. "I can't bear the thought of you being taken away from me."

With his eyes glassing over, too, Thomas took Jackie's hand and, looking deep into her eyes, said, "Distance is the only thing that could ever separate us."

Overpowered by her love for him, Jackie threw her arms around Thomas and squeezed him tight, her tears flowing down her cheeks. Jackie felt her love for Thomas stronger than ever. The more she thought about Rebecca taking Thomas away, the harder she clung to him. She hated anything that took Thomas away from her. Thomas belonged to her. Damn anyone who tried to come between them. Damn Rebecca Swanson most of all.

Thomas and Jackie turned off all the electronic devices in their borrowed home as if they were back on their farm. They were inseparable over the three days leading up to the trial.

Pleading with the President's personal secretary Larry Baker said, "I understand that he doesn't want to be disturbed. But, believe me, when he hears this he'll be glad you interrupted him."

The President's secretary looked at Larry Baker skeptically. She knew President Dial didn't want to be disturbed, but Larry Baker was the President's closest friend, and the President could use a friend about now.

Reading her mind, Larry said, "Tell him I have the poll results from his speech. He could use some good news."

Utterly self-assured in front of the cameras, behind closed doors President Dial questioned his decision to evoke his presidential power to close the stock market. His enemies were calling him reckless and heavy handed. Even those who put him in power weren't happy with the decision, derailing his prospects for re-election.

After a hushed call, the President's personal secretary led Larry Baker into the Vermillion room where he found President Dial fuming in an armchair.

"The verdict is in. The poles show that 74% of Americans agree that the market should be closed until legislation can be established."

Haggard and stressed, Dial forced a smile and said, "What's the accuracy?"

"Better than 80%. You did it. Don't you see? It's not so much about safeguarding the markets as it is about alleviating fear. Americans have confidence in your decision. They believe in you and have new hope for their economic future."

"I also wrote my re-election death sentence. Main Street casts votes but Wall Street decides the winner."

Larry always felt a sting at times like these when he witnessed how power-hungry his friend was. He wrote it off as a necessary personality trait for the most powerful person in the world. Anyone ascending to that height must desire it more than anything else.

"Please consider the importance of what I'm telling you. You have stemmed the tide, at least temporally. The American public believes that the government is taking the right steps in dealing with the stock market crash."

"Let's hope the public keeps thinking that way. Any hope for recovery depends on pulling off the veil of fear blinding us."

Sensing the President was coming around, Larry smiled to himself and said, "Let the critics stomp their feet while Congress moans. Tonight, Americans will go to sleep believing that tomorrow will be a better day."

Looking out the backseat window, Thomas and Jackie smiled as they watched the rising sun slowly color the wispy clouds in the frost-blue sky. Following Simion's wishes, their two body guards, Hank and Staple, took the front seat as they drove the 68 miles from Taos to Los Alamos. To fight his budding anxiety, Thomas told himself that the day's events were simply a play with no ramification other than to entertain.

Reaching the outskirts of town, Thomas and Rebecca were amazed to see cars parked on either side of the road. As they got closer to the court house it became clear that the number of supporters flanking the streets far exceeded the town's population of twelve thousand.

Two blocks away from the court house, crowds filled the streets. Uncertain what to do next, one of the body guards said, "We can't go any further; we will need to wait here until we can get a police escort."

Thomas smiled and shouted back, "Police escort, are you kidding me? Our escort is surrounding us! Come on Jackie, let's go."

Taking Jackie's hand, Thomas got out of the car and raised their interlocked hands to the crowd. Thomas shouts out, "We shall overcome. We shall overcome." Like a rippling wave over a sea of human bodies, the crowd began to shout out the chant louder and louder.

Abandoning the car Staple, the larger of the two body guards, got out and made his way to Thomas and Jackie with Hank in tow. With Staple in front and Hank bringing up the rear, they shielded Thomas and Jackie as they made their way up to the courthouse. All the while the massive crowd kept cheering and jostling to get close. Thomas and Jackie could feel supporters jostling to reach out to touch them as they made their way to the courthouse while overhead newsroom choppers captured the footage.

Confronted with the same crowd, David Mulland and Rebecca Swanson feared for their safety and waited for five motorcycle policemen to slowly escort their car to the courthouse.

Inside the courtroom the chants of the crowd could still be heard as the jury, along with the rest of the courtroom, waited for the prosecution to arrive. Nearly thirty agonizing minutes ticked by before David Mulland appeared with Rebecca Swanson at his side. Completely calm and at ease walking down the center of the courtroom, David Mulland and Rebecca Swanson looked as if they were making their way to a table at the Ritz. To complete the effect of power and stature, several steps back marched nine polished lawyers carrying attaché cases looking ready for battle.

Looking at Rebecca, Thomas furrowed his eyebrows. He could not believe her metamorphose. The clumsy skinny kid wearing black army boots that he knew in high school now appeared as a sophisticated power executive. Rebecca's riveting dark gray tropical wool jacket and skirt looked as if it was welded onto her. Her tight walk in stiletto shoes and dark nylons gave off a sexy yet refined vibe.

The impressive parade had a visible effect on the jury. They were looking at a highly polished professional legal team. Soon after, the courtroom rose as the judge entered. Wasting no time, the judge quickly addresses the prosecution. "I take it in future the prosecution will take appropriate steps to not keep this court waiting again."

David Mulland quickly stood to attention saying, "We apologize for the delay Your Honor; the crowds outside impeded our arrival. We will make appropriate preparations to prevent such an occurrence in the future."

Behind the bloodhound-like cheeks of the judge, no doubt a by-product of excessive consumption of cheese burgers and bad moods, crept an indistinguishable upward turn to the corners of his wide mouth in response to his keen appreciation for obedience.

Addressing the jury, Judge Becket continued, "Before I call this court to order, it is my duty to remind the jury that their sequestration will be for the duration of the trial. The court demands the jury's cooperation in order to prevent any prejudice by external contact. Furthermore, the jury must make their judgments based on events that took place eighteen years ago. As such, I am asking the jury to disregard any positive or negative preconceived notions they may have of Thomas Quinn, and base their judgments solely on the testimony and evidence presented in this case.

"Make no mistake: this jury is called to do a difficult task. Thomas Quinn is famous, as evidenced by the crowds and helicopters that have already disrupted these proceedings. I implore you not to take his current notoriety into consideration. Thomas Quinn is to be judged on the events that took place eighteen years ago.

"The court is now in session. David Mulland, you may begin with the prosecution's opening statement."

Standing slowly and approaching the jury with mild consternation, David Mulland addressed the jury.

"Ladies and gentlemen of the jury. During the course of this trial you will hear testimony and be provided evidence that Thomas Quinn raped Rebecca Swanson on the night of their Senior Prom eighteen years ago."

His face growing harder as his voice grew louder, David Mulland continued.

"On the night of May 16th, 1994, Thomas Quinn's raped Rebecca Swanson. In this unforgivable brutal act Thomas Quinn stripped away Rebecca Swanson's desire to live a full life. He stole her innocence, her pride, and her self-respect. Thomas Quinn crushed Rebecca Swanson's very soul. At the tender age of eighteen, Thomas Quinn took from her everything that makes life worth living.

"Think back to when you were in high school. It was a time of great hope. You planned your futures. You believed anything was possible. Your futures were bright.

"For most of us, the night when all these dreams were at their fullest was Prom Night. On that special night we, as hopeful young adults, celebrated our youth. We danced with joy for the future yet to come.

"On that very night when every dream was possible, Thomas Quinn destroyed Rebecca's life. He killed her hopes for her future.

"For eighteen long years, Rebecca Swanson has suffered. Stripped of all self-respect, Rebecca has lived a life of poverty and degradation.

"Ladies and gentleman of the jury. Over the course of this trial you will bear witness to Rebecca Swanson's suffering and you will come to know its cause: Thomas Quinn. When Thomas Quinn raped Rebecca Swanson on March 16th 1994, he destroyed her life. You will find him guilty and punish him accordingly."

David Mulland turned and took his seat. Judge Becket stared hard at Thomas Quinn and then at the jury before puffing out his baggy cheeks and saying, "We will now hear the opening statement from the defense."

Looking like a scaled down version of Clark Kent, William Emmings stood and walked to the area in front of the jury box.

"Thank you, Your Honor. Ladies and gentlemen of the jury, you know an innocent man sits before you today. Thomas Quinn did not rape Rebecca Swanson.

"It is so easy to accuse someone of a crime they did not commit. Yet we do it every day. You and I and everyone you see here today passes judgment on people without even knowing anything about that person. We judge them for the color of their skin, their hair, the clothes they wear, and even on how they walk. It is so easy to pass judgment on people. As we all know it is far, far easier to judge someone as being bad than being good.

"I need you to see past the hype and base your judgment on the facts set before you during this trial. The man before you, Thomas Quinn, has been falsely accused."

Emmings turned with his head high, nodded respectfully as he passed before the judge's bench, and took his seat next to Thomas Quinn.

The judge announced, "The prosecution will now call their first witness."

"Your honor, we call Manny Hernandez to the stand."

While Manny was not obese, he had a prominent beer belly that made him sway as he walked. His balloon-like cheeks seemed to be stapled down by his thick bristly mustache. With a sour expression, David Mulland approached the witness and said, "Manny Hernandez, what was your profession the night of May 16th, 1994?"

"I was an on-call limo driver during the evenings and a stock clerk for Arney's Market during the day.

"Describe the limousine you drove the night of May 16th."

With pride, Manny said, "It was a black double-stretch Lincoln with seating for ten: black leather seats, a mini bar, a video screen, the works. It was decked out."

As if nothing could be more important, Mulland asked, "Did it have a glass barrier between the driver and the passengers?"

"No sir."

"Did it have any barrier whatsoever that could obscure the driver's vision?"

Standing, Emmings calmly said, "Objection Your Honor."

Barking, Judge Becket snapped, "Grounds?"

"Argumentative, Your Honor."

"Sustained. Mr. Mulland will re-phrase his question."

"Were there any objects between the driver's seat and the passenger compartment?"

"No."

"Describe to me the route you took to pick up the students."

Cocking his head to one side, searching his memory, Manny said, "There were a total of six stops. The first stop I picked up the five boys, followed by a stop at each of the girl's homes."

"What time did you start and when did you drop them off at the dance?"

"We left at three in the afternoon and arrived at the hotel at 6:30."

"Was it still light out then?"

"Yes."

"Could you make out the faces in the seats behind you?"

"Yes."

"What were the students doing?"

"You know seniors. They're always noisy, having a good time."

"Who was the last student you picked up?"

Clearly rehearsed, Manny said, "I didn't know her name at the time, but she is here today: Rebecca Swanson."

"Why did you pick up Rebecca Swanson last?"

"She lived off Trinity Drive near the airport, on the border of the city, furthest from the school. After picking her up I took the interstate to the dance."

Facing the jury, Mulland said, "So you picked up Rebecca Swanson last because she lived furthest away. Tell me, what were the students doing as you drove them to the prom?"

"High school kids are always loud. When they are not shouting at each other they are cracking up. But you could tell they were having fun."

"Did you see any of the students drink?"

"No."

Walking to the witness stand and turning to look back at the jury, Mulland raised his voice and asked, "Are you absolutely sure?"

Offended, Manny said, "Yeah, I'm sure. I didn't see anyone drinking."

Louder, now addressing the jury directly, Mulland stated, "So, you did not see anyone drinking on the way to the prom."

Before Manny could reply, Mulland asked in a voice soft enough to make the jury strain to hear, "What was Rebecca Swanson's condition when you picked her up after the prom was over?"

"The way she staggered I was afraid she was going to get sick. She was really hammered. She kept swaying back and forth and knocking into everyone."

So Rebecca Swanson was definitely intoxicated. Were there any other students who had too much to drink?"

"You know high school students, they always seem to be a bit juiced, but Rebecca was definitely drunk."

Walking toward the prosecution's table but stopping halfway, Mulland asked so loudly Manny was startled, "Who was in the limo when you dropped Rebecca Swanson off?"

"Just her, me, and Thomas Quinn."

A hush fell over the courtroom.

"How much time passed from the time you dropped off the last couple to the time you dropped off Rebecca Swanson?"

"At that time of night? About twenty minutes."

"Describe for me what you saw during those twenty minutes."

"By the time I dropped off the last couple, Rebecca looked as if she was sleeping. Her head was against the back head rest." Then he paused, embarrassed, and said in a solemn voice: "About ten minutes away from Rebecca's home, I saw Thomas Quinn get on top of her."

Standing directly in front of the jury Mulland shouted out, "What was Thomas Quinn doing?"

Manny hung his head and answered, "Raping her. His pants were down and her dress was pushed up. I was in shock." Looking up, Manny said, "Then Rebecca shouted out, 'You Bastard!' And she started kicking her legs and swinging her arms trying to get Thomas off. I saw him scoot over to the corner of the backseat and Rebecca started to cry."

Clearly disgusted, Mulland threw up his hands and shouted, "What did you do next?"

Pleadingly Manny said, "Rebecca was crying and I didn't know what to do. Since I was almost at Rebecca's home I figured I'd get her parents to help."

In two steps Mulland was at the witness stand and shouted accusingly into Manny's face: "So you did not do anything to help this poor crying young woman!"

Turning back to the jury, Mulland asked, "What happened when you reached her home?"

Distraught, Manny said, "We reached her house but she just sat in the backseat, sobbing. I went around and opened the door. I thought she was going to fall on me. I helped her get out. She was still really plastered so I walked her to the door. I was expecting her father or mother to come running out and jump on Thomas, but no one was home. I tried calling out but no one answered."

"So what did you do next?" Mulland asked angrily.

Manny said, "I left."

Mulland shouted, "So, after seeing this poor girl be raped, you just left?!"

"Objection!"

"Sustained."

"So after seeing what you saw, you simply left?"

"I didn't know what to do. I figured the girl's parents would take care of what happened." Sitting up a little, Manny said, "Look, I knew Thomas Quinn crossed the line, but I didn't know how far."

"So what did you do next?"

"I went back to the car and saw that Thomas Quinn had left. I turned the limo around and saw Thomas Quinn running in the direction of his home."

Reproachfully, Mulland asked, "What made you think he wouldn't head straight for Rebecca's house to hurt her again?"

Manny stammered, "He looked like a scared kid, he just wanted to get away."

Mulland stared hard at Manny Hernandez before looking at Judge Becket.

"No further questions Your Honor."

Now it was William Emmings' turn to question Manny Hernandez. Approaching the witness stand, Emmings said, "Mr. Hernandez, based on the testimony you just gave, you stated that Thomas Quinn's pants were down. Exactly how far down were Thomas Quinn's pants?"

Manny answered smugly, "Not that far down, but I could see some of his butt showing."

"How do you know that what you saw was Thomas Quinn's bottom? I mean, after all, you were driving at night. How can you be sure you saw Thomas Quinn's bottom?"

Smiling with amusement Manny said, "I know an ass when I see one."

Emmings said, "So you are something of an ass expert, being able to see one at night speeding down the road at 45 miles per hour. Just how do you know that it wasn't Rebecca Swanson's arm across Thomas Quinn's bottom?"

Still enjoying his joke, Manny said, "I can tell the difference between an arm and an ass."

Sensing he was losing control of the jury, Emmings snapped, "Oh you can, can you? Tell me: what is the length of the super stretch Lincoln limo you were driving that night?"

"I don't know."

"Well, what is the luminosity of the interior of the super stretch Lincoln limo you were driving that night?"

"I don't know."

Taking out a poster size illustration of the limo, Emmings addressed the judge: "Your Honor, I would like to enter into evidence exhibit 12B, an illustration of the limo."

Judge Becket announced, "Proceed."

Emmings first showed the illustration to the prosecution, and then he set it down in front of Manny in full view of the jury and said, "Mr. Hernandez, how long had you driven a limo before picking up Rebecca Swanson on the night of May 16th?"

"Almost three years."

"So you spent almost three years driving a limo. Would you say you are an expert regarding limos?"

"There's not much I don't know about them."

"I see. What is the distance from the driver's seat to the back of the super stretch Lincoln limo?"

"I don't know."

"You don't know. Well, let me ask you this: what is the wattage of the two interior lights?"

"I don't know."

"I see. For being an expert there seems to be quite a few things you don't know about super stretch Lincoln limos. You don't know that ten feet separate the driver seat from the backseat. You don't know that the interior cabin is lighted by two five watt light bulbs that have the same luminosity as one candle each." Turning to the jury, Emmings said, "So I ask you again, as you were speeding down the road traveling forty-five miles per hour, seated ten feet away peering through the dark, how can you be sure beyond any reason of a doubt that what you saw was Thomas Quinn's exposed buttocks?"

"That's not something you can mistake. I saw his ass."

Turning back to Manny, Emmings asked, "Mr. Hernandez, where

did Rebecca Swanson and Thomas Quinn sit when they got into the limo when you drove them home?"

"Rebecca Swanson was sitting on the far backseat. I don't remember where Thomas Quinn was sitting when he got into the limo but I know where he ended up."

"You don't remember? You don't know? Let me ask you, Mr. Hernandez, do you consider your memory to be good?"

"Objection."

"Sustained"

"What exactly do you remember about Thomas Quinn getting into the limo?"

"Like I said, I didn't notice, but when just the two of them were alone back there I saw Thomas Quinn slide up next to Rebecca."

"You don't remember. No further questions, Your Honor."

"The prosecution will call their next witness."

David Mulland called Susan Torres to the stand.

In stark contrast to his disdainful approach to Manny Hernandez, Mulland asked cordially, "Ms. Torres, please tell the jury your full name and your relationship to Rebecca Swanson."

Susan's voice shook as she answered, "My name is Susan Torres. I was Rebecca Swanson's friend during my senior year in high school."

"Describe your friendship with Rebecca Swanson. What did you do together?"

"We talked on the phone, mostly. I went to her house a couple of times and we went to the movies."

"So, would you say you were typical high school friends?"

"Yes, I guess so."

"What did you talk about on the phone?"

"We talked about boys and school."

"So you talked about boys. Did you talk about Thomas Quinn?"

"No. We were not friends at the time of the prom; we were friends around the holidays."

"Would you say Rebecca Swanson was a normal high school student?"

"Objection."

"Sustained."

"Let me put it this way: please describe for us your impression of Rebecca Swanson."

"Rebecca was a loner. Like me, she did not have many friends. I was busy helping raise my two younger brothers. I didn't have much time for socializing."

"Why did you stop being Rebecca's friend?"

There was a long pause before Susan replied, "I was just too busy. After telling her a couple of times I couldn't go out, Rebecca stopped asking."

"The prosecution has no further questions Your Honor."

Approaching Susan Torres, William Emmings smiled and asked, "How did you and Rebecca Swanson meet?"

Her eyes darted over to Mulland and back before Susan answered, "We met in the school cafeteria during lunch."

"Did you have any classes together?"

"No."

"Were either of you members of any club?"

"No."

"Did either of you play after-school sports?"

"No."

"Were either of you in a play together?"

"Objection, Your Honor. I do not see the purpose of this line of questioning."

"Your Honor, the prosecution has presented Susan Torres as a character witness for Rebecca Swanson. I am simply trying to establish what kind of relationship they had."

"Over-ruled. Answer the question."

"We didn't do any organized activities."

"Why not?"

"Like I said, I was too busy taking care of my younger brothers. I didn't have time for fun."

"Most high schools students hang out together in groups known as clicks. There are jock clicks, nerd clicks, and popular clicks. Which click were you and Rebecca in?"

"None. I stayed mostly to myself."

"How about Rebecca Swanson, was she part of any click?"

"If she was, she never mentioned it to me."

William Emmings brought forth a large poster-size photo of Susan Torres and showed it first to the judge, then the jury and lastly to the witness.

"Is this your senior year high school photograph?"

Seeing the overly plump, pimple-faced photo of herself made Susan blush.

"Yes, that's my yearbook photo."

Taking out another poster-sized photograph of Rebecca Swanson, the amused expression of the jury vanished. Rebecca's photo looked more like a mug shot. She looked like she was going to pick a fight with the cameraman. Her pale skin and dark, black-rimmed eyes made her look sick.

"Do you recognize the person in this photo?"

"Yes: it's Rebecca Swanson."

Taking out another full length photo of Rebecca with her hair bunched up on top of her head, dressed in a black tank top, black jeans and black boots, Emmings continued.

"Have you seen this photo before?"

"Yes. It's Rebecca Swanson's yearbook picture."

"Did Rebecca Swanson ever mention that she liked the subculture known as Goth?"

"Goth? I never heard of it before." Looking around for help, Susan stammered, "She never talked to me about Goth."

"Goth is a subculture that celebrates the grim and ghastly aspects of death; they dress predominantly in black. Why do you think Rebecca never talk about being Goth?"

"I don't know. We did listen to Judas Priest."

"What kind of music is Judas Priest?"

"Heavy Metal."

"Did you like Heavy Metal music in high school?"

"Not really."

"Did you like things grim and ghastly, did you dress in black?"

"No."

"Did you have anything in common with Rebecca Swanson?"

Looking at Rebecca Swanson, Susan shook her head and said, "Not really."

"Then why were you friends with her?"

Susan looked shaken.

"We were friends for a while, that's all."

Emmings waited a moment for the tension to permeate the courtroom before he said, "The defense rests, Your Honor."

"Mr. Mulland?"

"No further witnesses, Your Honor."

"Then the defense will call its first witness."

"The defense calls Mark Adel to the stand."

Thomas didn't recognize Mark at first because the thick brown hair of his youth was all but gone and his stomach stuck out like he'd swallowed a basketball.

"Mr. Adel. You were one of the students who rode in the limo the night of May 16th. Did Thomas Quinn sit next to Rebecca Swanson in the limo on the way to or from the dance?"

"No."

"Did you see Thomas Quinn and Rebecca Swanson dance together during the prom?"

Smiling, Mark said, "No, I didn't see them dance, but I was dancing a lot so they might have."

"When you were seated at the table with Thomas and Rebecca, did they look like they were having a good time?"

"That's the main reason my friends and I kept taking off to different tables. They weren't talking or even looking at each other. They were just sitting there."

"Did you see them showing any affection towards each other?"

"Like I said, they weren't even talking, let alone being affectionate. It's like they were forced to sit next to each other."

"In the limo driving to the dance, did any of you have alcoholic drinks?"

"Yeah, we were drinking in the limo, and at the dance."

"Did you see Rebecca drinking?"

"Yeah. She had a pint of Vodka she was drinking from."

"At any time that night, either in the limo or at the dance, did you see Thomas Quinn drink?"

"No."

"Did either person seem upset or angry?"

"They didn't look angry, they looked bored stiff. A guy Thomas knew came over and talked to him for a while, but other than that they looked as if they wanted to leave."

"No further questions, Your Honor."

"The prosecution may cross-examine the witness."

"We have no questions, Your Honor."

"This court is now adjourned until tomorrow morning at 10:00 AM."

Rising, Thomas looked at Emmings as the jurors were lead from their stand and out a side passage.

"Is that it? Why did the judge adjourn so early?"

"It's not unusual. The judge wants to allow the jury time to deliberate."

"They sure don't have much to go on."

"Come tomorrow, they'll have plenty to consider. In the meantime, get some rest. You need to be at your best tomorrow."

With that, Emmings headed down the aisle, ignoring the desperation on Thomas's face.

Chapter 13

Each morning Detric got worse. Laline, his wife of twenty-eight years, stood at the kitchen sink with her arms folded across her large breasts, watching Detric sit stiff as a board at their small round dining table like his soul had left his body. He starred off into the distance, his sunken gray eyes unaware of the steam wafting up from his untouched coffee.

She sat next to him anxiously and placed her hand on his shoulder. Using her sweetest, most charming voice, she said, "What is the matter, Detric? It can't be your health, my dear. You would tell me if anything was wrong, wouldn't you?"

He did not respond. Gripping his shoulder, she pleaded, "Please, Detric! What is going on?"

Turning his head slowly, in a voice without expression, Detric said, "I'm not hungry, Laline."

Drawing herself up, Laline stuttered, "Have you found a lover?" She put her hand on her cheek and cried, "Oh, what am I to do? How could you, Detric?"

A smile crept into the corners of his mouth. The smile grew until Detric started to laugh. The laugh grew louder and louder, as if Detric was possessed by a demon. He opened his mouth wide and laughed a loud, ugly laugh.

Laline became hysterical. Frantically shaking Detric's shoulder she shouted, "Detric...Detric you scare me! Detric, you stop, stop it right now!"

Repressing the torrent of bile that threatened to erupt, Detric stopped laughing, took a few deep breaths and said, "My sweet Laline. You know I could not do anything to hurt you. You are my one and only."

Standing, Detric wrapped his arms around her and said, "I love you, Laline."

Hugging her made his world come into focus. Detric squeezed her tighter and said, "Don't worry about me. I'm not ill. I sure won't die anytime soon. I'm just a bit pre-occupied about something that happened at work. That is all."

Still shaken, Laline pulled back and looked him in the eye.

"Is everything okay at the bank? Are they cutting back? Detric, you've been with them for so long."

"No, Laline, nothing like that. Everything at the bank is fine. There's nothing to worry about. This will all be over soon."

With that, Detric kissed Laline's cheek and left to catch the tram. Walking to the stop, he thought to himself: "Banca Zabin in trouble? That will never happen."

After a night of tossing and turning Thomas was jolted awake by a dream; he struggled to remember it but he couldn't. Making his way to the bathroom, he bent over the sink and splashed cold water on his face. His haggard reflection in the mirror reminded him of what six years in prison would do to him. As it was, his sunken dark rimmed eyes made him look ten years older. He tried to recall how many days had passed since he left the farm. Would he be able to do all the things he wanted to do with Jackie by the end of this ordeal?

Feeling like a diver running out of air, Thomas ran back to bed and held Jackie as if it was his last chance for a very long time. His fear dissipated as he pressed his nose against Jackie's neck and breathed her in.

Eating stale bagels on the way to the courthouse, Thomas again wondered what it would be like to be locked up. Gazing at the side of her face as she watched houses go by, Thomas realized how much Jackie's spirit sustained him. No matter what happened, thoughts of her would make it all bearable.

As the car approached the courthouse, they were surprised to see the crowd had grown from yesterday. Thomas was thankful that Staple and Hank were there to help them make their way up the courthouse steps.

Fully prepared following yesterday's chaos, police barriers held back the crowds. Halfway up the steps, Thomas turned to take a moment to address the throngs of supporters.

Even with the prosecution arriving on time, Judge Bates elected to have the courtroom wait fifteen minutes for the chanting to dissipate before making his entry into the courtroom. If possible, he looked even more miserable than usual. With a frown cut short by the baggy folds of his cheeks, Judge Becket addressed Thomas Quinn angrily.

"This court is not a grandstand for you to voice your opinion on current issues, Mr. Quinn. The court fines you $250, and bands you from addressing the public within one hundred yards of this courthouse."

Thomas leaned over to William Emmings and spoke into his ear for a few second, then sat erect and stared straight at the Judge.

"My client is enjoying his constitutional rights to Freedom of Assembly and Speech as granted in the first Amendment of the Constitution."

Visually perturbed, Judge Becket spat back, "A permit is required by statute to assemble and $250 is the fine for violating that statute. Mr. Quinn can enjoy his rights so long as they do not disturb the proceedings of this court. Now, without further interruptions, the prosecution is to bring forth their first witness."

The morning was a long, drawn out affair. Over the next three hours one character witness after another were sworn in to verify that both Rebecca Swanson and Thomas Quinn were outsiders in high school. Although Rebecca barely passed, she was never suspended or even reprimanded for bad behavior. And though Thomas's teachers were quick to praise his scholarly merits, they knew little about him personally.

After a much appreciated lunch break, the court resumed to hear testimony from Burt Vargas of CTR DNA Labs.

"Mr. Vargas, state your full name, profession and the length of time you have worked for your current employer."

"My name is Burt Vargas. I am a lab technician at CTR laboratories. I have been employed at CTR for over three years."

"What do you do at CTR?"

"I analyze DNA samples."

Holding up a black silky dress, David Mulland continued, "Do you recognize this dress?"

"I believe so."

"Describe it for us."

"This appears to be the dress I extracted a DNA sample from."

"Who requested this DNA sample?"

"Rebecca Swanson."

"Were you able to extract a DNA sample?"

"Yes."

"At the time of the extraction, did you know the DNA sample would match Thomas Quinn's DNA?"

"No."

"So you had no idea who this DNA belonged to. The only thing you knew was that it was, in fact, someone's DNA. Tell me, Mr. Vargas, what is the accuracy of the DNA test you took?"

"CTR Labs videotapes the entire process, from the time a sample is submitted until the DNA is extracted, providing visual documentation that the sample was not altered. This results in 100% accuracy."

Affecting an exaggerated slow cadence, Mulland proclaimed, "100% accurate! Not 80% accurate or even 99% accurate, but 100% accurate. Are you quite certain, Mr. Vargas, that your DNA test is 100% accurate?"

"That is correct, 100% accurate. DNA testing has advanced to the point where results are proven to be 100% accurate."

"No further questions, Your Honor."

"The defense may question the witness."

Looking confused, Emmings approached the witness stand and said, "Mr. Vargas, how long have you been testing DNA samples with CTR?"

"I began working for CTR laboratories when I graduated from college. I was a Junior Lab Tech my first year and now I'm an Assistant Lab Tech. I've been testing DNA samples for CTR for over two years."

"Would you say you are an expert in DNA testing?"

With confidence, Burt Vargas stated, "I perform three to five test per day, performing well over two-thousand DNA extractions, so yes, I would say I'm an expert."

"Do the tests provide any information other than DNA identification?"

"What do you mean?"

"Can the DNA test tell if the sample is, say, a few months old or 18 years old?"

"Objection."

"Sustained."

"Can you decipher the age of the sample?"

"No."

"So the sample could be a few days old or decades old, you have no way of knowing, is that correct?"

"That is correct."

"So what you said earlier, that the DNA test is 100% accurate, that only pertains to verification of the DNA sample. Your test produces no other information."

"That's correct."

Turning to the jury, Emmings raised his voice: "In fact, you don't know any other crucial information, do you. For example, you have 0% accuracy in determining just how old the DNA sample is, correct?"

"That is correct."

Turning back to the witness, Emmings stated: "Please tell the jury why CTR doesn't bother to test the age of their DNA samples."

"Because it is impossible to determine a sample's age using our current methods."

"Explain why it is impossible to determine the age of a DNA sample."

"Carbon dating has limited accuracy in determining the age of carbon based matter. Results can vary as much as one to several decades or more."

Turning to the jury once again, Emmings threw up his hands and said, "Several decades? So you don't know if this sample came from 30 years ago or if it was produced just a few months ago!"

"Objection!"

Judge Becket shouted out, "Sustained!" Pointing his bent finger at Emmings, he said, "Mr. Emmings, you are hereby warned."

"No further questions, Your Honor."

Pounding his gavel once, Judge Becket barked, "This court is adjourned."

Whenever President Dial called for a cabinet meeting, he was reminded of King Author calling his knights to the Round Table. As he scanned each somber face, he realized the task before them was more daunting than any they had faced before.

"I appreciate your sacrifice in arriving here on such short notice. As you realize, Kimball Industries has just announced that they are converting into a hui corporation. With P&G, that makes a total of 200,000 hui employees. More ominously, there is mounting pressure on corporations to convert into huis.

"Ladies and gentlemen, we are at a crossroad more crucial than any in America's history. For the first time since the Vietnam War, the desire of the population is in conflict with the actions of the government. The bulk of Americans believe that working for a hui corporation will improve their lives. As we speak, the congress is debating whether or not to make hui corporations constitutionally illegal. We are here today to examine the political and economic ramifications of such legislation.

"I ask that we begin by hearing what the Secretary of the Treasury, Robert O'Neil, has to say."

Robert O'Neil slowly stood up and, clearing his voice, said, "In less than one year, Vorbine is already the size of America's largest coal-based energy plant. The economic advantage of hui corporations is staggering. Reduced cost and increased efficiencies has allowed Vorbine to produce energy cheaper than coal.

"There is no question that Vorbine's dominance in the energy market is simply a matter of time. P&G and Kimball Industry will follow in Vorbine's footsteps and soon dominate their markets. It is evident that, given time, all major industries will need to be converted into hui corporations in order to remain competitive.

"The essence of economics is competition. In order to compete with hui corporations, non-hui corporations will need to convert or they will be forced to close. Make no mistake about it, if we allow the formation of hui corporations, the socio-economic landscape of the world will change, dramatically and rapidly."

President Dial turned to the Secretary of Commerce. "Ms. Hamilton, does your department concur with these findings?"

"Once the genie is out of the bottle, there's no saying just how fast huinomics will spread. I concur. Without preventative legislation, tax revenues will be insufficient to keep our government afloat within a few years."

Turning from Hamilton, President Dial addressed the entire Cabinet: "If we amend the constitution we will face wide-spread social unrest. Think of Viet Nam on steroids. Concurrent with this legislation we must strategize how to win back the hearts of Americans."

The Secretary of the Interior's voice rose above the others: "We must fight fire with fire. We are weeks behind the curve in getting our message out to the American public. We need a media blitz to convince people that huinomics is a utopian fantasy that will destroy the American dream.

"We've been sitting on the sidelines watching the opposition bombard the American public with propaganda that huinomics is the answer to all their problems. We need to launch a counter campaign to win back the hearts of America, and that is going to require a significant re-allocation of resources."

Larry Baker, the White House Chief of Staff joined in. "Too conventional. A media blitz won't change anything because a media blitz didn't give them their edge. This isn't about protesting in the streets, this is a virtual protest. Since it went viral, the hui movement did more than fan the dreams of the American public, it encouraged participation in the process. Our only hope to turn the tide is by connecting with Americans through social media."

Raising her hand, Francine Plymouth, the Secretary of Labor, stated, "We need a response to the hui movement beyond traditional public relations rhetoric. We have 45 million Americans on food stamps. One out of five children suffers from insufficient nutrition. For the first time in history, the nation's offspring will have a shorter lifespan than their parents. Over 70% of Americans say they strongly dislike their jobs. 66% of Americans are overweight. Unemployment is higher than it has been since the great depression, and the elderly are being forced back into the work force to survive. If you want to combat the spread of huinomics, you need to improve the lives of the average American. We can't keep making empty promises to the American public and expect this tide to turn. We need tangible solutions."

The president turned to her and said, "I agree with you, Ms. Plymouth, America needs more job programs. However, that is a discussion for a different time. We need to address the immediate threat of what will happen when the government disallows the formation of hui corporations."

Lisa Clintock, The Secretary of Health and Human Services, said loudly, "There is another alternative, Mr. President."

"What alternative are you speaking of, Ms. Clintock?"

"Thank you for hearing me out. More than one person in this room has confided in me that they believe huinomics has it merits. I may lose my position by saying so, but I agree with the majority of Americans. I believe huinomics is the solution. As Ms. Plymouth has so bravely pointed out, Americans are suffering. Huinomics provides an answer to their problems. Our duty is to devise ways to help huinomics flourish."

Among the many voices rising in protest came the strong southern accent of the Secretary of Defense, Robert Chatsworth. "I cannot disagree with you more. Huinomics will set this country back 100 years. Widespread unemployment, hunger and suffering are at our doorstep. The founders of huinomics cast their propaganda net and captured the imagination of the American People. They have corralled Americans into believing a false reality. What they are peddling is nothing less than economic romance.

"If we do not make our move now, and make it quick, we will lose the reins of this great country."

President Dial turned to the Secretary of Home Land Security. "What civil retaliatory consequences do you anticipate?"

Dorothy Hendricks swallowed hard before stating, "The hui belief that social evolution by definition must be peaceful is so ingrained into its followers that our forecast does not anticipate violent outbreaks, only peaceful demonstration.

"While non-violent transformation sounds harmless, a united retaliatory stance can have devastating effects. For example, there is growing support for a nation-wide refusal to pay taxes. If this concept gains more traction, our government will be rendered powerless."

The Secretary of Defense was quick to respond. "I for one do not believe in social evolution. It is just another tactic to get people to believe in huinomics. I do believe, however, that man is inherently violent. There is a fine line that separates a peaceful demonstration from one that turns violent. We need to anticipate angry mobs of one hundred thousand or more rampaging through our cities. We need to deploy the National Guard at hui demonstrations to keep the peace. I trust I don't need to remind you what happened at P&G."

President Dial cut in. "We'll consider placing the National Guard outside city centers where protests are scheduled to take place, but the last thing we want is to provoke violence by having a military presence. The hui movement is founded on government mistrust. I won't fuel those flames by flexing our military muscle. What we can do is step up our efforts to change public opinion about huinomics.

"Each of you has an operating budget for public relations. I want to channel those funds into a campaign to get the message out that the American government has grave concerns about huinomics. We need to show our side of the story. We need to let America know what will happen to the elderly and our veterans when people do not pay their taxes. We need to let people know that work stoppages will harm our nation. We need to hire the best social media experts or we won't be able to compete with the hui movement. I realize that certain individuals will be up in arms about diverting funds from Appropriations. Let me tell you right now: if we don't act strong and act fast, there won't be any funds to appropriate.

"We are engaged in a battle for the very ideas this country was founded on. Should we fail, the America we know today will no longer exist. The future will be vastly different and I fear we will slide considerably in our global standing. Our only hope is to unite and shift the tide of support for huinomics. I am asking each of you to join me in this fight." Adjourning the meeting President Dial felt moderately relieved hearing his cabinet members applaud.

Directly following the cabinet meeting, President Dial called Larry Baker to the Oval Office.

"I wasn't expecting dissension within my own staff. Did you know about this? Who else supports huinomics?"

Baker sat down and said, "Look, I understand your concern. I was just as surprised as you. If Lisa and Francine had the guts to speak publicly in favor of huinomics, no doubt there are others."

Staring at the presidential seal plastered to the ceiling, Dial sighed and said, "We must plan for every contingency. Let's assume that huinomics is allowed to flourish, and the government's operating budget is cut in half. What could we cut and still survive?"

Taken by surprise, he answered, "I don't know. What a sobering thought. The military, Medicaid, Medicare…"

"We need to look into every possibility. In the meantime, let's get Ross Hamilton on the phone. I want to know how his Bloodhound tracking program is progressing."

A few moments later Ross Hamilton appeared on the video phone looking startled.

"Mr. Hamilton, I apologize for the impromptu phone call. I'm here with Larry Baker. We were discussing your progress with Bloodhound's ability to detect algorithmic trading. As you know, New York passed a law prohibiting this nano-trading. We need the SEC will follow suit."

"I wish I had better news, but the nation's best physicists have yet to find a plausible way to detect high speed, high frequency trading."

The President retorted, "Then the best physicist work for the nation's top investment firms, not us."

"Not this time. At considerable expense, we recruited several physicists from the private sector, but they're coming up with the same results. Stealth artificial intelligence programs are too hard for Bloodhound to detect. Their complexity and speed is far too great. It's like trying to stop the rain using a screen."

"Are you telling me it's impossible for us to police the buying and selling of securities?"

"Yes. We can enact laws, but if we don't devise ways to force radical changes, we can't enforce regulatory statutes. We can punish those who get caught, but the big players know how to evade detection. It's kind of like giving a master thief the keys to your home and telling him if he takes anything he'll go to jail."

"What do you propose?"

"I don't like this expression, but I don't know how else to say it. We need to dumb down the market. In short, we need to take computers out of the equation. The only way we can do that is by requiring stock exchanges to issue users an exchange code that will only be valid for ten minutes per stock symbol. Requesting and entering exchange codes will force stock trades to take place in real time."

"How will eliminating high-speed trades effect Wall Street?"

"The days of nanosecond stock trading and using sophisticated artificial intelligence programs to beat the odds will be over. In turn, we should see the market flatten out; the days of huge market swings will end."

"Stability will come with a price; what is it?"

"Considering that the New York Stock Exchange alone has over one billion trades taking place every day, reducing the volume of trades by ninety percent will greatly reduce profitability in the financial sector."

"What's the big picture?"

"The financial industry will take a big hit, but in the long run it will help individual investors who have put their life savings into 401k programs."

"Why wasn't this changed before the stock market loss 18% of its value? No wonder why the American public has lost faith in the government."

A long pause took place before Ross Hamilton said, "Regan and every president after him deregulated everything they could get away with. Wall Street has profited at the expense of Middle America for some time. Legislation like this will reverse the tide."

"The governor of New York has already pushed through state legislation regulating the stock market. Have your staff study what they did in New York and draw up similar legislation. Let me know as soon as you have it ready. The SEC will have to submit when the Congress signs it into law."

Hanging up, president Dial looked across his desk to his long-time friend, Larry Baker, and smiled.

"It looks like we may be making history."

Larry Baker said, "From the ashes, the Phoenix rises."

After another sleepless night, Thomas was thankful Judge Becket ordered a public assembly ban. He barely had the energy to dress and climb into the waiting car, let alone make an address to the thousands of supporters thronging to the courthouse every day. Holding Rebecca's hand, Thomas simply waved to the crowd before quickly climbing the steps and sweeping through the tall double doors.

Leaving Rebecca at her aisle seat right behind the audience barrier, Thomas hurried over to Emmings, who greeted him with a jerk of his head. Without ado, Judge Becket announced that court was in session and told the prosecution to call their first witness.

A stillness settled over Thomas as Mulland called Rebecca Swanson to the stand. She took her time rising and walked elegantly to the witness stand, was sworn in, and took her seat in the box.

In an understanding voice, David Mulland asked, "Ms. Swanson, tell me, how did you first meet Thomas Quinn?"

Rebecca gave the impression that she was trying to look brave, and looking directly into David Mulland's eyes said, "It is difficult to say. It began sometime after the holidays, during our senior year. Thomas Quinn always seemed to pop up when I least expected. After a while, I got used to Thomas approaching me. He did it all the time, when I was walking to class or eating in the cafeteria…he just started hunting me down."

"What was Thomas like during these impromptu meetings?"

In a shy voice that retained a sense of refinement and confidence, Rebecca said, "At first I found it flattering. You know, being a young woman and having a boy's attention like that. But Thomas was always, you know, fidgety. His little visits became very uncomfortable."

"Uncomfortable? How so?"

"Well, for one thing, he always spoke too loud, and fast. And he stood too close and put his face really close to mine." Embarrassed, Rebecca said, "I had to lean backwards when he spoke to me or he would have been close enough to kiss."

Watching the jury soak in Rebecca's performance, Thomas felt completely alone, like drifting on a raft in a frigid ocean.

"Did Thomas ask you out on any dates? That is, other than prom?"

"I think he wanted to but never got up the courage. Right before spring break he did manage to ask me for my phone number."

"Did you give it to him?"

"No. I told him our phone was disconnected because my mother didn't pay the bill. In part it was the truth. She often ended up paying the bill in-person to get it turned back on."

"You could have given it to him anyway, for when it was working. Why didn't you?"

"I didn't really like Thomas. I certainly didn't want to give him the wrong impression, like I wanted to be his girlfriend or anything. I guess you could say I wasn't attracted to him."

"But you agreed to go to the prom with him. What changed your mind?"

Rebecca looked as though she were far away as she said: "I always dreamed about going to the prom. I wanted to dress up and dance with a good looking guy, like Cinderella. I didn't expect anyone to ask me during my sophomore year, but when I got passed by in my junior year, I was afraid I would never get to go to prom."

Rebecca paused and looked down, giving the impression she had revealed more than she had planned to.

"When Thomas asked me to go to the prom, I told him I had to think about it. I was praying someone else would ask me, because Thomas was pretty much my last choice. But no one asked me so, two days before prom night, I let Thomas know that I would go with him on one condition. I told him it was only a date; I would not be his girlfriend."

"So you were not emotionally involved with Thomas."

"Exactly. Like I said, I didn't even like him. I went with him because no one else asked me and I just had to go. I had dreamed about it for four years."

"Did you ever meet with Thomas outside of school, before the prom?"

"No."

"Did you ever talk on the phone with him?"

"Never. Thomas knew where he stood with me. I never even gave him my phone number. He had my address to pick me up in the limo. I knew there would be other kids with us the whole time. I was hoping I wouldn't have to deal with him that much."

"When the limo came did he go into your home to meet your mother?"

"No."

"Why not?"

"We were poor. We lived in a rundown rented house. I felt ashamed. I just wanted to get to the dance. Besides, I had already come to terms that my 'dream date' for the prom wasn't going to happen. You know, pinning the corsage while your folks took photos. I just wanted to get the ride over and get to the prom."

"So you got into the limo without Thomas meeting your mother. Tell me what happened on the way to the prom."

"I was the last one to get picked up so I sat on the jump-seat. Thomas was sitting across from me."

"What do you mean by jump-seat?"

"We called the side seats, the ones where only one person can sit, jump-seats. All the other couples sat side by side, but we were separated, which was fine by me."

"What happened during the drive to the prom?"

"Everyone was laughing and talking and having fun. Like most of the guys, Thomas had a flask of Vodka and he started drinking."

"Did you drink with Thomas?"

"Yes. We were all drinking. I wanted to be part of the fun, so yes. I had some drinks off Thomas's flask."

"Had you ever consumed hard alcohol before that night in the limo?"

"No. I had a few sips of wine from my mother's glass, but that was it."

"How much did you drink on the way to the prom?"

"I'm not sure, maybe two or three gulps. I remember it burned like hell. I also distinctly remember that it didn't have any effect on me at first. I thought, why do people like to drink? This isn't doing anything."

"Did Thomas try to hold you or make physical contact with you on the way to the prom?"

"No. We were sitting across from each other. Once we got out, Thomas held my hand and we went into the gym."

"Tell me about the dance."

"We found our assigned table but I didn't stick around. I went to see friends at other tables. I was hoping someone besides Thomas would ask me to dance. When it was clear none of the other guys were going to ask me to dance, I got upset and went back to our table. Thomas looked unhappy. He asked me if I would dance but I didn't feel like it. He was sneaking drinks off the flask and I joined him, thinking it would cheer us up."

"How much did you have to drink?"

"I wasn't keeping track, but towards the end of the dance all of a sudden the vodka hit me. When I closed my eyes I felt like I was falling backwards."

"Would you say you were intoxicated?"

"I was defiantly intoxicated. It crept up on me. One moment I had a burning sensation in my stomach and the next I couldn't walk straight."

"Was Thomas intoxicated?"

"No, I don't think so; anyway he sure didn't act like it."

"What happened during the limo drive home?"

"I was feeling sorry for myself. Everyone in the car had a great time except Thomas and me. They were all happy and goofing around. I just wanted to get home and forget the whole thing. I felt miserable. I just wanted to close my eyes and go to sleep."

"Did you fall asleep?"

"After the first two couples left, the back seat was open so I sat back there. I fell asleep soon after that."

In a somber voice Mulland said, "Tell me what happened next."

Rebecca looked down and stammered, "He did it to me."

Raising his voice, Mulland said, "I know this is hard for you, but you must tell me exactly what happened next."

Fighting back tears, Rebecca looked at Mulland and said, "I think I must have passed out because I woke up with him inside of me. At first I couldn't believe it. I thought I was dreaming. But when I felt a sharp pain down there I was jolted awake. Only then did I realize what was happening to me. I shouted out but he quickly covered my mouth. I tried to get away and hit him with my arms but he was too powerful." Tears rolled down Rebecca's cheeks. In a voice wracked with despair, Rebecca said, "He did it…I felt so horrible. I put my hands between my legs and rolled up into a ball and cried. I felt so hopeless. I wanted to die."

Unable to continue, Rebecca buried her face in her hands and cried. She tried to stop, only to be consumed by another tremor of grief welling up from deep inside her.

Allowing her sorrow to cast a dark cloud over the courtroom, Mulland waited a while then said, "Tell me what happened next."

Wiping away her tears Rebecca answered, "The driver didn't do anything. He shouted something but just kept on driving. He didn't care. The car stopped seconds later and I got out and ran for my front door. The door was unlocked but my mother wasn't home. I slammed it shut and locked it. I went to my room, threw myself down on my bed and rocked myself to sleep."

"When you awoke, was your mother there? Did you tell her what happened?"

"Yes, she was home making breakfast like she always did Sunday morning. I knew I should tell her but I couldn't. I just couldn't. I was so shocked and traumatized. So I pretended it was all just a bad dream."

"Tell the jury what happened next."

"I took that dress, the one he ruined, my prom dress, and buried it in the back yard so no one could ever find it."

"Why didn't you go to the police?"

"I was afraid of what people would think. I didn't really have any close friends or family. My mother was all I had in the world. I wanted to be her little girl like always. I couldn't bear the thought of her looking at me differently. I made-believe that it never happened."

"But it did happen, didn't it? Can you tell the jury how your life changed after the prom?"

"I didn't want to go back to school. I was so afraid that Thomas would be bragging to his friends. The very thought of seeing Thomas again made me sick. I felt students were looking at me funny as if they knew what happened. I felt so horrible."

With tears beginning to flow again Rebecca looked at Thomas and with loathing in her voice she said, "He made me hate myself."

The courtroom went silent. Then Mulland asked, "What happened to you after high school?"

"My life just got worse. I was really unhappy and began to argue with everyone, including my mother. I was planning on attending a junior college, but I moved out that summer. I moved to Phoenix. I worked as a clerk at a dollar store. My dreams were gone. The only thing Thomas Quinn left me was alcohol, and that was the only thing that made the memory of what he did to me go away."

"Why did you wait so long before bringing Mr. Quinn to trial?"

"It took some time for me to realize I needed to stand up for myself. It took me years to build the courage. I didn't have any money. It was only after Thomas Quinn became famous that I began to think maybe a law firm would take my case."

"So you contacted the law offices of Baker, Smith and Hines."

"Yes. I figured they would have the expertise to ensure that Thomas Quinn is punished for what he did to me."

Turning to the judge, David Mulland said, "No further questions, Your Honor."

"This court is hereby adjourned until 1 PM."

With a regal defiance, Rebecca stepped down from the witness box and walked right past Thomas, whose quizzical look seemed to say, "You're kidding me, right?"

Staying while the courtroom emptied, Thomas motioned for Jackie to stay in her seat as he whispered to Emmings, "My God, they're buying her act! Every word she says is a lie. And the tears! It's all crap! She deserves an Emmy!"

"I knew they would coach her extensively, but this is ridiculous. We're going to trip her up on cross-examination, though. Right after lunch."

"All I can stomach right now is coffee."

The three of them returned to the Italian place where a table was waiting for them. They sat in silence until it was time to head back to the courthouse.

Rebecca was called back to the stand and was sworn in. William Emmings approached her politely, as if she were an alien life form, and began his questioning.

"So, if I understand you correctly, according to your testimony you did not ask Thomas Quinn to the prom. You maintain he asked you, correct?"

"Yes, Thomas Quinn asked me to the prom."

"You said that prior to the night of prom, you never drank before. I think you said, 'Just a few sips' from your mother's glass, is that correct?"

"Yes."

"How many times would you say you drank from your mother's glass?"

"I don't understand the question."

"Did you taste alcohol once before prom night? Or are we talking more like two or three times?"

"I don't recall."

"Did you ever have more than a drink from your mother's glass?"

"Never. The first time I drank was on prom night."

"Did you drink after prom night?"

"Yes."

"How much?"

"A lot."

"Ms. Swanson, would you call yourself an alcoholic?"

Jumping to his feet, David Mulland said, "Objection, Your Honor. Events after the night of May 16th are not relevant."

"Sustained. The defense will confine themselves to the events surrounding the night of May 16th."

"We took a look at your transcripts and found that you were frequently tardy. In fact, you were tardy 18 times during your senior year and absent eleven times. Why were you tardy and absent from school so frequently?"

"Objection. Irrelevant, Your Honor."

"Your Honor, I am establishing a pattern of behavior."

"Over-ruled. Ms. Swanson, please answer the question."

"My mother was always busy at work, so I had to help out around the house."

"That cannot be the truth, because the school bus records show you were on the bus, so you had to be tardy later in the day. Which periods were you tardy for?"

"I don't remember; it must have been 5th Period, after lunch."

"So you took long lunches?"

"I told you, I can't remember."

"Did you smoke cigarettes during your lunch period?"

"Objection."

"Over-ruled."

"Yes, behind the school, off of school grounds. It was cool back then. A lot of kids smoked."

"Did you smoke marijuana during lunch?"

"No, I never smoked pot."

"So you smoked cigarettes on a daily basis, even though there was a strict ban against smoking at your high school, but you say you never drank. Oh, except for a few sips from your mother's glass. You say you never smoked marijuana, but you dressed in Goth clothing and listened to heavy metal music. All the other Goth kids were certainly drinking and smoking pot, I wonder how you resisted?"

"Objection!"

"Sustained. The jury is to disregard the defense's last question. Mr. Emmings, you are walking a thin line."

"Tell me, Ms. Swanson, are you a sentimental person?"

"No more than anyone else."

"Do you have a collection of things from your childhood, any dolls or other possessions?"

"No."

"So why did you keep the dress? Why not just throw it into the trash?"

With a tinge of malice in her voice Rebecca said, "Like I said before, burying the dress was the act of a young, frightened woman trying to forget her past."

"So you dug a hole in the back yard and threw the dress in it and buried it, correct?"

"I didn't just throw it into the hole. I placed it in a plastic bag, put that into a cardboard box and buried it."

"Is that so? How deep did you bury it?"

"I didn't measure it but I guess it was two to three feet deep."

"Uh-huh. What tools did you use?"

"A shovel."

"Are you familiar with the word caliche?"

"No."

"Caliche is a type of soil that is formed by hardened deposits of calcium carbonate. The soil in your back yard in high school is caliche. Did you know that caliche is so dense that workmen use jack hammers to break it up? Yet you were able to dig a hole two to three feet deep using a mere shovel. Can you describe to the jury just how that was possible?"

"It took me a long time and I got blisters on my hands but I didn't care. I had to bury that dress to forget what Thomas Quinn did to me."

"Is that so? And tell me, Rebecca, just what was the condition of the shoe box and the dress after being underground for 18 years?"

"The shoe box was destroyed, but the dress was not damaged."

"So the dress was just the same as when you buried it 18 years ago? No water stains? No worm holes?"

"I wouldn't say it was exactly the same but the plastic did a good job of preserving it."

"So let me get this straight, you dug a three foot hole in rock hard soil with only a shovel, to find a dress that looks absolutely new despite it being buried underground for eighteen years. I guess next you want us to believe that you donated the purse and shoes to the Salvation Army?"

"Objection."

"Sustained."

"The Defense has no more questions for this person, Your Honor."

"Then call your next Witness."

"The Defense calls Thomas Quinn to the stand."

Feeling lightheaded, Thomas made his way to the witness stand, was sworn in and climbed into the box.

"Mr. Quinn: who asked you to prom your senior year?"

"Rebecca Swanson."

"You didn't ask her?"

"No."

"So, Rebecca Swanson's testimony is false?"

"Totally."

"Describe to the court when and how Rebecca Swanson asked you to the prom."

"It was three days before prom. I was sitting in the library during my free period when Rebecca sat down across from me and said, 'You wanna go to prom?' I thought she was joking. We'd never even spoken to each other before. We had no classes together, or any social contact. We were two completely different people."

"What did you say?"

"I asked her why she wanted to go to the prom with me. She said no one else would take her. I told her I wasn't planning on going. She just said, 'Please.'"

"So you agreed to go to the prom with Rebecca Swanson."

"Yes. I felt sorry for her. She had no friends. I mean, not one. She dressed like the Grim Reaper. I escorted Rebecca to the prom out of kindness."

"Were you fond of Rebecca?"

"No. She wasn't a very nice person."

"Were you from the same social circle?"

"No. Rebecca hung out on the cafeteria loading dock where kids smoked. I hung out in the computer lab or at the library. Socially, we were on opposite sides of the fence."

"Were you sexually attracted to Rebecca Swanson?"

"God no. Look, we were about as far apart as two people could be. I was not attracted to Rebecca Swanson."

"Did you have girlfriends in high school?"

"When it came to romance, I was a late bloomer. I met my first girlfriend my senior year of college. It was the first and only sexual relationship I ever had." Lifting his head and smiling, Thomas gestured to Jackie and said, "She's here today. My first girlfriend, the only woman I have ever known, is my wife, Jackie Quinn."

Emmings paused to allow the warmth between Thomas and Jackie permeate the courtroom.

"Describe the events that took place the evening of May 16th."

"I got dressed around five o'clock. I remember being hot in that heavy tux without air conditioning. I regretted saying yes. But my parents had fun taking pictures of me in that tux. They were disappointed that my date wasn't there, but they knew that Rebecca was not my girlfriend and that I was taking her out of kindness. Around six, the limo arrived. Two couples were already in there. We picked up one other couple before heading out to pick up Rebecca."

"Did you drink with the students in the limo?"

"No. I was in college before I had my first drink. I've never been much of a drinker."

"So you did not have a flask of vodka with you?"

"Correct. I never tasted alcohol until college."

"When you arrived at Rebecca's home, did you go in to meet her mother?"

"Before I got halfway to the door, Rebecca came walking out from around the side of the house, which was strange but no one exactly expected normal from her. I asked her if she wanted me to pin on the orchid corsage I had bought for her but she walked right past me without saying a word and got into the limo. It was obvious that if her mother was home, Rebecca didn't want me to meet her."

"At that time, how did you make sense of Rebecca's behavior?"

"I could smell alcohol on her, so I knew she had been drinking. But she drank a lot, she must have had a high tolerance because she didn't look or act drunk, she just acted perturbed, as usual."

"What do you mean by perturbed?"

"Rebecca had one hell of a chip on her shoulder, like she was carrying the weight of the world on her back. We all knew deep down something was terribly wrong but she wouldn't open up to anyone about it."

"Did Rebecca have any alcohol with her?"

"Yes, Rebecca had a pint of vodka."

"Was she drinking in the limo on the way to the prom?"

"Yes, she was drinking from the pint she had with her."

Shaking his head, William Emmings picked up a black dress from the evidence table and held it up for Thomas to see. "Is this the dress Rebecca was wearing prom night?"

"I don't know. I remember that Rebecca was wearing a black sleeveless dress, but if that's it, it's been remarkably well-preserved."

"Indeed. Describe what took place once you got to the prom."

"Not long after finding our table, most of the other kids who were sitting there left. I don't really blame them. I tried to engage Rebecca in conversation; I even asked her to dance once or twice, but Rebecca wanted none of it. She just sat there with a gloomy look on her face, like she was disturbed."

"Did she leave the table?"

"Yes, for most of the evening, in fact. I sat by myself for most of the prom."

"Did you go and talk to other friends?"

"I talked to Matt Simon, a computer club friend of mine, but other than exchanging niceties with the kids originally sitting at my table, I didn't talk to anyone."

"How did that make you feel?"

"Out of place. But I was used to feeling out of place, unless I was with my nerdy friends and believe me, none of them ever went to prom, for obvious reasons. They didn't want to experience what I was going through. Even my sky-blue tux looked nerdy next to all the guys wearing black."

"Did you see Rebecca Swanson drink from the pint of vodka?"

"A few times I remember her pouring some into a cup of punch, but like I said, most of the time she wasn't near me."

"Where did she go?"

"She didn't say, but by the time we climbed back into the limo she smelled like cigarettes. So I figured she was off smoking somewhere."

"If Rebecca Swanson avoided you the entire prom, why do you think she went with you in the first place?"

"I'm not sure. Maybe she thought she would have a good time. Maybe she had her eye on someone else. I truly haven't the slightest idea."

"What was Rebecca's condition by the time you all got back into the limo?"

"Everyone could tell she was drunk. She was weaving. I thought she was going to vomit in the limo."

"Describe the events that took place during the drive back."

"We all took the same seats. Rebecca was on the jump-seat. I sat across from her. The other kids were getting really rowdy. All the other guys got out with their dates. I guess they were going to walk home. I stayed in the limo to see Rebecca to her door. I was dropped off last."

"At any time did Rebecca change her seat?"

"No. She stayed slumped over in the jump seat. I don't think she could have moved if she had wanted to. She kept nodding off. Every time she nodded off she threw her arms out like she was falling."

"Did you change seats?"

"No. I kept an eye on her. I kept thinking she was going to hit her head or something."

"So neither you nor Rebecca Swanson moved to the back seat."

"Correct. We kept the same seats all the way home."

"After the other students were dropped off and it was just you and Rebecca, did you have any physical contact with her?"

"I never had any physical contact with Rebecca Swanson the entire night, except when we held hands walking into the prom."

"What happened when you arrived at her home?"

"I had to shout her name to wake her up. Her eyes were bloodshot. I climbed out and held the door for her. She never said a word to me. She got out, stood still to get her balance, and walked to her house."

"Did you help her to her door?"

"No. I said, 'Rebecca, let me walk you to your door,' but she scowled and waved me off. She clearly wanted me to leave her alone so I did. I just watched her stumble along until she opened her front door and closed it behind her, then I got back into the limo and that guy drove me home."

"Are you referring to Mr. Manny Hernandez?"

"Yes."

"So Mr. Hernandez was not telling the truth when he stated that you ran away?"

"No. Nothing he said was true, either. Mr. Hernandez drove me home. He had already been paid but he asked for a tip. I didn't have any money on me. I considered going in to ask my Dad but he said, 'Just forget it,' so I got out and he drove away."

"Did you talk about the prom with your parents?"

"A little. I told them I had a crappy time and that I was tired, so I went to bed."

"The Defense rests, Your Honor."

To Emmings surprise David Mulland stood and said, "The Prosecution has no questions, Your Honor."

"Tomorrow morning the court will hear your closing statements after which the jury will deliberate. This court is adjourned."

At 10:00 AM William Emmings began his closing argument. Rising slowly, he walked over to the jury and stood directly in front of them.

"Today you are faced with the decision of a life time. The fate of an innocent man is in your hands. It's as simple as that: Thomas Quinn is innocent.

"We may never know what drove Rebecca Swanson to accuse Thomas Quinn of a crime he did not commit. We may never know why Burt Vargas claimed to have seen Thomas Quinn commit an act that he never committed. We may never know how Thomas Quinn's DNA sample ended up on that black dress.

"But we do know one thing: Thomas Quinn did not rape Rebecca Swanson. You know that truth from the credibility of his testimony, from the credibility of his life, his dedication to his wife and his community. That is beyond doubt.

"What is in doubt is the circumstantial evidence the defense has presented you with. Are we to believe that a dress, that has been buried underground for 18 years can look new? Not to mention that a young girl of eighteen is willing and able to dig at least two feet underground in rock-hard caliche using a mere shovel. Moreover, there is no way of proving if the DNA sample is three months or eighteen years old.

"Ladies and gentlemen of the jury, the case the prosecution built just doesn't stand up. There is clearly more than a reasonable doubt of Thomas Quinn' guilt.

"I ask each one of you to search within yourselves and recall when Thomas Quinn took the stand. Remember how he looked, the sound of his voice, the words he spoke. There you will find the truth. You will see that Thomas Quinn is innocent."

Emmings turned and took his seat.

Getting up and shaking his head, David Mulland walked over to the jury and held out his arms. "The defense wants you to think that this is all just a figment of your imagination. That it's all make-believe. That, simply based on the sound of someone's voice, this rape did not happen.

"Rape, ladies and gentlemen, is not make-believe. It is real, it is brutal and it devastates people's lives. It devastated the life of Rebecca Swanson.

"I'm not asking you to base your decision on the sound of the victim's voice. I'm asking you to base your decision on the facts.

"Fact: Thomas Quinn's DNA matches the DNA on the dress. Fact: Burt Vargas witnessed Thomas Quinn rapping Rebecca Swanson. Fact: for eighteen long years Rebecca Swanson suffered from being brutally raped by Thomas Quinn.

"No amount of emotional grandstanding can obscure these facts. They prove Thomas Quinn rapped Rebecca Swanson on the night of March 16th.

"Rape is brutal, it is ugly and it brings out the very worse in men. All rape victims have mental damage, but when a young girl of eighteen is raped on prom night, the mental trauma is immeasurable.

"Thomas Quinn stole Rebecca Swanson's innocence, her self-respect, her hopes and dreams!

"Ladies and gentlemen of the jury, Rebecca Swanson waited eighteen long years for this day. Rebecca Swanson has suffered all of her adult life. You can't return to Rebecca Swanson all the years she has lost. All that is gone now. But you can give her some measure of peace knowing that justice has been served. You can do your duty as citizens of this great nation and convict Thomas Quinn of rape."

David Mulland took his seat with an air of self-righteous indignation. Judge Becket glanced at the papers on his desk before lifting his head and said, "This court is now adjourned. The jury will begin its deliberation."

Emmings, Thomas and Jackie went to an outer office to wait. When the phone rang two hours later, all three of them jumped. Shocked that the jury reached a decision so quickly they hurried back to the courtroom.

The judge called the court to order.

"Has the jury reached its verdict?"

"Yes, Your Honor."

Accepting the folded piece of paper from the Head Juror, Judge Becket read it silently then handed it back. The Head Juror took his place in the front row of the jury box and read: "In the charge of third degree sexual assault, the jury finds Thomas Quinn guilty."

Silence reverberated through the courtroom louder than a gunshot. Thomas clenched his fist so tight his nails bit into his palms. Then he took a deep breath and let go. He was prepared for this outcome and now that he was facing it, he found he was able to accept it gracefully, as he had hoped he would.

"Due to the perpetrator's age at the time of this event, and based on the fact that he has no previous arrests or convictions, I hereby sentence Thomas Quinn to four years in prison."

Standing, Thomas swallowed hard, vowing not to let go of his spirit. Jackie made her way over to Thomas on uncertain legs. Clutching his arm she said, "This can't be happening." Thomas smiled and brushed away the tears running down her face. "It's going to be Okay. This is all part of the journey. Everything will be fine." Duty bound, two clearly sympathetic officers cuffed Thomas the escorted him out through the back of the courtroom, to be transferred to the state prison in the morning.

Senator Bates shouted, "Max." Even louder, "Max, come in here! I got some news for you."

After being evolved with bringing Thomas Quinn to court, Max Harvey's perspective of working for Senator Bates took on an entirely new light. A conservative to the core, 'safe and secure' was Max's mantra. He wouldn't think of getting behind the wheel of a car after having a drink, let alone toying with the law in such a grievous manner. It far exceeded his risk tolerance.

When he heard about Blake's death, Max's fear shifted into overdrive, prompting him to buy a sixty dollar audio/video pen camera with a sixteen gigabyte memory chip. Max would be damned if he would allow Bates to make him the fall guy. Sensing the time was right, Max nervously turned on the camera, stuck it in his front shirt pocket and walked into Bates's office.

Bates excitedly waved Max over to his desk and barked, "Close the door behind you." With the door securely closed, Bates said, "Was I right or was I right? Thomas Quinn is in jail."

Frantically thinking that he did not want to be the next person going to jail Max replied, "How much time did he get?"

"Four years. Sure, he'll walk in two or three, but by that time he'll be ruined."

"I heard his sentence created a backlash."

"Damn it, there will always be naysayers. But this is the opening we have been waiting for: the conservative Christian coalition is turning on Quinn. The pendulum is beginning to swing in our favor."

"If we get the Conservatives, our overall support will top thirty percent."

"More like forty percent. Once that happens, it's only a matter of time before huinomics becomes a blip on the radar."

"What about Senator McCormick? His case may have some validity. Hui supporters may gain footing in making a martyr out of Quinn."

"McCormick has his head up his ass. There is no way a man found guilty of a crime, especially rape, will ever be looked at in the same light."

"I see your point." Talking softer, Max leaned in and asked, "Do you think anyone will be suspicious of Rebecca Swanson's new found fortune?"

In anger Bates snapped, "Don't you worry about Swanson."

Knowing it was now or never, Max said, "I'm worried that somehow this could get back to you. Are you certain that Baker, Smith and Hines can be trusted?"

Bates looked at Max as if he just stepped in dog shit, and as usual, his anger got the best of him.

"Damn it! What else do you want me to do? I told you there is no possible way any of this could come back to me. Look, untraceable cashier's checks went directly to Hine who placed them in four different banks before it stopped in our friend's account. I'm not an idiot, Max."

Smiling assuredly, Max pulled back, thinking, "I got you, you slimy bastard." But to the Senator he said, "You're right, of course. I don't know what I was thinking. I'll never mention it again."

"Good. Now get back to work on Sunday's interview with Meet the Press."

Chapter 14

Detric Ehrlich's anxiety grew. At first Detric tried his best to push it aside but like a leaky faucet, images of Rebecca Swanson and Thomas Quinn kept dripping into his mind.

When the court found Quinn guilty, Detric began to fall apart. Getting off the tram he took home every night, Detric was appalled to find his left foot dragging spastically like it was bound by an invisible bungee cord causing it to scrape against the pavement every time he took a step. Taking off his shoes as soon as he got home, Detric looked down in disbelief at the strange scuff marks along the top of his left shoe.

Disgusted with himself, Detric took out an old flat tin of black shoe polish. Polishing in tiny feverish circles, he frantically worked to remove the small scratches on the left shoe. With every stroke, Detric summoned what little strength he had left to rid his tormented mind of Thomas Quinn and Rebecca Swanson.

Vowing to vanquish his newly acquired spastic gate only made things worse. Detric took to lifting his left knee abnormally high, causing his foot to dangle momentarily like a lump of meat at the end of a pole before he untrustingly set it on the ground.

A single number was like a cybernetic virus physically morphing Detric into a paraplegic. This number, 7895-4278-69550, was the root of all Detric's misery. To anyone else the number was just like any other random string of numbers, but only Detric knew it was the number linking Rebecca Swanson's trust account drawn from the account of Baker, Smith and Hines via a transaction of the Cayman Islands.

Over the years, hundreds of names and interlinked numbers crossed Detric's desk. Corrupt politicians, drug lords and thieves all placed their trust in Banca Zabin. Without realizing it, they were actually placing their trust in Detric Ehrlich. Detric held the keys to open all of the doors.

To men like Detric, the thought of betraying a client's confidence was unbearable. Coming from a long line of men just like him - precise, meticulous men who would rather sever an arm than expose a client's identity - Detric found himself drowning in moral quicksand. Relieving his conscience would mean betraying his employers, and possibly being jailed.

With every thought, Detric sank further into the abyss.

It wasn't the coarse prison clothes or being shackled to a steel bar on the reinforced transport bus that tortured Thomas. It was the bright yellow plastic paint coating the prison walls. It made him feel his life was being squeezed out of him. Walking down the state penitentiary hall, Thomas felt he was entering an enormous lifeless plastic pit. Windowless walls illuminated by sharp white florescent lights guided their path as the guard led Thomas deeper and deeper into the prison. Feeling lightheaded to the point of fainting, Thomas prayed for relief. When they finally made it to the Warden's office, Thomas inwardly rejoiced when he saw that the Warden had a window.

The Warden looked mean. Thomas hoped their conversation would be short.

In a voice that was used to getting its way, the Warden barked, "Sit down." Thomas took a seat, the guard standing at attention behind him. Taking his time, glancing over a file flipped open on his green steal laminated desk the Warden looked up at Thomas.

"You're the first celebrity we've had in this prison for a long time."

Waiting for a response that did not come, he said, "I don't know if I like that or not. You probably think you're better than everyone, including me. Well, that'll change. You'll quickly discover that the only thing that matters is survival. Your fellow inmates don't give a damn who you are. Men like you have only one function in this world of ours, and I don't think you'll find that much to your liking."

Still waiting for a reply, the Warden grew impatient.

"There are arrangements that can be made. A man of your fame must have unknown millions at his disposal. Money can make the hazards of prison life more, well, let's just say 'secure.'"

The attempt at extortion did not anger Thomas so much as the Warden's pleasure in being a bully. Suppressing his fear, Thomas said, "I'm confident that the $49,700 the state pays for each and every one of your prisoners is sufficient to make me feel secure."

The Warden jerked back his arm to hit Thomas and he probably would have, if Thomas had been within striking distance.

"Now I'm damn sure I don't like you. For being such a fucking smart ass, your fee just doubled. The only way you'll find any safety behind these walls is through me. Now get the fuck out of my sight."

Opening the door, the guard looked at Thomas and cocked his head before escorting him down the hall. After clearing the first security gate the guard said, "We were hoping we'd get you. Most of the men here are hardened criminals, but a whole lot of people here believe you were framed, including me."

Thomas looked into the guard's eyes and saw sincerity there.

"Thanks. The Warden said I need to make a contribution to keep safe in here, is that so?"

The guard frowned and snapped, "I don't know shit about that and you best not mention it to anyone. Keep your mouth shut." Easing up some, he said, "But don't worry. The men like you."

Entering the main cell block, Thomas understood what the guard said. Word of his arrival was spreading along the cells on either side of the corridor faster than they could walk. Thomas felt relieved as he heard shouts of encouragement as they passed. Opening the door to a cell and nodding for him to enter, Thomas was greeted by a black man about Thomas's age. He raised his hand high and said, "My man! Shiettt."

Thomas grinned and high-fived his new cell-mate, thinking, "At least something is going my way."

"I'm Marcus, Marcus DePaul. Damn! Ain't I the lucky one. Shiett."

"I'm Thomas Quinn."

"Hell, man, I know who you are. Shiett. Everybody knows you. You're the man. And here you are in my cell. Ain't that the shit?"

"The Warden tried to scare me. Like I should expect trouble."

"Hell, man, the Warden should know better than to pull that shit on you. You ain't going to find no trouble here. Even The Band is calling you their brother."

"The Band?"

"The Aryan Brotherhood, man. Now those are some mean-ass mother fuckers. When you got them on your side, ain't nobody going to mess with you."

"I thought the Aryan Brotherhood was a white supremacy gang. I'm about bringing people together, not driving them apart."

"Don't believe all the shit you hear. The AB are brothers with La Ema… the Mexican Ma-Fee-Ah. Hell, the Outside wants you to believe we're just a bunch of animals butt-fucking poor white boys. Shiett. It ain't like that. We're just like anyone else, man. We want what is good for us. There's gotta be a better way and Mr. Quinn, you are it."

Surprised by the unexpected support, Thomas said, "I just had the idea. Thousands are making it a reality. What're you in for, Marcus?"

"Armed robbery. Held up a pawn shop while high on crack cocaine. Got four years for stealing $43 and an electric guitar. I wasn't any chronic-lag crack-head, either. Just wanted to party, man; just wanted to party."

"I'm less than impressed with our judicial system myself."

"Ain't that the truth."

"I need to make some calls. How much phone time do we get?"

"Fifteen minutes twice a day. But you don't need to worry about that, man. You can have all the phone time you want, starting with mine."

After a night haunted by the strange sounds of a strange place, Thomas woke to the sound of a guard shouting, "Thomas Quinn. Simion Ruzart is on the line, wants to talk to you."

Marcus sprang from his bunk. "Simion Ruzart! Damn, man, give me the phone. I need a loan! Shiett."

Thomas cracked a smile and, rubbing his eyes, shuffled over to the bars to grab the phone. Thanking the guard, Thomas took the phone back to the edge of his bunk.

"Hi Simion."

"The New York Stock Exchange opened 45 minutes ago."

"That was quick. What's going on?"

"New legislation was just rolled out. Whenever a stock is bought or sold an exchange code must be issued to authorize it. This will slow the market down to what it was thirty years ago."

"Who would have guessed that Dial would have the courage to enact change?"

"That's the good news. The bad news is that the market is still dropping. Even taking computers out of the equation, the market has already lost 3% of its value."

"What about P&G?"

"P&G is down 13%."

"P&G pledged to buy back their stock at the pre-boycott rate of sixty-nine dollars a share. Why would anyone continue to sell at a loss?"

"Just like anything else: fear. How are you holding up?"

"I'm hanging in there. God knows my time, or anyone else's for that matter, could be better spent than sitting in jail."

"Keep your spirits up. We're all counting on you."

"How do my prospects for an appeal look?"

"We still have a detective investigating how your DNA fell into the prosecution's hands. But it seems our adversary is much too cleaver to make simple mistakes, so don't get your hopes up. Our best bet is a Presidential Pardon."

"A Presidential Pardon? I'm not too high on his list."

Marcus' shoulders began dancing up and down and from the background he chimed in, "A Pardon? Shiett. You gotta get me one of those. Damn, tell Simion, no problemo, I'll keep those free minutes flowin', just get me a Pardon, too."

Thomas covered the mouthpiece. "Marcus."

Marcus threw up his hands in acknowledgment that he was being a pain in the ass and would stop. Thomas returned to the call.

"That's your cell mate, I take it?"

"Yes."

"Glad to see you're making friends. We need to talk about Maria Salazar."

Maria Salazar was the first person ever fired from Vorbine. She wrangled herself into a front page tabloid spot with the claim that she was fired from Vorbine for being an 'overweight Christian.' Peter Sadinski deflected the initial media storm but right wing radio personalities were starting to cash in.

"The opposition is getting far too much mileage from the Maria Salazar issue, so Peter has arranged for Susan Tang to interview you in prison."

Susan Tang was a new breed of political talk show host. Having worked as a news anchor for years, her authority sanctioned the show's title: 'Between the Lines'.

"A show I admire. Susan Tang draws a large crowd. When is it scheduled?"

"Tomorrow."

"As much as I like the idea, it doesn't give me much time to prepare. Not to mention I don't have a thing to wear."

"You know your best work is impromptu. Just be yourself, but remember your audience. Be casual, like you were talking to Jackie."

Despite Simion's confidence, Jackie threw questions at Thomas during visitation hours and on the phone for the better part of the day. With nearly twenty inmates granting him their phone minutes, Thomas was exhausted by the end of the day.

News of the interview electrified the prison. For a softer touch, they held the interview in the prison library. Susan Tang and Thomas Quinn faced each other in heavy metal chairs upholstered in red plastic, their legs crossed casually. After a few cues from the camera woman, Susan Tang began.

"Mr. Quinn, thank you for agreeing to meet with me under such trying circumstances. I'd like to begin with something that's on everyone's minds. We've heard many versions of what happened to Maria Salazar at Vorbine. What's your version?"

"I appreciate this chance to meet with you and please, call me Thomas. I really don't have a version, but I know what lead up to Maria Salazar being fired. Your viewers may or may not know that, unlike conventional corporations, an employee is expelled from a hui corporation democratically. Each member has a vote. Members are provided factual information about the incident. Then they take an online test to evaluate if they have any bias toward the person in question. Then they cast their vote. The hui voted to expel Maria Salazar. They have the right to do so, as all members know before they join."

"But there are three thousand Vorbine employees. Testing them all hardly sounds efficient."

"It's not efficient, but it's fair. And being automated, it is surprisingly fast; the data is transmitted via smart phone to a cloud-based program for tabulation. All members must participate before getting to work. In Maria's case, the entire voting process took an average of ten minutes from beginning to end. It does take some time and effort, but it's the only way to reach an unbiased conclusion."

"It sounds regimented. So why did the hui vote to have Maria Salazar expelled? She's making a pretty good case that she was thrown out for sharing her Christian views."

"To answer that question, your viewers must first understand that hui corporations place as much importance on social skills as cognitive or craft skills. You see, hui corporations strive to be free of unproductive social pressure. Mutual acceptance and respect are the guiding principles of huis. Accordingly, the back-stabbing and brown-nosing that is so much a part of existing corporate culture is grounds for expulsion in a hui corporation."

"But everyone gets the same reward working for a hui corporation… why would anyone bother to try to improve their position using politics?"

"The answer is multifaceted. First off, a member's reward for work performed is based on the type of work they do, just like a conventional corporation. Initially, monetary reward is the main incentive to work hard but over time it becomes less and less important. Factors like personal satisfaction and camaraderie become primary motivators. In other words, the work itself and one's perception of their coworkers is more valued than monetary gain whether you work for a standard corporation or a hui corporation. Because politics erode effectiveness by decreasing overall job-satisfaction, it is grounds for expulsion in a hui corporation."

"You still haven't answered my question: Did Maria Salazar get fired from Vorbine because of her religious beliefs?"

"Nothing could be further from the truth. One of the core beliefs of huinomics is to experience life to its fullest. That's why Vorbine built a multi-denominational spiritual center for worship on-grounds, though folks can go anywhere they wish to worship.

"Maria Salazar was not expelled for her religious beliefs; she was expelled for being so confrontational. She made it hard on those around her to work."

"How so?"

"Maria worked as a frame fabricator on the shop floor. It's a tough job with a lot of physical requirements. Her last fabrication task entailed moving six-foot lengths of aluminum pipe from a conveyor belt onto an extruding press that stretches and shapes the pipe.

"Maria admitted that she was not happy with her job because of its physical requirements. She systematically began to criticize her foreman in an attempt to get her job."

"So Maria Salazar was fired because she criticized her foreman? Rather extreme, don't you think?"

"Yes, if that was all there was to it, I would agree. But that was not the case. Maria had counseling over the course of three weeks prior to the vote. Even with counseling, Maria still chose to be disruptive in her department.

"You may think, so what if Maria caused waves? It's not a big deal to put up with someone's bickering. The problem is that resentment leads to the degradation of that person's work and it brings down the morale of every worker who is exposed to her. In short, political back-stabbing is like a virus that, if not cared for, can ruin a company."

"So, would you say Maria Salazar was fired because she was unprofitable?"

"We like to use the word 'expelled' because it captures the harmonious group lifestyle of a hui. For people to work in harmony with each other, the environment must be non-confrontational and apolitical. Maria's tirades disturbed the peace, making everyone around her less happy and less profitable."

"But Vorbine has over three thousand positions. Why didn't Maria Salazar get transferred to a job she liked?"

"Again, there is a concept out there that hui corporations are some kind of happy commune, obligated to care for every member whether they are good workers or not. This concept is totally false. Hui corporations exist, and will proliferate, because they are highly competitive. Vorbine is growing faster than any energy corporation in history, a success based entirely on the productivity of its workers.

"Maria Salazar could not be transferred to another position just because she didn't like her job. It wouldn't be fair to the other employees. If Vorbine had gone against hui principles and just transferred her to avoid controversy, then any employee wishing to be transferred would only need to be disruptive. It would have also undermined the voice of Maria's coworkers, while subjecting another group of people to her negativity."

"So Vorbine employees are stuck forever in the same job?"

"Members can leave any time they like. They can apply for other positions inside Vorbine as well. But please don't confuse manual labor with something distasteful. Vorbine factory workers take pride in their work. In fact, manual labor has many benefits over white collar work. Also you need to keep in mind that people perceive work differently in a hui corporation. Since there are no lawns to mow, no meals to cook, no laundry to do, and in the case of Vorbine, no commute, employees have a great deal of time to pursue other interests outside of work. Work is not the focal point of their lives. To fully understand what I am saying, ask yourself this: does my work occupy the majority of my life?"

"I've never given it much thought. I guess I would have to answer yes, but my work is definitely rewarding. So tell me, what is your response to those who say you created the concept of social evolution just to support your huinomic theory?"

"Sentient species must evolve socially to circumvent extinction. If we do not shift to a sustainable economy we will become extinct just like the inhabitants of Easter Island. The inhabitants of Easter Island became extinct because as their population grew, they exhausted their natural resources. This is unlike the Hawaiians who had a far denser population, but thrived because they had a strict set of environmental laws."

"So you believe that mankind will perish like the people of Easter Island if we do not work in groups?"

"It is not a belief. It is a mathematical equation. The amount of $co2$ the planet can absorb is a finite about. Thirty gigatons of carbon thrown into the atmosphere every year is not sustainable. If we do not bring carbon emissions down to zero within fifty years, the planet's temperature will continue to rise and much of humanity will not survive. The question is, will we do something about it or fling ourselves off the cliff like lemmings?"

"Bringing carbon emissions down to zero within fifty years is a another story. But back to Maria Salazar. Maria has stated that being a member of Vorbine stripped her of her freedom. She said that Vorbine members don't even have the freedom to buy their own clothes. What is your response to that?"

"Vorbine provides its members a clothing allowance. There are on-site stores, and of course members are free to drive to retail stores whenever they have time can to buy whatever they have the money for. But you will never see a Vorbine member with a closet full of shoes. In a self-serving world, people want a closet full of shoes. In a group-serving world, people want to see every person on the planet owning a few good pairs of shoes."

"But the desire to impress others by owning things is part of human nature. We all want to have more than our neighbor has. It's only natural to want more."

"I disagree. We are programmed to want more. We are programmed to believe objects are a reflection of our sense of self-worth. That is, of course, absurd. Belongings are sorry replacements for the connectedness and meaning we all desire."

"There are those who say your utopian optimism is unrealistic. People are base; they're self-serving. They act in ways that help themselves, not others."

"People join huis because they want more out of life, not to get a closet full of shoes."

Susan Tang shook off her predatory questioning and smiled. "I believe in your cause, like so many others, but I'm not willing to give up my shoes…at least, not yet. Thank you, Mr. Quinn."

Turning to face the camera woman head-on, she said: "This is Susan Tang reporting live from New Mexico State Penitentiary."

"What do you mean, move to the country? Oh Detric, what has happened to you?"

Looking at the small potted plants on the kitchen windowsill, Detric turned and said, "Laline, I can't go on like this. I've got to get away."

Seeing her husband collapse like a windblown tent, Laline stammered, "The pills. The pills the doctor gave you…you're taking them, aren't you Detric?"

"The pills?" Detric snorts in disgust, "Damn the pills, they do not help. I can't take it anymore! I am trying to tell you Laline our lives are about to change. I tried to stop it. I have suffered so, but I cannot take it any longer. I must let you know the truth."

Seeing tears well up in Laline's eyes, Detric said, "My dear Laline. Sometime ago I took care of a five million dollar trust fund. This trust fund was established for a very famous person. An infamous person. I tried not to care, to pretend that the fund doesn't exist, but I couldn't. This fund has been haunting me. I can't sleep, I can't eat…this secret is sucking the very life out of me, Laline."

"What is it, Detric? Tell me. I will understand."

"Thomas Quinn is innocent. A five million dollar trust fund is being held at my bank for Rebecca Swanson."

Having feared much worse, Laline wiped the tears from her eyes and said: "Is that all? No problem, Detric. You just tell the truth."

In despair, Detric said, "It's not so easy. I will lose my job. I will lose my pension. Twenty-six years at Banca Zabin and they will take away our retirement pay. We will have nothing."

The room became icy quiet. Laline's soft mouse-like voice broke the silence.

"Nothing, nothing at all?"

"Worse than nothing. Zabin will press charges against me. They will sue me for everything we own. I will be blacklisted. No bank will ever hire me again."

Putting her hands on the table and lowering her head down on them to stop the room from spinning, Laline took a moment before straightening up. Then she leaned forward and looked Detric in the eye and said, "You do it. You do it, Detric. Don't care about Zabin. You free yourself from this hell. We will get by."

Helping Laline to her feet, Detric hugged his wife of twenty-eight years, feeling closer to her than he ever had before. Then Detric pulled back and said, "I have a plan."

"Zabin will come after me, but I'll be ready. First, this home and everything we own will be put in your name. Legally, I will own nothing. Second, I will sell the story to an American media network. They will pay me a lot for the story. This is our only way out. I will be free from Zabin and we can retire to the country."

What Connie Phen lacked in flair, she made up for in friends. Good friends. The kind of friends who will be there when you need them.

One such friend was Milton Kirkpatrick. A throwback from the era when art and craft dictated print quality, Milton had operated printing presses for some of the largest magazines for nearly thirty years. Today, Milton was obsolete, as presses practically run themselves. From typesetting to cut and bind, modern high speed printers are a marvel of automation, which was just fine by Milton, as he was getting soft. Milton's belly, tight as a snare drum, was expanding with every passing year.

Occasionally, after everyone was gone, Connie would navigate the factory's labyrinth of stairs and descend into the press room to drink single malt scotch with Milton.

Although a loner, Milton liked Connie. Sure, she wanted the scoop like everyone else, but she was different. Connie didn't ask Milton for breaking news. If he wanted to give her a story it was because he liked her. Neither wanted to do anything that might mess up their friendship. First and foremost, Connie and Milton were friends.

At 8:30 in the evening Milton gave Connie a call. She was just putting up dishes in the small studio she shared with her son when he called.

"Hey Connie, how's it going?"

"I wish this rain would stop. I feel like a wet chicken."

Milton smiled. He had been skeptical about Asians before he met Connie. He couldn't read them, there were too many differences. But as he got to know Connie, he began to cherish those differences. Like the image of a wet chicken. So Taiwanese.

"I got something for you."

"Let me call my sis to come watch Brian and I'll be right over."

"This is too big to wait. I'm sending you the file."

"No Milton, it's not worth it. It's safer for you if I come over. No big deal. I can be there in an hour."

"Too late. I just sent it. Don't worry about me. This old dog knows a few tricks. We'll catch up tomorrow." And with that, Milton hung up.

Opening the file on her phone, Connie realized her life was about to change. It was the story of the century and it was hers. True to form, Connie did the first thing she always did when confronted with obstacles: she called a friend.

Alex Baker was an Assistant District Attorneys working in New York. He had given Connie her first real break with a human trafficking story because he liked her. They became friends, giving each other work back and forth over the years.

"Alex, I just got the story of the century."

"Are you talking this century or last century? You know, you got some stiff competition if it was last century."

"Alex, stop fooling. Have you heard of any action against Baker, Smith and Hines? Listen. You are not going to believe this: Thomas Quinn is innocent. Milton is printing a story proving that he was framed. It will be on every newsstand by the morning."

"My God. Who's behind it? What does Baker, Smith and Hines have to do with it?"

"They paid off Rebecca Swanson, or at least that's where the money trail stops."

The phone went quiet before Alex asked, "Can you give me the story?"

"What do you plan to do?"

"Catch a thief. As soon as the story hits, Baker, Smith and Hines will cover their tracks. We need to investigate their office before they have a chance to destroy any evidence."

"I'll give you the story, Alex, but no leaks. I want signed confidentiality agreements. People could get hurt."

"Connie, I'm going to hand the story over to the District Attorney.

I don't think Neil Cummings will have any interest in leaking the story before it hits the stands."

"I don't care if you give it to the Pope. Whoever gets the story, including Neil Cummings, they must sign an affidavit."

"Okay, you have my word."

Without hesitating, Alex called his boss, who picked up after the ninth try. Within minutes, Neil had the district judge on the line, who issued a search warrant for Baker, Smith and Hines. Ever loyal, Neil's next call was to the Mayor, Joe Hinkle.

Unlike the string of Mayors before him who rode to power on the coattails of their Wall Street connections, Joe Hinkle rose from the rough streets of the lower east side, becoming the youngest Mayor of New York through his connections with the common man. Shear tenacity and unstoppable determination got Joe Hinkle elected Mayor of New York. As an outspoken proponent of huinomics, Joe Hinkle was grateful that Neil called him so quickly.

"Does the police commissioner know about this?"

"I just got off the phone with him. He's meeting me with ten of his best plainclothes detectives. Two men will be stationed at every floor."

"Why such a low profile?"

"We were tipped off. To protect our informant we are sworn to secrecy until the news story breaks. Our main objective is damage control…make sure evidence isn't destroyed."

"When does this go down?"

"I'm on my way there now."

"Good call, those bastards never sleep. When does the story break?"

"Distribution begins at 4:00 AM."

"I'll be there at 5:00 AM with a camera crew."

Neil was impressed by the opulence of the Baker, Smith and Hines building. Situated in the heart of Lower Manhattan, the entrance doors opened onto a massive foyer whose floors were a Romanesque mosaic of polished black granite inlaid with white marble. Rising out of the jet black floor was a floor-to-ceiling Dale Chihuly sculpture. It was breathtaking.

Shaking his head, Neil thought: "The money supply is soon to shut down for this pack of thieves."

At 9:15 the police commissioner simultaneously sent up detectives in five elevators to secure the top five floors. A bold lawyer on the top floor refused to open the door was finally persuaded only after a detective took his photo as evidence of obstruction of justice. Within a few minutes each of the floors were secured. The employees, all 127 of them, were given the option to wait in the main conference room or return home. Despite arguments by some of New York's top lawyers, no data or documents could leave the premises.

Within minutes, Michael Simmons along with the other partners at Baker Smith and Hines learned about the search. Michael Simmons called the last remaining senior partner Mathew Hines.

"Michael, this better be good. You know I go to bed early."

"I doubt you'll get any sleep tonight."

"What is the problem Michael?"

"The police commissioner is at the firm. He just expelled the remaining staff and closed the doors pending an investigation."

"Yeah? Well, they won't find anything."

"We don't know where they got their information."

"You mean Bates had a leak? Why would anyone want to stick their foot in a bear trap?"

"You know what a big mouth that man has. Who knows who he pissed off?"

"Easy now; we don't know all the facts."

"The D.A. is down here; they seem pretty confident."

"There's nothing to find, correct? Michael, you did follow all our security procedures, yes?"

One reason for Baker, Smith and Hines' success was the diligent destruction of any information connected with any infraction of the law. The inner circle at Baker, Smith and Hines held firm to the belief that you have nothing to hide if you destroy the evidence. No documents, emails, receipts, recordings…nothing, nothing was ever kept.

"Yes, of course, but I can't help wondering why our building is swarming with detectives."

"Call Bates. Let him know what's going on. Tell him to use his contacts inside the police to get over to the office and fix this thing."

"I'm not sure that's our best option. I don't even know if I can reach him."

"That's my last word on the matter. You do what you need to do. Now, good night, Michael."

Michael didn't bother trying to call Senator Bates. He knew his only chance was to see him in person. So, for $4680, David chartered a jet to Washington DC, departing at 10:30PM.

By 11:45 Michael stood on Senator Bates's doorstep. Giving up on the doorbell, he pounded on the door and shouted until a police cruiser drove up and a police officer verified Simmons's identity and called Bates to give him the all-clear.

"What the hell just happened? Why did you call the cops on me?"

Fuming, Bates replied, "I did not call the cops on you. It must have been the neighbors. Now why are you pounding on my door in the middle of the night?"

"The police are searching the firm. All activities at Baker, Smith and Hines have been halted pending their investigation."

Senator Bates looked like he was about to throw up all over his padded silk robe. Breathing heavily, Bates leaned menacingly toward Michael.

"How the hell did this fuck up happen?"

"I left New York 52 minutes ago to ask you precisely the same question."

They glared at each other. Bates's breathing became more labored as his eyes narrowed in fury.

"Senator, take it easy."

Realizing he was on the verge of fainting, Bates closed his eyes and tried to control his breathing. Michael helped him inside to a chair in the foyer. He began turning red.

"Get my blood pressure meds…bedroom…night table. Fucking can't believe…you're in my house! Get the meds!"

Guessing the bedroom to be on the upper floor, Michael ran upstairs and after opening two doors he found the master bedroom, surprising a young woman who sat bolt upright in the Senator's bed. Clutching the bedspread to hide her naked body, she opened her mouth to scream but before she could make a sound Michael said, "I'm a friend of Bates. He needs his blood pressure meds, now!"

The young woman quickly reached over to grab the bottle on the night stand, exposing her slender torso. Michael diverted his eyes as he approached to take the pills from the young woman's outstretched hand. Tearing down the stairs, Michael realized he had to save Bates and get the hell out of there.

Bates swallowed two and said, "Get me to my study. I'll be fine in a minute."

Waiting for the medicine to kick in, Michael couldn't help but wonder what he would gain if Bates's heart gave out. Looking around the dimly lit room, it was clear that Bates's brand of politics paid well.

When Bates's breathing was under control he said, "This is your problem. I have nothing to do with what is going down at your firm."

Hoping to avoid the need for medical attention, Michael moderated his approach to Bates.

"Whoever sent the D.A. to our doorstep knows otherwise. We need to consider every possibility. If we know where the leak came from we might be able to protect ourselves."

"Really, why you are here? What do Baker, Smith and Hines' legal issues have to do with me?"

"What makes you think the leak came from us? It is quite possible the leak came from your side of the river. Look, right now the NYPD is searching our firm; if you get Homeland Security involved, you could muddy the waters."

Peering over at Michael, Bates regained his cocky disposition.

"And just why would I want to do that? I see no reason why I should stick my neck out for you boys."

Sick or not sick, Michael had enough of Bates's arrogance.

"Ah, for one, I know about your involvement. Ever hear of a little thing called State's Evidence? Secondly, what makes you think the leak came from us? You need to engage Homeland Security to protect yourself, Senator."

"Impossible. Only your firm knows; no one else. That grants me deniability."

"So you never told anyone, not even a bed companion, of this affair?"

Remembering the woman in his room, Bates grimaced.

"Don't be ridiculous. I hardly need to impress a woman with stories."

Looking at the haggard fat old man in front of him, Michael thought the Senator's self- deception bordered on delusion.

"So you want me to believe that you never spoke of this matter with anyone?"

Bates remembered his conversations with Max and briefly questioned Max's loyalty. But he knew that Max was totally devoted to him. In fact, Bates believed Max loved him like a father. Puffing out his chest, Bates said, "The only one I spoke to is you. So if I go down, you go down."

Michael knew Bates was lying, but this line of questioning was getting him nowhere so he changed his tactics.

"I see. We still need Homeland Security. Even with extraordinary caution, you never know what fragments of information might be missed."

"Fine. I'll call in the troops, but understand, I'm cleaning up your mess."

Simmons walked back out the front door with the image of Bates's smug smile etched on his memory.

Surprisingly, Stephen Alerkson picked up on the fourth ring.

"Stephen, Bates. We have a problem. The New York police

commissioner, along with God knows who, has quarantined the offices of Baker, Smith and Hines. I need you to send in a team to investigate."

"Investigate what?"

"You know what. To investigate why they're investigating!"

"What? This is the first I've heard about this. Call your contacts at the firm, confirm your information and call me back."

"My contact, Michael Simmons, just left my house 30 seconds ago. Consider my information confirmed! The police escorted his staff from the building about 90 minutes ago and sealed the building. Now get your boys in there and tell me what's going on."

"There's no way I'm going to send a team over there to cover your ass. I'm not laying my career on the line for you."

"Get a fucking backbone. You are the Vice Deputy of Homeland Security. Say you got a tip that a terrorist infiltrated Baker, Smith and Hines and you needed your own eyes on the situation."

Barely controlling his anger, Stephen hissed, "This is a police affair."

"Do I need to remind you just how precarious your position is? I heard about what happened to James Blake. Now that wouldn't be murder, right? Manslaughter?"

Stephen Alerkson didn't normally have violent thoughts but just then he imagined putting a gun to Bates's head and pulling the trigger. Swallowing hard, Stephen answered, "Look. I'll make some calls, see if there's any intel on the investigation. After that I'll assemble a team, on location. Once we have intel, we'll move quickly."

As Michael was waiting for a cab outside Bates's front door to bring him to the Intercontinental Hotel, Detective Danny Thompson stood inside his office wondering where a man like Michael Simmons would hide his darkest secrets.

Danny's skills did not come from studying forensic science, but rather from tough knocks street smarts. Growing up as a short pudgy kid in the inner city, Danny had shark like instincts in reading the worst in people. It is hard enough being a butter ball when you were a kid back then, but when your mother had the reputation of having the milkman in for coffee, kids could be absolutely cruel. Unlike most kids Danny fought back. Danny did not fight with his hands but with verbal abuse. Danny went far beyond swearing at bullies, in a flash Danny could unleash a torrent of personal insults against his assailant. By trial and error Danny could read the very worst in people and verbally cut them down to the bone. More often than not Danny would get the shit kicked out of him the first time a bullies picked on him but the verbal abuse he inflected on them kept them from coming back.

Looking at the expensive antique Persian rug laid carefully over the office's exquisite walnut plank flooring, Danny easily imagined Michael's life of elegant socializing and ruthless legal manipulation. Thinking, 'the geek hounds won't find anything here,' Danny took in the contents of the room. Italian leather sofa, two matching easy chairs, a wet bar, priceless paintings, and a grand ebony desk filled the room.

Circling behind the desk, Danny felt that tiny tingle, like a sixth sense sounding an alarm, and he knew an important clue was within his grasp. Then he spied it.

Under a pink crystal cube was a blue and white Memo note. Smiling, Danny moved the fancy paperweight and picked it up. Name, Phone Number, Time, Date and Message, all neatly filled in.

"Of course! You don't listen to voicemail. How mundane. Your secretary filters your calls and your voicemail, capturing only the most important for you to review at your leisure. She's the key," Danny thought.

Neatly stacked in the back of the deep bottom drawer of the secretary's desk were six used phone message books. Feeling like he'd unearthed the Dead Sea scrolls, Danny set the oblong books on the desk and began flipping through their flimsy yellow carbons.

At 5:05 AM, Larry Baker was lying half-awake when his phone rang. Seeing his aide's number, he picked up the call.

"Hi Ellie, what's going on?"

"Turn on Channel Seven. Thomas Quinn was framed."

Turning on the light and grabbing the remote, Larry flipped to Chanel Seven and saw a photo of Detric Ehrlich standing in an urban neighborhood with a woman clinging to his side. He heard the reporter state that this brave banker stood up for what was right and informed the authorities that the law firm of Baker Smith and Hines had paid Rebecca Swanson to file the spurious suit. Police were searching the law firm's offices for proof.

"Ellie, are you still there?"

"Yes. This is unbelievable."

"I knew he was innocent. Look, we need to act quickly. Get the Attorney General on the phone. I want a full pardon drawn up for the President to sign."

Larry realized it was Wednesday, the day President Dial attended mass so he wouldn't be available until 8:00 AM. Unlike his predecessors, who used Christianity as a political widget, Dial kept his religious practices hidden, even converting a small room off the kitchen into a chapel known only to a few of his Cabinet.

"You have it drawn up and bring it to me, Ellie. I'll get the President to sign it."

Placing the thin phone back on his nightstand and laying back down, Larry began obsessing about the National Intelligence Director's probable involvement in what would surely be the Scandal of the Millennium.

At 5:06 AM, Joe Hinkle stood in front of the Chihuly sculpture with a vibrant female newscaster facing him.

"Mayor Hinkle, can you tell us if the law firm of Baker, Smith and Hines is responsible for framing Thomas Quinn?"

"I assure you that the hard working men and women of the New York police department are conducting a thorough investigation into the affairs of Baker, Smith and Hines as we speak. Acting on an anonymous tip, NYPD has labored through the night, collecting information to aid the investigation. We will not rest until we get to the bottom of this."

"Have any charges been brought against Baker, Smith and Hines or any of its employees?"

"It's too early for arrest warrants. However, the business activities of Baker, Smith and Hines, along with the firm's financial accounts and other associates, have been suspended."

"What is your view? Do you believe that Thomas Quinn is innocent?"

"Yes. As you know, I've gone on record months ago questioning the entire trial. This new evidence has proven that Thomas Quinn was framed. Now we have to find the people who did this and bring them to justice."

"But don't you have them? Clearly, Baker, Smith and Hines were named by Mr. Ehrlich, the Banca Zabin whistle-blower. We know they deposited the money in Rebecca Swanson's Swiss bank account."

"Of course, this law firm was involved, but we don't know who. Those responsible for framing Thomas Quinn will be brought to justice. If anyone is with holding information they need to do the right thing and step forward, just as Mr. Ehrlich did."

Just as the Mayor was ending his plea for information, shouts came from the regal front doors of the Baker, Smith and Hines Building, where two plainclothes policemen were struggling to deter entry to what looked like a pack of rabid executives.

With cameras rolling, the Mayor shouted, "This is a quarantine crime scene! Any unauthorized entry is prohibited."

Unaware that they were being filmed, a man from the back of the pack stepped forward and said, "As we were trying to tell these police officers, we are authorized! We are Homeland Security agents, acting on the behalf of the Director of National Intelligence."

Unmoved, the Mayor stated, "As the Mayor of New York City, I am here to inform you that this is not a National Security issue; you have no jurisdiction here. The building is locked down. NYPD has secured the crime scene, heading off any potential cover-up." Then the Mayor stepped aside to reveal the rolling cameras.

Upon seeing the cameras, the agent balked.

"Mayor Hinkle, in all due respect, the Director of National Intelligence's authority supersedes yours in this matter. We would appreciate your cooperation in turning this case over to us."

"And you are agent…?"

"Barns, Sir."

"Agent Barns, unless I receive a direct order from the Commander in Chief, no federal agent will have access to this crime scene. Now, you and your officers will need to vacate these premises immediately or our officers will remove you. Do I make myself clear?"

Sneering, Barns turned and headed to the door with his men in tow.

Invigorated, Mayor Hinkle turned to the cameras.

"There is no evidence that the firm of Baker Smith and Hines is connected to a terrorist organization in any way. What is clear is that this law firm is directly involved in monetary transfers to Rebecca Swanson and Manny Hernandez.

"Exactly why Home Land Security agents were sent to investigate a local crime scene needs to be answered. But you can rest assured that the hard working men and women of the New York police force will bring justice to all of those involved in framing Thomas Quinn."

Excusing himself of any more questions mayor Hinkle felt his power expand knowing this live news coverage was airing around the world and that he was at the center of it.

At precisely 7:30 AM, Larry called the president away from his chapel to bring him up to speed.

"My God. What a mess. Have the attorney general draw up Quinn's pardon. I want his release to be swift and silent."

"The documents are ready and here for you to sign."

"Good job. I can always count on you to be on top of things."

Signing the document, the president said, "Have the Attorney General do what needs to be done to have Thomas Quinn released before noon. Make sure the press knows about the pardon."

"Already on it."

"Now we need to answer the big question. What role did Homeland Security play in sending Thomas Quinn to jail?"

"You know how I feel about the Director of National Intelligence. General Wiley has been flying beneath the radar for a long time. We should assume he played a role in framing Thomas Quinn."

"The blowback from such a covert government operation will be catastrophic. We could be looking at anarchy, rioting, and widespread distrust of the government's ability to govern."

"You need to see the New York footage with Mayor Hinkle. He made it clear to the American public that Homeland Security was somehow involved in the fame."

"Get the Director of National Intelligence General Anthony Wiley on video."

Five minutes later, the general's face appeared on the screen.

"General Wiley, why wasn't I notified of Homeland's proposed actions?"

"This morning, Sir?"

"This morning, last week, last month…yes, General Wiley. ALL of your department's actions."

"Sir, Stephen Alerkson, the Vice Deputy of Homeland Security, acted on his own authority. I have requested his resignation, effective immediately. I have people I personally trust conducting an investigation into any possible connection between the department of Homeland Security, Rebecca Swanson and the law firm of Smith, Baker and Hines."

The President gathered himself and calmly stated, "Trust is hard to come by these days. Contrary to the principles of democracy, there seems to be a prevailing theory in your department that it's best to keep the people, and their President, in the dark. I will go on record to inform you, General Wiley, that I must be informed immediately of all past and present Homeland Security involvement in framing Thomas Quinn. Withholding information will result in immediate court martial by your Commander in Chief as treason."

"Yes, Mr. President. I understand exactly what's at stake here and I will keep you abreast of all activity. To begin, we have pulled Alerkson's team from the Baker, Smith and Hines Building and are interrogating them."

"Good. Lieutenant General, I have no doubt your department was behind this. I want to know who, and when, and why, and I want to know today. Have I made myself clear?"

"Absolutely clear, Sir."

Signing off, the President looked at Larry, too tired to be furious.

"President Dial, what makes you think General Wiley can be trusted?"

"What choice do I have?"

Hanging up, Lieutenant General Anthony Wiley wore a smirk. As the Director of National Intelligence, Wiley commanded an educated and trained army of 230,000 men and women, all serving in the United States Intelligence Community. Before 9/11and the creation of the Department of Homeland Security, the President controlled the CIA. The CIA was the President's private army, ever ready to follow his command to topple foreign governments, assassinate rivals and wreak economic havoc on his enemies without the consent of Congress, without the knowledge of the American public.

9/11 ended all that. The intelligence community was no longer under the president's control. Lieutenant General Wiley had control and he knew how to use it. If the president was too weak to keep the country safe, Wiley would. His love for his country, the United States of America, was as strong and steadfast as bedrock.

An hour before Alerkson sent his fools off to the Baker, Smith and Hines crime scene, Wiley had sent an elite team of CIA operatives to observe and report on the activities of the NYPD and Mayor Hinkle.

Rebecca refused to shed the new personality that Harris Thompson had crafted for her. She loved feeling as if she could be someone. Rebecca wore her new persona as tightly as her Neman Marcus suits. No longer the antisocial pessimist with nothing good to say about anything, Rebecca became a reserved, caring person, who, for the first time in her life, actually began to like herself.

Over and over Rebecca pledged not to return to her old life. She would break free from the chains of alcoholism. She would go to California, get a job in a small town convenience store, and wait out the two years before claiming her pot of gold.

She would walk with the sun on her shoulders and a breeze in her hair. She would become a new person.

With a heart full of joy, Rebecca drove off to California in her dusty old Jetta the same day the trial ended. With long shadows slipping over Shiprock, the high desert monument that guided the Pueblo people north, Rebecca looked for a motel in the little town of Teec Nos Pos. A rusting red and yellow motel sign caught her eye and she pulled into the gravel parking lot. Sighing, Rebecca tried to forget the posh hotel rooms of the past three months, telling herself that she could stand one night in the rundown motel. After all, she had stayed in much worse.

Trying to work the old tarnished key into the handle of her hollow core motel door, Rebecca focused on not thinking about the small adobe building down the road with a flashing sign in the window. With hands shaking, Rebecca shook the door open, walked in and closed the door behind her, feeling for the light plate near the door.

She flipped the switch and gasped. The room smelled like a dirty rag and looked like a glorified jail cell. She set her small suit case on the dresser and pulled the red musty curtains closed. Slumped on the corner of the bed, the old Rebecca was drawn to the flashing sign down the road. The new Rebecca was content to watch television, get some sleep, and rise early to get the hell out of town before sun up.

But the sign kept flashing. Over and over it flashed in Rebecca's mind. Bar. Bar. Bar.

Going to the bathroom Rebecca looked at her reflection in the mirror. Squeezing out some toothpaste Rebecca admired her new look, but noticed how her hand was shaking. In an attempt to calm herself she said to her reflection.

"Come on Rebecca, those days are over." With a half assured smile Rebecca clenched her teeth tight as she brushed her front teeth with short quick up and down strokes.

Returning to the bedroom, Rebecca lay down on the sagging bed and stared up at the popcorn ceiling.

"Take off your clothes; just take off your clothes. You won't leave this room in your underwear."

Feeling childish, Rebecca sat up and looked at her reflection at the mirror across from the bed. She liked how she looked in her prim business suit. She admired her cream manicured nails. With growing confidence, she willed herself to believe that the new Rebecca no longer needed to drink.

But a familiar, hypnotic voice crept into Rebecca's mind. For several minutes she looked at her reflection, convincing herself that she was beyond the temptations of the past. She could relax and have a drink like any other weary traveler.

Time stood still. At first it was simply an odd sensation, but it grew until the walls evaporated and the silence was so deep that her ears began to ring. Truly afraid, Rebecca grabbed her purse and headed out the door, thinking that if she could just make it to the car she could find safety, drive away from her demons.

Stepping outside, Rebecca felt a rush of cold air and like a dog in heat, she found herself walking in the direction of the old adobe building with the flashing light. Nothing seemed to matter anymore. Rebecca's frosty breath took form under the old parking lot lights as she made her escape, her spiked heels twisting in the gravel. As if in a trance, Rebecca found herself at the door of the old adobe building.

A fleeting moment of realization flashed through her mind and for an instant she felt like running back to the hotel. But it was too late. Rebecca's hand gripped the tarnished handle. Pushing the door open, Rebecca saw her former self in the glassy raccoon eyes of the patrons staring at her as she stood in the doorway. The desire to flee grew weaker as the soft petal-green halo emanating from the illuminated bottles coaxed her to venture inside. With her arms clenched at her sides to stop the cold shivers racking her body, Rebecca walked over to the first heavy bar stool and took a seat, trying her best to be modest in her trim skirt. Ordering a gin and tonic, Rebecca's eyes were transfixed on the deep green bottle with its crisp white label. Inhaling the aromatic alcohol right before the blissful liquid slipped down her ravenous throat, Rebecca realized it was all over. The charade was over. She was back home.

Three days later, Rebecca was polishing off a fifth of gin in her hotel room at five thirty in the morning when two Albuquerque police officers knocked on the door to take her away.

While the bulk of his fellow detectives sloshed through reams of electronic data, Danny Thompson sat at Michael Simmons' secretary's desk, thumbing through old phone memo books. After hours of patiently turning page after page, Danny finally found what he was looking for: a phone memo from Senator Bates.

Like a shot of whiskey on a frosty night, Danny felt a warm sensation run through his body. With renewed vigor, he flipped through the last five books finding three more messages from Bates. Danny tore out the pages, folded them and tucked them into the inside pocket of his worn leather jacket.

Looking like he could use a pot of coffee, Danny Thompson approached the police commissioner and said, "It's been a long night. I'm going home to get some shut-eye."

Like most others on the force, the police commissioner had a special reverence for Danny Thompson. The job devoured most detectives in half the time. All the same, Danny was a wreck. Afflicted by high blood pressure, high cholesterol, and high blood sugar, Danny relied on medications to keep him alive, but he solved practically more high level cases than any officer on the force.

"Of course, Danny. Take all the time you need. Get some rest. Just check in with me sometime tomorrow."

But Danny wasn't interested in rest. Hurrying from the elevator to his car, Danny smiled when he remembered he filled up his car just yesterday; plenty of gas to drive to Washington. The sun was just rising and he pulled onto the highway. Thousands of inbound cars crawled down the opposite side of the highway as Danny headed out of town, dreaming of ending his career with the biggest bust of his life: the arrest of Senator Bates.

He imagined his picture in the paper, hauling the esteemed Senator Bates from the backseat of his car. But that's as far as his imagination could take him. Every time he pictured himself confronting the senator, the scene ended with Bates literally kicking him in the ass. Danny imagined various scenarios of him confronting the senator, none that worked: the senator was sure to use his power to steamroll Danny.

Unperturbed, Danny drove on. He knew he'd find the handle to get to Bates; he just needed to find the door.

After two hours of running on pure adrenalin Danny struggled to keep awake. Desperate to keep his eyes opened, Danny pinched the flabby flesh of his cheeks before finally spotting a towering sign of a highway fast food restaurant. Cursing himself for breaking the solemn oath he made to his doctor, Danny ate three one dollar breakfast sandwiches, reclined his seat and fell instantly to sleep.

An hour later, Danny was jolted awake. Breathing hard, he sensed something out there, something evil. Certain it was more than a bad dream, Danny opened the car door and, using the steering wheel for leverage, hoisted his heavy frame out.

Visually shaken, Danny scanned the parking lot for signs of danger. Dizzy with fright, he told himself to get to the bathroom. He walked to the bathroom in the back of the restaurant and rested his hands on the sink for a moment to catch his breath.

"Calm down. Take it easy, Danny Boy. Everything's okay."

Seeing the blood pulse in the veins of his neck, Danny splashed cool water on his face and sat down on the toilet to practice the breathing techniques his doctor taught him. Inhale while counting to eight, hold your breath for the count of five, and exhale while counting to eight. After twelve breathing cycles Danny began to settle down.

Stopping at the stone tables at front of the restaurant, Danny sat down, put his elbows on the table and rested his heavy head in them. Almost falling asleep it came to him. If he couldn't reach Bates, there must be someone else who he could reach…someone who had something to lose if Bates got away, maybe someone who worked for Bates.

Knowing it was a long shot, Danny went back to his car. Like watching a movie unfold in his mind, Danny cast everyone employed by Bates in the role of Betrayer, assessing each scenario's likelihood of success as he barreled full speed toward Senator Bates's office.

By the time Danny walked through the glass doors leading into Bates's office Danny had convinced himself his plan would work. Looking more like a pug than a boxer behind his graying mustache and thick glasses, Danny used his most serious tone of voice as he pulled out his New York Detective Badge and addressed Bates's receptionist.

"Miss, I'm detective Danny Thompson with the New York City police department. This is official business."

Bending lower to improve eye contact with the woman he said, "I'm here to see…You know, the name has completely slipped my mind. I hate it when that happens. One minute it's on the tip of your tongue and the next it's gone. Poof."

In a most helpful manner the secretary said, "Maybe I can help, what does the person do?"

"I'm so embarrassed. He's Senator Bates's assistant, or media man, confidant, some job like that."

"Oh, do you mean Max Harvey, Senator Bates's public relation manager?"

"That's it! Max Harvey. Thank you very much."

"Should I let him know you're here?"

"No, better not. See, I'm investigating a sensitive matter and it's, well, very hush hush. I don't want to alarm anyone. Just point me to his office, I'll introduce myself."

But before she could pick up the receiver Danny was making his way to the offices saying, "It is no bother, I'll find my way to Mr. Harvey's office."

Clearly feeling as if she was not doing her duty, the receptionist got up to follow Danny saying, "I really must announce your arrival. Please take a seat."

Ignoring her and walking down the hallway he turned and pointed saying, "It is this way right?" Not waiting for a response he continued walking.

Flustered the secretary quickly walked ahead of Danny past the outer offices to Max's office. Not bothering to let Max's secretary know what is happening, she sprung open Max's door saying, "I tried to make him wait outside, but he insisted in coming here himself, this is Detective Thompson from the New York Police Department."

Peering in from the side of the door Danny was just able to see Max's face turn pale and in that instant, knew he found his man. Brushing past the secretary Danny said, "The receptionist is right she did want me to wait outside." Taking two steps closer to Max, he continued in a hushed tone, "You see I need to be discreet about this business, it has to do with a sensitive issue that occurred in a law office last night."

In a tone not heard before Max quickly said, "That will be all Cathy. I will meet with detective Thompson."

The tension hung in the air for a moment before Cathy closed the door. Once they had some degree of privacy Max said, "I am a very busy man detective, I don't see why you are here."

"What I have to tell you will not take up too much of your time."

Aggressively Max reflected on his status and continued, "You do realize I could delay this meeting almost indefinitely."

Danny smiled saying, "I don't think you will want to do that, sir. You see, I am here for your safety."

Max's lower lip quivered and with a shaking voice said, "What do you mean, my safety?"

Stepping closer so that he could lower his voice to almost a whisper Danny said, "You see, during my investigation last night I found some rather incriminating evidence regarding your employer in one of the offices of Baker Smith and Hines. I don't want discuss it here, because, you know, for security reasons. Why don't you and I go out and get a cup of coffee somewhere?"

"I dddonn't bbelieve you."

Taking out the phone memo sheets from his inside pocket and holding them up for Max to read, Danny said, "I took this memo from Michael Simmon's office last night. You know, he is one of the big shots at Baker Smith and Hines. I was so hoping to avoid that for you."

Max clenched his teeth tighter, stifling a scream that came out like a squeak. Panicked he grabbed his jacket and nearly ran out the door, running into his secretary Cathy who apparently had been lurking nearby.

"Goddamn it Cathy! One of these days your eavesdropping will be the end of you!"

Max pushed past her, ran to the elevator and banged his balled fist against the Down arrow while Danny put a reassuring hand on Cathy's back and whispered, "Nothing's gonna happen to you, Max is just upset. You did good."

Trembling in silence, pantomiming that the elevator was bugged,

Max waited until they were in the parking garage before shouting, "What the hell do you want with me?"

"We know Senator Bates was behind the Thomas Quinn affair. We presumed that you aided him."

"Fortunately, Bates's sees me as too insignificant to perform all but the most menial of tasks. Mainly, I just listen to his interminable yammering about his two favorite subjects: his greatness, and saving this country from Thomas Quinn."

"You know about the death of James Blake?"

"Of course I do, why do you think I'm talking to you? Senator Bates was always a conceited bore, but when I found out about Blake....you need to put me in some kind of protection program. I'm not worried about Bates. You don't know who all is involved or what lengths they will go to keep this from being exposed.

Inwardly Danny knew he was in way over his head. Wondering where they should go Danny pulled out of the garage and said softly, "We're going to be alright."

"We? We?!"

The car went quiet. Danny drove while Max fumed.

"Who else knows about the memos?"

"Just the two of us."

"You mean it's just you and me? We are screwed!"

"Nobody knows…"

Just then a UPS truck ran through the intersection and smashed into the driver's side, flipping the compact car into the air like a Killer Whale playing with a seal.

A few seconds later, Max gained consciousness: he was upside down with his head pinned against the roof of the car. He heard the wheels still spinning and felt a warm wet sensation on the side of his neck. Panning, he took in the broken glass on the upside down pavement. Next he recognize Danny. His neck was bent unnaturally to the side. As if recognizing a familiar shape in muddy waters Max realized that Danny was probably dead.

Hearing sirens muted in the distance like a far off fog horn, Max recalled his conversation with Danny. Someone tried to kill him; his killer could be approaching. Max began to struggle, causing a bolt of pain to reverberate through his body. He heard a song begin playing in his mind and he willed himself to remain conscious. There was a pedestrian kneeling beside him saying, "Hang in there. An ambulance is on its way."

Max managed to croak, "Get out of here. Murder. Thomas. Quinn."

Moments later a police car arrived, followed by an ambulance and a rescue fire truck. Hearing the Jaws of Life splitting the car open, Max felt a sense of relief: the assailant must have fled.

In minutes, Max and Danny were out of the car. They lifted Max up and laid him on a gurney and as they slid him into the back of an ambulance he saw a paramedic pull a sheet over Danny's face. Max came to his senses and pathetically cried out.

"Murder. Police! Police!"

Two officers came running.

"Take it easy guy. You have been in an accident. We are taking you to the hospital."

Shaking his head, Max said, "I work for Senator Bates. That man was NYPD. They're not going to let me live to tell this story."

One of the officers stepped away and radioed his superior. Max heard him say, "Yeah. Two cars. We're leaving in the ambulance now."

While the medic took Max's vitals and hooked him up to an IV, Max told the officers about the memos in Danny's pocket incriminating the Senator and Baker, Smith and Hines in the framing of Thomas Quinn.

Without a word the policemen looked at each other and one touched the transmitter at his left shoulder.

"Stop the ambulance with Detective Danny Thomson's body and recover all personal items. Get his coat. Consider yourself on high alert… someone killed him to get what's in that coat."

Moments later the officers' captain was patched through to the New York police commissioner.

"I'm afraid I have some bad news. Danny Thompson was just killed in the line of duty."

"How? Where did you say you are? Washington? He was supposed to be home, in bed, getting some sleep."

"He was rammed on the driver's side by a UPS truck. The press secretary for Senator Jonathan Bates, a Mr. Max Harvey, was his passenger at the time. Danny was killed instantly but Harvey survived. He's the one who tipped us off."

"Where's he now?"

"He is in an ambulance on his way to the ICU, St. Joseph's. We have two men riding with him."

"Did they catch the driver?"

"No. Detective Thompson had evidence he took from the Baker, Smith & Hines crime scene. Guess he didn't trust anyone else to do it and I can't say as I blame him. He used it to convince Max Harvey to turn State's Evidence against Senator Bates for the Thomas Quinn frame."

"That sonofabitch. Issue a warrant for his arrest."

"Already done. I have two cars at his house as we speak. I don't know if a statement from his aide and a couple of phone memo carbons will be enough to hold him, but after the media circus that's sure to hit town, something is bound to turn up."

"You know, there's a good chance that the person who drove the truck is a government operative. Some higher up is pulling the strings, trying to hide their involvement in framing Thomas Quinn."

"FBI? NSA?"

"I'd bet NSA."

"Then we've got to go big quickly if we want to save innocent lives. Call the Times. Let's have the cameras rolling when your officers bring Bates in. Have a statement ready revealing the link between Senator Bates and Baker, Smith and Hines. Flap those memos at the camera so they can't be denied. That should help prevent any more unfortunate deaths."

Later that morning Thomas received a call from Simion.

"Thomas, I tried to reach your earlier but the guards couldn't patch me through."

Smiling, Thomas asked, "What's the news? Has a Zurich banker turned over evidence against Senator Bates and Baker, Smith and Hines?"

"I knew it. You can't keep news like this from leaking, even in prison. How did you find out?"

"The guards stay up all night watching TV. I had a blissful awakening around three am."

"Senator Bates is in custody."

Inwardly Thomas rejoiced. Of all the people Thomas struggled not to hate, Senator Bates was at the top. Repressing his desire to tell Simion he's keeping Bates's bunk warm for him, Thomas simply said, "The harder they come, the harder they fall."

"Jimmy Cliff, right? Very apropos. Peter Sadinski says we couldn't have bought better publicity if we spent ten billion dollars. The seas have parted. I'm sending Staple and Mack over to pick you up."

"What, now? I figured it would take at least a week for the wheels of justice to turn."

"Thanks to you, the wheels of justice are moving faster. We need you. You should be out by noon. Peter Sadinski is stationing camera crews as we speak."

"Leave it to Peter not to let an opportunity slip by."

"Peter says your three days in jail will be the most effective time you'll ever spend promoting huinomics."

"He's probably right, but this is one road I never want to walk down again. By the way did they arrest the banker? He was following his conscience…he should be rewarded."

"Highly unlikely any charges will be made. We posted his bail and we will pay for his legal counsel, if he in fact needs it. He's a national hero."

"It's all coming together."

"Wait until you see the news coverage. Americans are loosing faith in their government. You should have seen the Mayor of New York blocking Homeland Security agents from entering Baker, Smith and Hines. Even better, Americans watched Senator Bates being hauled off to jail."

"Have you spoken with Jackie?"

"No. Do you want me to call her?"

"She doesn't watch the news. Let's see how long I can keep this a secret. I want to surprise her."

"Nice. Look, when Mack and Staple pick you up, I want you wearing that vest."

"Simion, you know I hate that thing."

"You put Mack and Staple in danger when you don't wear it. You put the nation in danger. Thomas, the nation needs you. Wear the vest."

"Will do. Hey, the guard is here, I gotta go."

"They are releasing you."

"The guard says I'm going to see the warden."

"See you in Washington."

"Washington?"

"I'll explain later. Give Jackie my best."

Thomas turned to his cell mate, Marcus.

"Well, looks like my time is up. I'm glad you were my cell-mate, Marcus DePaul."

"Don't forget about us now. We're counting on you, brother."

Giving Marcus a hug, Thomas looked him in the eye and said: "Looks like my legal counsel's out of a job…no appeal. Can I ask them to drop by and look into your case?"

"Uh, sure. Shit yeah man."

As Thomas walked away with the guard Marcus started chanting "Quinn…Quinn….Quinn." Soon the entire cell block took up the chant.

Seeing the window in the warden's office, Thomas thought how wonderful it will be to breathe fresh air outside the prison walls. Sitting behind his desk, waving off the guard, the warden looked as smug as ever.

"Well, it looks like our little celebrity bought himself a ticket out of here. But, you and I both know you're just like every other guilty piece of shit sent here."

Thomas looked at the warden like he was a tormented child.

"You know, I can forgive you for delighting in harming others. I can forgive you for being pompous. But I will never forgive myself if I let you hold this position. You'll be hearing from me, warden." With that, Thomas turned and walked away.

Yelling out at Thomas's back, the warden said, "I'm not finished with you. Come back here, you piece of shit. I'm not signing your release forms!"

Unwavering, Thomas continued on to the guard's station. After standing for what seemed like an eternity, Thomas heard a loud buzz and pulled open the heavy steel door to find another set of double-chamber security doors. Again, he waited for the buzz and pulled it wide, loving the clanking of the door pulling itself closed behind him. He was finally striding across the courtyard. Ducking through another double-fenced doorway, he was met by the cheers of a small group of supporters and a camera crew.

Still in his prison jumper, Thomas waved both arms high over his head and shouted, "We did it! We did it! In just three days we were vindicated. Now, let's get to work. Huinomics will strengthen us all in the long run. The politicians will do their best to derail our cause, but huinomics will prevail because mankind will prevail. Billions of people go hungry every day while the rich lay waste to our planet, with the rest of us living meaningless lives of consumption, forever burdened with debt and an uncertain future. We refuse to live in their world any longer. We have a better way. Our time has come. Our time has come!"

Thomas refused to respond to the barrage of questions that followed, except one: "What do you plan to do next?"

"I'm going to Washington to join the fight for hui corporations. The tide is turning. My release today is proof that united, we can accomplish anything. We hold the power. All of us around the globe. People like you and Detric Ehrlich will change the world. Together we can accomplish anything."

Waving off further questions, Thomas allowed Mack and Staple to escort him to the waiting car. Once inside, Staple turned around and asked, "Where to, boss?"

Thomas grinned and said, "Home, James."

Chapter 15

After a sleepless night and four hours of interrogation, Bates was too depressed to sense the saliva trickling from the side of his mouth.

When they brought Bates in last night, head held high, he threatened every police officer within earshot. He shouted "I will have your job" so many times that, if his words had any power, half the Washington police force would have been sent home. Initially, Bates refused to believe that Max Harvey rolled on him. Bates desperately tried to convince himself that the police had made a mistake. He thought, "Sure, I'm tough on my staff. That's the only way to get things done. They understand that, don't they? Deep down, they love me. Max stood by my side all these years out of devotion. He would never do anything to harm me."

Over and over Bates told himself that this was a circus created by the Thomas Quinn camp to see what he knew. Gaining strength by the power that hate brings, Bates pledged that heads would roll in retribution for this disgrace.

Only after threatening then pleading with three of the most powerful lawyers in Washington, none of whom would take his case, did Bates finally realize he was lost in a barren desert. With no one left to turn to, Bates called their family lawyer, Tim Scott, to bail him out. A Family Law attorney, Tim knew little about criminal law but he was all Bates had.

After stewing all night in a private cell, Bates was hauled into the interrogation room. Relieved to see Tim Scott's familiar face, Bates glared at the detective who manhandled him into the hot seat with bile in his heart. Distraught but not beaten, Bates said, "I want to know your name, officer. You will take priority in my personal quest to see that every man involved in this fiasco is punished."

The hardened detective shook his head at the naivety of the congressman's threats as years of interrogation experience kicked in.

"So, you want to know who I am? Okay. My name is Detective Robert Burns. I was a close friend of Danny Thompson...you know, the detective you had murdered yesterday? He was riding with your personal assistant of twenty years, Max Harvey. You've probably heard that the hit didn't go right and that Max Harvey is on life support at St. Joseph hospital. What you don't know is, on the ride over to the hospital, Max Harvey provided us with a tape recording of a conversation he had with you."

"You don't know what the hell you're talking about. I was at home when that accident occurred."

Speaking slowly and clearly, without emotion, the detective said,

"We know you are guilty. We have your admission on tape. You will be impeached and go to prison for a very long time. That is unavoidable. But what is avoidable is having more innocent people like Danny Thompson killed. Frankly, you are neither cleaver enough or connected enough to have pulled this off on your own. Who are you working with? CIA? NSA?"

As if surfacing from the depths of a dark lake, Senator Bates drew in a deep breath and said, "I see your game. You want a pay-off don't you? I know how inner city police work: rough 'em up to get a pay-off. Well, it won't work on me. Play your dirty tricks on someone else."

Incredulous, the New York detective asked the police officer in the room, "Has this man been drugged?"

"No sir."

"Did he take any pills last night or this morning?"

Sitting up straighter, Senator Bates said, "What the hell are you inferring? I haven't been given a thing since arriving here last night, and I'm due for my blood pressure medication. My God boy, I am a third term senator. Now release me."

Realizing Bates's ego had long since swamped the rational part of his brain, Barns stated, "The judge is deliberating if bail can be posted for your release. My report that you have cooperated will go a long way in influencing the judge's decision. Tell me who you worked with and she may set you free until your trial."

"You sit at your little desk with your little gun and think you know all the answers. You know nothing of this world…what it takes to keep peace and order. Its men like me who keep your world safe. You would have nothing if it wasn't for men like me."

"Right. And its men like you who must make the tough decisions, like who lives and who dies, who gets framed and who goes free. Where are these 'men like you' now? Why aren't they helping you?"

"They are willing to make the big sacrifices. You have no idea what it takes to keep this world safe."

"It must be someone in government who helps you make the tough decisions; perhaps someone in Homeland Security? Do yourself a favor and tell me now: who helped you, Senator Bates?"

"I'm afraid that information is above your pay grade," Bates retorted with scorn.

"Look, if you didn't order the hit, who did? And how do you know they aren't planning something else? Who's next. Your wife? Your kids? Perhaps your mistress? Because at this point, it won't be hard to make it look like you've lost your mind. Then all they have to do is tie up any loose ends you have hanging out there, like Max Harvey."

Refusing to answer, Bates looked down at his hands. He realized they looked old and fat. He clenched his eyes so tight he looked like he was bracing for a blow. For a moment the room was still. Ever so slowly Bates forced himself to lift his head to face another lashing from the detective.

Instinctively knowing Bates was weakening, the detective said, "An innocent man died today. Another is lying on his death bed. The killing will continue until you confess who you worked with to frame Thomas Quinn. If there is any good left inside you, stop the killing, Senator Bates."

The senator looked down and mumbled softly, "I want clemency."

"What's that senator?"

Much louder, Bates said, "I want clemency, damn it. I tell you what you want to know but I want clemency."

"I'll do what I can to get you released on bail."

Looking older than his years, Bates looked up at the ceiling and exhaling loudly, said, "Stephen Alerkson."

"Stephen Alerkson. Who is he?"

"Stephen Alerkson is the Vice Deputy of Homeland Security. He sent agent James Blake to cut a deal with Rebecca Swanson. James Blake was killed while serving his country in Afghanistan."

"What about the money? Where did the money come from, Senator Bates?"

"That's it for today. You have enough for the judge to let me go. I'll give you the financial backers after I cut a deal with the DA."

Bates was led back to his private cell and within an hour Tim Scott was cutting a check for $500,000 to post bail. Feeling like his mind just went through a meat grinder, Bates wracked his brain for someone in his life who loved him unconditionally. On the steps of the police station in the late afternoon, in a wrinkled suit and a day's growth of gray beard, Bates called his wife.

"Evelyn, you need to believe me. I did what I did for the sake of the country. Someone had to act. I am the only one strong enough. I really need you now, Evelyn. Please come and pick me up."

"Jonathan. You call me for photo shoots, you call me for political fund raisers and you call me for campaign appearances. Picking you up at the police station is not part of the deal. Call one of your mistresses to pick you up."

Then and there, Jonathan Bates did something he promised himself at age ten he would never do again: he began to cry. Wiping away his tears with a mixture of self-pity and self-disgust, he accepted a ride from Tim to his Georgetown brownstone.

Flipping on a light and securing the door behind him, Senator Bates shuffled like an old man down the hall to his dining room credenza.

Planting one fat hand on top of it to steady himself, he reached the other into the middle drawer and took out his most prized possession: a Henry Derringer.

One of the first compression fired guns, the Henry Derringer was John Wilkes Booth's weapon of choice. Bates loved the feel of his Henry Derringer. There was something eternal about its hand-cast steel set in polished hickory. Sometimes late at night when he couldn't sleep, Bates held the gun, wondering how many lives it had taken over the course of its two hundred years. All too frequently, Bates had imagined taking his own life with the Derringer. In fact, it was such a constant fantasy that Senator Bates looked almost casual when he placed the gun in his mouth and blew out the back of his skull.

Although phones were echoing throughout his sprawling thirty-eight hundred square foot mansion, Andrew Baxter was awakened by one of his three chocolate Labradors licking his hand. Inserting his hearing aids while glancing at the clock, he wondered who could be bold enough to disturb his sleep at 9:15 in the evening. Everyone important knew that the Speaker of the House was in bed by 8:00 and was not to be disturbed.

"Sorry for the interruption, Andrew, but there's been a new development. We need your guidance."

Recognizing the voice of the Majority Leader Ely Baron, Baxter said, "Talk to me, Ely."

"Senator Bates took his life about an hour ago."

"Do we know which government agency was involved in the frame?"

"My sources believe he fingered someone from Homeland Security."

"Yes, but whom?"

"We don't know."

"Bates may be the hit that sinks our ship. Call the Members to meet at the Club at 10:00 AM tomorrow morning. This is our final hour. If we don't act now, we won't get another chance."

A stone's throw from the Capital Building, the Capital Hill Club is an exclusive club for members of the House of Representatives. From its intricately matched wall paper to its elaborate code of conduct, the club reeked of political power. Walking over the hand-scrapped solid oak plank floors, passing portraits of past presidents as they traversed the hallway leading to the Presidents' Hall, Club Members have gathered for centuries to discuss the affairs of state in private.

Despite the bitter cold, the limos began to line up First Street all the way to Independence Street. By 10:15, the Speaker of the House pounded his gavel, calling to order the hundreds of members filling the President's Hall. With a thunderous voice, the Speaker began.

"A call has gone out in the night and you have responded. I would thank you for your presence, but there is no need, for each one of you would gladly do whatever is necessary to serve your country. At this very moment, more so than any other in our history, the country needs your strength and wisdom. Our nation is adrift in the fog of conflict and is destined to crash on a reef unless we steer her clear.

"There are those among us who do not understand what we are facing. Some of us gathered today believe that this ship can weather the reef. I encourage them to take a look around at the portraits of the presidents on the walls. Enjoy being an American and living in this grand country as it was envisioned by our founding fathers while you can, because if we fail to act, if we take the easy road and become complacent, the America you know now will no longer exist. Should we enter these waters, the reef will crack the hull and our ship will sink. We must drop anchor and act now while we still have time.

"First Vorbine, then P&G, now Kimball Industries. Who's next? General Motors? Wal-Mart? Ladies and gentlemen, unless we stop them, you will witness an avalanche of companies converting into hui corporations.

"If we do not act now, it will be too late. This isn't some future possibility; it is reality, taking place right now. Today there are over two hundred thousand employees that are not paying taxes. What will happen when two hundred million employees do not pay taxes?

"Where will the money come from to run our government? Who will provide for the hungry and care for the sick? Who will pay for Social Security and Medicare? Who will protect our shores from invaders? Who will keep peace in the world?

"If we do not stop huinomics now, if we do not answer the call to act in the best interest of the nation, we will see wide spread suffering the likes of which have never been seen before. Millions of Americans will become homeless. Invaders will swarm our shores. Our nation will crumble.

"And yet, with certain destruction at our doorstep, there are those among us who are intent on turning their backs on this great country of ours. There are those who place their own self-serving interests before the interests of this great country, whose only goal is to improve their own selfish desire to gain more power.

"If you fail in this most noble duty to faithfully serve your country for the sake of being re-elected, you will have no country left to serve. The seeds of discontent are sown. As we sit in our chambers and quibble over details, distrust of the government is growing exponentially. Our inability to act is choking the life out of this nation. We must act and we must act now.

"As all of you know, we have lost one of our members. Senator Bates took his life. He was involved in the framing of Thomas Quinn, the leader and founder of huinomics. I believe it is safe to say that there is not one among us who praises Senator Bates's actions. However, I for one understand his motivation. Senator Bates foresaw the grave consequences of huinomics. He understood that huinomics would impoverish this nation allowing our enemies to run roughshod over us. Senator Bates understood the importance of passing legislation to prohibit the formation of hui corporations.

"The American public does not understand. They have been persuaded by the likes of Xavier Lamont to believe that there is a euphoric community out there just waiting for them to join; a world where all their dreams come true.

"Americans across this great country of ours are losing faith. Is their distrust justified? Is it true that we are not acting in their best interests? Yes! We are failing, because we have failed to pass legislation prohibiting hui corporations.

I ask you to join me in marching to the Capital Building where we will not rest until we pass a resolution. No more deal making. No more holding out. Today we will not be grandstanded. Today we will capture the spot light. Today we will go down in history as the first congress to march to Capitol Hill to pass legislation prohibiting the formation of Hui corporations. Are you with me?"

Thunderous applause and cries of support came from the hundreds gathered. As if sounding a battle cry, The Speaker slammed his gavel over and over, shouting: "Let's march! Let's march!"

President Dial stared at the Washington Post's photo of Senator Bates being dragged out of the back of a patrol car. Shaking his head, president Dial had an unwelcome feeling; a feeling that he had conquered long ago, yet there it was. Anger was growing inside him, once again clouding his judgment.

"Two hundred and thirty thousand intelligence employees under my command and I have to find out that Senator Bates took his life after being arrested for framing Thomas Quinn from the Post. Preposterous. Beyond preposterous. Criminal."

Throwing the newspaper to the coffee table in disgust, president Dial turned to Larry Baker.

"We have no control. Zero."

"It's got to be Wiley. I never trusted him. The Director of National Intelligence knew all along."

Dial turned and walked over to the oval window and peered out at a gardener working. Dial focused his attention on the worker's frosty breath. Standing below a mature maple, the gardener calmly raked the large auburn leaves into a pile. Dial longed to have a moment, however fleeting, where he could relax and enjoy life's simple tasks, like raking leaves.

Larry respected the president when he drifted off. He knew the quiet lapses functioned like a pressure relief valve. Looking at the president, he could almost see the anger venting from the top of his cranium.

Coming out of his stupor, Dial turned to Larry.

"There was a time when the president had direct control of the intelligence community, when honor and loyalty were paramount and people told the truth. Today, the intelligence community has grown into a myopic Cyclops, incapable of rational thought. The agencies are so large they spy on each other. We have spies spying on spies."

A voice came over the intercom: "The Director has insisted that I let you know that he would be happy to come back at a later time."

Smiling, Dial replied, "That is quite alright; tell the director to wait."

"The tragedy is we let 9/11 become a complete success for the terrorists. It's not just the three point seven trillion dollars spent thus far on the wars in Afghanistan and Iraq, money which could have provided free health care to every American. It's the proliferation of the Intelligence community and the sweeping powers it's been granted since the attack. It's bankrupting the country, financially and morally, and it has severely eroded the powers of this Office."

Larry knew better than to encourage the present to continue his discussion of the cost of war, so he made a detour.

"We can only hope that Donald Ashbury will be less secretive than his predecessor."

"I'm afraid hope is one of our few choices." Turning to the intercom, Dial requested Wiley's presence.

Standing in front of his desk with his arms folded across his chest, wearing an expression that clearly indicated his dissatisfaction, the president waited for the Director of National Intelligence to enter. Keeping his distance from the president, stopping a few steps inside the door, Lieutenant General Anthony Wiley looked as defiant as ever.

"I see you are not in the mood to shake hands with me. Quite a different position from when I gave you this job, for both of us."

The general puffed out his chest and said, "I don't suppose I am, sir."

"What?"

"No sir. I'm in no mood to shake your hand."

"That is the only thing we can agree on. Mr. Wiley, why did you disobey my orders and withhold information from me?"

"For your own protection, sir."

"Lieutenant General Wiley, what is the punishment for not obeying orders from your Commander in Chief?"

Without hesitating, Wiley responded, "The minimal punishment is dishonorable discharge, forfeiture of pay and privileges of rank, along with a prison term of five years."

"As your Commander in Chief, what do you believe is the appropriate punishment?"

"Sir, before I answer that question, I would like to explain the reasons behind my actions."

"Proceed, general."

"Sir, I did not issue the command for Homeland Security agents to entrap Thomas Quinn. As you may realize, Senator Bates persuaded Stephen Alerkson, the Vice Deputy of Homeland Security, to proceed covertly. Alerkson used a federal agent by the name of James Blake to proposition Rebecca Swanson. In an attempt to cover up this plot, James Blake was sent to Kabul. Three weeks after his arrival he was allegedly killed by sniper fire. A formal investigation into the death of James Blake has begun."

"General, I have that information, no thanks to you. What I want to know is who was driving the UPS truck that killed detective Danny Thomas?"

"They were intelligence officers acting on my orders, sir."

"So we live in a country where federal agents are given orders to commit murder by the Head of National Security?"

"Sir, it is exactly for this reason that I did not provide you with the information regarding Senator Bates's influence over Homeland Security agents. I was protecting you. I am protecting you from the tough decisions; the decisions no one wants to make, but must be made, to protect the freedom of this country. We are at war, sir."

"And just how is this war going, General? How did your attempt to save the country pan out?"

"Not as planned, sir."

"What will happen when the American public finds out that the Director of National Intelligence assigned an agent to assassinate a police officer and an employee of Senator Bates with a UPS truck in order to cover-up the government's involvement in framing Thomas Quinn?"

"That cannot happen, sir."

"And how will you stop it this time?"

"Sir, I will abide by your decision."

"I'm relieved to hear that I'm not next on your hit list. Or am I? Just where do you draw the line? What criteria do you use when deciding who to assassinate, General?"

"Sir, huinomics will destroy the American way of life. I acted to protect the liberty and freedom of the citizens of this great country of ours."

"No general, the American way of life is being destroyed by people like you, who stop at nothing for power, who rob American's of the very freedoms you are supposed to protect."

"I acted as any soldier would in times of war. I am not sorry for my actions. Given the same circumstances, any good general would have acted exactly as I did."

"The tragedy is that I cannot have you stand trial for the murder of Danny Thompson. I cannot even have you court marshaled. If I don't keep this quiet, the resulting social unrest would cause irrevocable harm. My only consolation is that your punishment will be delivered on the Day of Reckoning. But I can do one thing; I expect you have anticipated this, correct General?"

"I have my letter of resignation with me, sir."

The president accepted the envelop and waited for Wiley to exit before turning to Larry Baker.

"Democracies believe there is knowledge in numbers. When I was elected to this office, I believed I was the right man for the job because the collective knowledge of the American public concluded that I was.

"If it is true that the voice of the many is wiser than the voice of the few then the government is wrong about huinomics. Polls indicate that huinomics has a 76% approval rate. That's 175 million Americans versus 430 congressmen, 100 senators, 9 Supreme Court justices and me. Our arrogance is unbearable."

"The founding fathers would not have supported the collective knowledge of its citizens if it meant the dismantling of the government."

"Are you sure about that? Would the founding fathers approve the innocent murder of its citizens? This is the 21st century. If we believe that our government was founded on the greatest principles known to man in 1791, we must consider how the constitution would have been written if it was written today."

Musing quietly, president Dial stated, "If Thomas Jefferson lived in the digital age, voting would be directly in the hands of the people with each citizen casting their vote over the Internet. After all, with lobbyist and other political pressures, just how often do congressmen vote to represent the people they serve?"

"I see your point, but what does this have to do with prohibiting the formation of hui corporations?"

"Larry, we must examine all possibilities. I believe that the government needs to evolve. It may be possible for governments and huinomics to exist side by side."

Jackie and Thomas spent the night intertwined in each other's arms. As the morning sun filled their room, Thomas stirred and, half asleep, reached for his cell phone on the nightstand. Jackie touched Thomas's shoulder.

"You promised. Today it's just you and me. No work. Think about what I've gone through: one minute you're spending the next six years in a cell and the next you're here in my arms. I can't let you go. Not today, Thomas."

Radiating kindness, Thomas smiled and said, "Of course I will spend the day with you. But even when I'm working, I'm always with you."

Cold to Thomas's kindness, Jackie pulled away.

"I wish that was true, but you aren't, Thomas. You get so wrapped up in the movement that I become invisible to you."

Thomas lay still. Wondering how Jackie could attack his devotion to the movement on this, the morning following his release, Thomas mustered his strength.

"Let's go for a hike. I'll pack some food and we'll go have some fun, just you, me and nature. That is, if you don't mind Miss Nature tagging along."

"I'm serious, Thomas. I feel lost to you. Do you know how hard it is on me? Now that I got you back, I'm not going to lose you to Simion Ruzart and the movement."

"Jackie, I wish it were that simple. I really do. But you know the movement is bigger than you and me. If I could, I would snap my fingers and huinomics would take hold and flourish. Then we could resume our former lives together."

"It's your ego that's talking. You've changed. You like the spotlight. I want the old Thomas back."

"Jackie, our thoughts are reality. Happiness, sadness, love, despair, jealousy, and joy are not spontaneous emotional feelings; they are created by thought.

Every day I have thoughts of my love for you. Because of this, I'm actively creating my reality of love for you.

"You're missing my point."

"No Jackie, I understand your point and I know you understand mine. But today I choose my reality to be happy. I will have happy thoughts of you and me together, and I will have fun on a hike. If you choose, you will join me and foster the same thoughts so we can be happy together."

Jumping out of bed, Thomas hustled to the kitchen. Still upset, Jackie rolled out of bed and headed to the bathroom.

Although it had only snowed an inch, the landscape was blanked in sparkling white, a striking contrast to the gray sky. It was the kind of still, windless day where you could hear a crow call from a mile away. Wearing hats and gloves, and boots with thick wool socks, Jackie and Thomas headed for a small stream behind their farmhouse.

Jackie met Thomas on a hike during college and ever since then Thomas and Jackie spent much of their free time outdoors. They both loved hiking for different reasons. Jackie loved to abandon the man-made world around her and connect with nature, while Thomas loved to abandon the thoughts in his mind and connect with his body through movement.

Walking along the creek they soon reached a larger stream that meandered away from the foot of the mountain. Jackie named the place Rocky Point after the Volkswagen-sized granite boulders ascending some three thousand feet. Grappling large boulders on the assent was sport, but the real fun cam leaping from bolder to bolder on the way down. After climbing steadily for thirty minutes, Jackie saw a dirt bike heading to the base of the mountain.

"Are you kidding me? Look, I think that's Staple, on a dirt bike. My god, what's he doing? Call him, see what he wants."

"Remember? I promised no phones today."

"Good for you, lets continue," she said sarcastically.

"Something is wrong Jackie. We need to get down."

"All Hail the King."

And with that, spry as a cat, Jackie began to leap down from boulder to boulder. About half way down they could hear Staple.

"Thomas? You gotta come down."

Catching his breath, Thomas said, "We're coming. Hold on." After another ten minutes of bolder-hopping they reached Staple at the foot of Rocky Point.

Being the first one down, Jackie said, "What the hell Staple? Do you know what day it is?"

"Come on Jackie, you know I wouldn't be here if it wasn't important."

"What is it?"

"You left your phones back at the house. Simion was frantic to reach you. Senator Bates was arrested for his involvement with your frame and he committed suicide after his attorney posted bail."

"My God."

"He gave up Homeland Security before he was released. The Speaker of the House called an emergency meeting. They staged a big publicity stunt, marched to the Capital Building and pledged to pass a legislation outlawing huinomics. Simion Ruzart, Xavier Lamont and a host of others are forming a demonstration outside the capital building. You need to be there Thomas. A jet is on the runway waiting."

Turning to Jackie, Thomas said, "Are you with me?"

"Of course, Thomas."

Quickly showering and packing, Thomas and Jackie found themselves sitting in the back of an SUV with Mack and Staple up front. But they weren't headed to Santa Fe.

"Are we taking a different route to Santa Fe?"

"We're flying out of Taos regional to save time."

As soon as they lifted off, Thomas called Simion.

"Staple tells me we'll be protesting in front of the Capital Building."

"The Capital Building will be the epicenter. Huinomic fans have organized protests at every federal building across America. We don't need to do anything anymore. It has a life of its own now. Everyone can see what's going on."

"What if it gets away from us? I don't like what happened at P&G. I don't want anyone hurt."

"We are conducting a positive media blitz. By the end of the day only hermits living off the grid will not know about tomorrow's protests. Peter Sadinski is calling it a National Day of Protest. Xavier Lamont is the front runner online."

"What kind of turn out are we expecting?"

"Peter believes we will top Europe's record breaking protest of the Iraq War that had over three million participants."

"Peaceful protest will be key."

"I know. We're sitting on top of a pressure cooker. The blowback from the Bates scandal has ignited America. I'll fill you in on the details when you land. You'll head the scene at the Capitol."

"I don't have a speech."

"Good. Your best talks are extemporaneous."

"Thanks for the vote of confidence, but all the same, has Peter's team come up with any guidelines?"

"Yes, I have them, along with some surprise guests, waiting for you."

"Will I see you at the hotel?"

"A hotel is too risky. You all will stay with me at my home in Georgetown."

"I hope you have ear plugs. Staple snores like a beast."

After hanging up Thomas turned to Jackie and before he could get a word out she said, "You could have checked with me to see if I wanted to stay at Simion's home."

Feeling as if someone has placed a spell on Jackie, Thomas continued saying, "Simion has concerns of our safety when staying at a Hotel. And you know how Staple and Mack feel about it."

"Thomas this is just another example of you putting yourself before me in everything you do."

Unbelieving that Jackie could be so selfish in such a critical time, Thomas continued, "I wish I could help you Jackie. That I could simply snap my fingers and you could become a happy person. But I can't. That is something you will need to do on your own. You decide just how happy or unhappy you want to be."

"Fine, blame it all on me. It's my problem right? It is, after all, always my problem, isn't it? Just think about it Thomas." With that Jackie got up and went to the rear of the plane and sat next to Mack.

With a hundred muddled thoughts rampaging through his mind, Thomas wondered how he would ever be able to pull off tomorrow's speech. Every time Thomas began to formulate the words to his speech his mind over flowed with a cascade of irrelevant and disjointed thoughts. Thomas had been there many times before; lost in the stormy seas of his mind.

Seeking clarity and coherence Thomas calmly steered his thinking to quieter waters. In his mind Thomas pictured black. A black so black no other image or thought could emerge from his mind. A black so deep and far reaching it consumed the hum of the jet's engines. Minute after minute Thomas's mind went black. No thought existed in his mind, simply black. Black that stretched on into infinity.

Then an image of an infinitely large body of perfectly calm water, illuminated by the faintest moonlight, appeared in his mind. From the depths of the still water came a luminescent blue light. As the light got closer to the surface it began to take shape. The shape formed letters and a word began to waiver in and out of focus. Hovering near the surface, Thomas was just barely able to make out the word: "speech." No sooner had Thomas recognized the word than it lost its form and became a luminescent blue light again, drifting slowly down into the depths of the infinite expanse of water.

Slowly and of their own volition new images and words rose and sank.

Only when Jackie came back and accidentally jostled him while fastening her safety belt did Thomas leave the depths of his mind. Like smelling a sweet perfume, Thomas's eyes met Jackie's. They linked smiles and Thomas knew that Jackie was once again at peace. Knowing that Thomas was not wanting to talk, Jackie was content to hold his hand while the Cessna Citation X eased up on its 700 mile an hour speed for the descent.

Looking at the city lights from the highway, Jackie snuggled closer to Thomas.

"It's hard to believe just four hours ago we were at Rocky Point. But I've made peace with it, Thomas. I'm good for the ride no matter where it takes me, so long as I'm with you."

Thomas gazed into Jackie's almond-shaped eyes and smooth skin.

"A bumpy road lies ahead of us, but along the way we will do things we never dreamed of and before you know it, it will all be over."

Without a care in the world, Jackie clung tight to Thomas as the car wound its way into Georgetown.

Entering the modest foyer, Thomas was surprised to see a group of people gathered around the dining room table looking at what appeared to be story boards. Thomas saw John Carter, the multi-billionaire media mogul, sauntering towards him.

"The man of the hour has arrived." Shaking Thomas's hand, he continued, "I have waited for this moment for quite some time."

Making his way to the dining table Thomas felt another rush when he saw Luke Baldwin. Luke amassed the world's fourth largest fortune by buying and selling stock. He worked closely with Simion's charities for years. Simion caught sight of Thomas and hurried over to hug him.

"I hope you don't mind me inviting a few friends over."

"This is quite the meeting. I wish I could have arrived sooner."

"Indeed. It's the first time we've all been in the same room. But you haven't missed much; we were just going over the presentation schematics." Then Simion leaned over and tapped someone on the back. "John, this is your baby, why don't you explain to Thomas what we have in store for tomorrow."

"We're collaborating with local TV crews to provide footage of the protests at two hundred capital buildings across the nation. The National Monument protest will be at center stage. Video feeds from each site across the nation will be spontaneously edited and fed back through my network to be televised across the globe."

"I can't believe it."

Like a youngster who can't wait to get to the really good part, Simion beamed.

"That's only the beginning. Luke has some great news."

"When Simion first told me about huinomics, I was skeptical, to say the least. I believed that people, for the most part, are like me. They want monetary reward for their work." Looking over to Simion, and smiling, Luke continued.

Speaking with his hands Luke said, "when Simion showed me Vorbine's one year growth projections, I told Simion that Vorbine would be lucky to achieve that in three years. I am afraid that I went on to say that long before that, Vorbine would go belly-up. Good thing I didn't put my money where my mouth was. When Simion announced that Vorbine completed their first astronomical twelve month projection in just eight months, I had to eat crow. No company in history has been so productive. I told Simion, 'this can't be right. Either Vorbine's getting outside help or else everyone is working eighty hours a week. Simion told me that I had to see it for myself to believe it.

"So I headed out to Boise, and Cliff, what a character he is, set me up in a guest apartment. Now, I have visited a number of factories in my day and have been given the red carpet treatment, but Cliff simply told me that I could go around and talk to anyone I liked. After handing me the day's calendar and a map of the grounds, he just left. I didn't know whether to laugh or cry. And do you know what? After six days at Vorbine I never wanted to leave. It was like I had been transported to another dimension: a dimension where people are happy, truly happy. And I realized that Vorbine's factories are efficient because everyone is dedicated and takes pride in their work."

Beaming, Simion interjected, "Get to the good part."

"Ahh yes. Well, you probably know that I have invested 1.3 billion in Simion's Global Development Program? Well, that figure will be going up dramatically. I have begun to liquidate my stock holdings. I will be investing in; I mean I will be giving a sizable portion of my wealth to establish Vorbine subsidiaries in Africa and Afghanistan.

"Simion, John and I are like-minded. We believe in creating a better world for the poor while preserving our environment. Poverty and energy are linked. When you spend half your day collecting cow dung to cook your meals and to heat your home, there's little time left for improving your lot in life. Free energy will be the economic ladder to help millions lift themselves out of poverty."

Simion could no longer contain himself.

"Afghanistan, like most countries in Africa, derives 95% of its energy from burning biomass. These are polluting fuels that directly correlate with high mortality rates. It is estimated that 1.6 billion people have no access to electricity. The level of human suffering and damage to the environment is catastrophic. Free energy will change all that."

Thomas looked a bit skeptical and simply said, "Free is non-sustainable; even 53 billion dollars is a finite number."

Turning to Luke, Simion said, "See? See what I told you about Thomas? With help from me, John, Luke and many others, we will build a total of eleven 600 megawatt factories modeled after Vorbine. These eleven factories will be located in Denmark, France and Germany.

In addition to building these eleven factories, we will be building sixteen Flexwing plants in Africa and two in Afghanistan. The raw materials and operational cost for the Flexwing plants will come from the European plants. Until such time that the African and Afghanistan communities can afford to pay for their own electricity, it will be subsidized by Vorbine Europe."

"You want to expand to Europe? With all the trouble we're having here, isn't it too soon?" Thomas asked.

John Carter chimed in.

"That's where I fit in. Simion enlisted my help a while back to get our friends across the pond to take part in the expansion of sustainable energy. I've met with so many prime ministers I can't keep them all straight. I can tell you one thing: we have the green light to build unlimited Vorbine factories in Denmark, Germany and France, with every other European country lining up behind them. The Europeans are ahead of the curve when it comes to Global Warming. They don't care who profits: zero carbon is their goal. It's not all rosy. France and Germany will only allow green energy hui corporations to become established. At least that is how they stand now."

Looking around at everyone, Thomas said, "I'm flabbergasted. But why Flexwing? The energy output to material and manufacturing is lower than Vorbine's."

Luke looked disappointed, either because of what he was going to say or because Thomas hadn't figured it out yet.

"It's the same age old problem. These governments are poor, so they're too corrupt for large scale energy production and have very limited infrastructure. Hell, in Kabul you have to bribe someone just to be permitted to pay your electric bill. Building an entire network grid is too costly but localized small-scale electric production using Saul Beckman's five megawatt thrust generator is ideal. Flexwings using organic flow batteries will power remote villages.

Simion added, "Like Vorbine, Flexwing will be completely vertical: local man power, local raw materials and local factories. The people of Africa and Afghanistan will build their own Flexwings."

"You do realize that I can't go on stage tomorrow alone," Thomas said.

Simion slapped Thomas on the back and said, "We wouldn't dream of it. In fact, we were just going over who was going on first. Maybe I'll open then John then Luke then you'll tie it all together for the grand finale."

They all talked for hours until Simion announced, "As much as I love everyone's company, we all need to be fresh in the morning, and I, for one, need my eight hours of sleep."

Thomas felt like he'd just run a marathon. Managing to shed most of his clothes, he climbed into bed and fell into a deep sleep.

Lying silently next to Thomas, Jackie's head was spinning. She was remorseful about reproaching Thomas for focusing on the hui movement, but she knew she had to make peace with herself. Realizing that many years would pass before she had Thomas's undivided attention, she vowed to let Thomas run with the line, content to wait for the day when she could reel him in and be the center of his world once again.

At the same time, another person had thoughts of Thomas Quinn circling in his mind. But the thoughts James Carver III had were far different than Jackie's thoughts. Sitting on a flat mattress with more than one spring poking out, James peered into an old corroded mirror. Unconscious of his ever-present shaking leg, James twisted his boney, calloused hands and admired his meticulously trimmed goatee.

Aside from the three years spent as a Marine in the Iraq War, James sported a goatee since he was sixteen. At seventeen, James's parents were only too happy to have their scrappy kid leave their backcountry shack. James was always getting into fights; being shorter than most guys never deterred James. With unmatched ferocity and a lust for inflicting bodily harm, James hospitalized two hell-bound hillbillies in a matter of moments when he was just a sophomore in high school. Whenever James got in trouble, his father would say, "I sure the hell don't know what got into that boy." If the disabled moonshiner had a video of each time he smacked James on the side of his head when he was growing up, his mystery would be solved.

Like his parents, James's drill sergeant was only too happy to send James off to battle. His propensity to fight was the only thing that kept him from being dishonorably discharged during boot camp. You can't teach courage, and James had courage, which he proved in battle at the Rumaila oil fields.

James's squadron leader turned a blind eye to the rampant crystal methamphetamine use in his platoon, and why not? Ever since the Viet Cong used crank to rebuild bridges overnight, it had been the high octane fuel running through many soldier's veins. Only after James's third tour did the drug become so embedded in his persona that he couldn't get clean to pass the mandatory combat drug test and was discharged.

Being discharged from the marines did not squelch James's thirst for crank. He believed he could harness the drug's power without being controlled by it. Never squeamish about needles, James prided himself on not destroying the lining of his nose or losing his teeth by snorting or smoking crank; he fed his body with precise amounts administered as well as any doctor.

Buying crank from back-country meth labs and running it to bigger cities to unload on small time dealers, James made enough money to live in cheap hotels and eat in diners. James's choice of transportation was a lightweight 600 CC speed bike capable of jetting from 60 to 140 miles per hour in a matter of seconds. On more than one occasion James needed to vacate quickly after emptying a clip from his 9mm.

Like so many with crank flowing through their veins, James Carver III developed a type of psychosis in which he believed he had invincible powers and abilities unsurpassed by any man. Looking far off into the mirror, James Carver admired his grand reflection.

Working out with his personal trainer in the West Wing, president Dial was surprised to see Larry. Smiling, the president said, "If you're serious about dropping some weight you'll need to put on some tennis shoes."

"Ohh, right, uh, good luck with getting me in a pair of those. No, I came here to show you the coverage of the demonstration."

"I thought it wasn't supposed to begin until 3:00 pm."

Turning on the television, Larry said, "That's when the speakers arrive. This is the pre-game show."

"Is that Elton John?"

"Yes, he just showed up. They say Bob Dylan and U2 are coming on stage next."

"How many people so far?"

"Still three hours to go before Quinn arrives and the national lawn is completely filled. The reporters are saying close to 600,000 have arrived so far. We have crowds extending all along the national mall."

"I got to see this for myself."

"You can't be serious."

"I'm not going out. I can see what's going on from the library, right?"

Practically jogging out of the gym and up the steps leading to the library, President Dial knew without looking that the number of protesters was greater than the number of supporters who came to his inaugural speech. Hearing the melody of a familiar song coming from his front yard, president Dial smiled as he watched people from every direction move towards the stage like moths to a light.

As the protesters gathered, James Carver III careened through the traffic on his bike, looking for limos. The midday sun did little to warm the frosty air, but the cold never bothered James. Plugged into the Ducati's super sport battery, James's honeycombed micro-wire bodysuit was set to 74 degrees. Gutter sniping along Independence Avenue, James spotted two stretch limos about three quarters of a mile ahead. As if the bike was hardwired into James's mind, in a flash it zipped between the snail-paced traffic to reach the limos just as they were pulling up to the curb.

Seeing five men wearing overcoats get out of the first limo, James's already fast beating heart kicked up another notch. Out of the second limo came four older men sporting long hair and sunglasses. James glanced in his mirror, put his bike in gear and sped off, thinking to himself, 'Fucking entertainers.'

On and on James willed his bike through the traffic. By the time he heard the music stop he felt his prize slipping away. Conjuring up hope in his tormented mind, James fanned out his search, looking for parked limos along the side streets off Constitution Avenue. Like a man with a turbo pack, zipping between parked cars, James spied two pewter gray Lincoln Town cars parked in front of the State Department Building on C Street. Seeing two men seated in the front seats of either car, James felt a spark of hope.

Riding to the side of the building, James popped the curb and left his bike, helmet and gloves, and headed over to the cars. Tapping on the passenger window of the first car he came to, James inquired as the electric window hummed, "I've been trying to make my way to the meetin', but I don't know if I'm headed in the right direction."

As the words came from his mouth, James instantly knew that the eyes of the driver and his partner were not the eyes of your out for a Saturday drive type; they were the eyes of a professional. They were the kind of eyes asked, 'Who are you and what's the best way to disable you?' In an effort to mask what his eyes had already revealed, the man said,

"You're almost there. Just keep heading straight for two blocks and you'll see it."

Not wanting to linger, James thanked the man, got back on his bike and headed in the direction of the assembly. When he was out of sight, he circled back and positioned his bike within sight of the limo.

Making his way across the stage to the podium, Thomas felt like a part of him froze with every step, creating a chain of luminous shadows transfixed by each passing moment. He was becoming a disembodied voice, a mixture of his being and the will of the millions standing before him.

"I applaud you. Today is your day. You have saved the planet for our children's children and you have revolutionized the lives of every man, woman and child living now. You, along with forty million other Americans who came out to support huinomics today have changed history. There are countless others around the world, from Cape Horn to the Gobi Desert who have joined us. We are now the strongest force on the planet. Together we can accomplish anything.

"Today will go down in history as the day humanity choose to create a society where all men prosper in harmony with the planet. As I speak Vorbine is reducing carbon emissions by 600 tons per hour. Within ten years Vorbine will replace all coal based electricity in America. Vorbine is expanding into Denmark, France and Germany with profits being fueled into Flexwing electric plants in towns and villages across Africa and Afghanistan. Together we will bring carbon emissions down to zero within 30 years and restore the planet to its former glory. The days of our slash and burn disposable economy are over."

Endless waves of cheering rolled up and down 15th Street, infecting those on F and G Streets watching Thomas remotely as he leaned into the podium.

"Our old economy, the economy of the self, is dying. As it passes away so too does human suffering and the unchecked depletion of the earth's eco system. With its passing comes a new age. This is the age of huinomics. A new economy, based on the group, is emerging. Soon we will join the nearly two hundred thousand Americans already employed at hui corporations. Soon all of us will experience what it is like to be truly free. You too will know what it is like to live without fear of the future and live free of debt. Soon you too will have the time to be with the ones you love and pursue your own dreams and desires.

"But just down the street from us a handful of old men want to stop us. They want things to stay the same. Your government desires a complacent nation. They created a society were its citizens are so over burdened with debt and so entrenched in the struggle to survive, that they believe no one has the strength to stand up to create a better world.

"And yet, here we are, forty million Americans and countless others around the globe who have the strength. We are no longer afraid to stand up and choose a better life. We refuse to buy into their fear propaganda. We refuse to be slaves of an economy that produces unimaginable wealth for a select few at the top.

"A handful of old men in Washington can not hold us back. Our unity is greater than any force on this planet. Our will decides our reality. We have chosen to create a better a better world. We have triumphed. Today we have changed the world."

As if being serenaded by a million angles, Thomas made his way off the stage. Embracing Jackie as Xavier Lamont took the stage, Simion shouted in Thomas's ear.

"Good work. Look Thomas, Staple and Mack are nervous, the crowd is getting out of control, we need to leave now."

"Wouldn't it be easier to stay until the crowd disperses?"

"I'm afraid not. The longer you're out here, the worse your exposure. We really need to get moving."

Taking Jackie by the hand, Thomas threaded his way to the back of the stage where they met Mack and Staple along with three other suited bodyguards.

"Great speech, Thomas," Mack said. "Now let's get you out of here. We'll be slicing through a sea of people. Those three gentlemen will go first, carving out a path, with the two of you close behind them and me and Staple right behind you. What ever you do, don't stop."

As soon as they left the stage area, Mack's quick escape plan was thwarted by a sea of people converging on Thomas. Grasping Jackie's hand across his chest, a jolt of anxiety passed through Thomas as the swarming crowd threatened to topple them. Wedging through the crowd, Staple took out his radio and called for backup from the two drivers. Even with three extra guards, they all felt swamped as the crowd frantically tried to reach Thomas.

After a hellish struggle, they finally made it to the two parked town cars. Two of the bodyguards were bleeding and Thomas was scratched up. Mack and Staple were on the verge of violence, literally growling at anyone hindering their decent into the safety of the town cars.

Focused like a jackal amidst the melee, James Carver III crouched over his bike half a block away with the town cars in his sights.

Thrilled to have escaped the crowds, Thomas and Jackie settled into the plush comfort of their car as it slowly wend its way down side streets and onto the freeway.

It took all of James's will power to creep along to stay just within eyesight of the limos. In all the thousands of miles James rode a bike, none were as slow as tailing Thomas Quinn.

Simion's Georgetown brownstone never looked so good. Exhausted, Thomas and Jackie didn't get out of bed until almost ten. Greeting them at the breakfast table, Simion said, "You are on every news station. I hate to say it, but Peter was right: to be released from jail in three days, in the wake of the Bates Scandal, was the best publicity we ever got."

"Really? Well, tell Peter not to get any ideas: from here on out, jail is not an option."

"Of course. Besides, Peter has new adventures in store for Thomas. From Saturday Night Live to morning talk shows, he wants you to get as much air time as possible."

Jackie shot an apprehensive look at Thomas.

Replying quickly, Thomas said, "I need to downshift for a while. I believe it's time to head back to the farm."

Simion looked exasperated. The world was on the verge of a breakthrough, but he knew not to push.

"Take some time off. You've both been extremely taxed over the past few weeks. Relax a few days. If you feel up to it, do the interviews next week."

"Any day now the house will decide to amend the constitution. I want to be at Vorbine when that decision is made. It only takes a couple hours from the farm."

"So you're returning to your farm today?"

"This afternoon, at one thirty."

"Did you make a reservation for Staple?"

"No. I really don't think it's necessary."

"Thomas, you know how I feel about this. You need to understand that you're a target. Make whatever plans you like, but Staple and Mack travel with you."

"Okay, Simion. If it makes you happy, Staple and Mack are welcome come along."

A few hours later, Thomas gave Simion a hug goodbye at the curb before stepping out into the sun with Jackie and Staple as Mack pulled the town car up to the curb. Thomas caught a dark shape in the corner of his eye as he was walking to the car. Turning his head to focus on the object, Thomas saw a young man swing his arm out from behind his back. A guttural moan of recognition issued from Thomas's open mouth as James fired a bullet point-blank into his chest, picking him off his feet and slamming him on his back.

When the gun went off Mack flew forward as James was swinging the barrel of the gun towards him. In a flash Mack caught hold of James's gun arm and lifted it above his head. Pulling his massive body downwards, Mack held on as James squeezed the trigger a second time, sending a bullet straight into the air. Wedging his shoulder under James's arm, Mack sprang up as he yanked James's arm down. An audible crack sounded as James' clavicle snapped and his shoulder was ripped from its socket. The upward thrust was so intense that James's legs cartwheeled in an upward arc an instant before his body was slammed to the concrete.

Unconscious before he hit the ground, Mack rendered James defenseless in a matter of seconds, but it didn't matter. Thomas had been shot.

Thomas grabbed his sides and rocked back and forth in an uncontrollable spasm. Jackie fell to her knees next to Mack and cried, "He's not breathing! God, Mack, he's not breathing."

"Don't touch him. He's re-setting."

"Mack! Do something!"

"Get back! The wind's knocked out of him. His body is re-setting."

Violent tremors shook Jackie as she cried, "Oh God, please no!"

Then Thomas sucked in loudly and started to pant.

"Yes! Thank you God, thank you." The tears flowed freely as Jackie caressed Thomas's face.

Wide-eyed, Thomas looked at Jackie and tried to sit up but he fell back instantly, wincing in pain. Mack leaned in and said, "Just hold still, Thomas. You're gonna be okay, but you have to hold still."

Seeing Thomas's understanding eyes, Mack turned his attention back to James. Taking out two long black zip ties, Mack secured James's ankles and wrist.

Staple gunned the town car to where Thomas lay and hit the brakes. Flying to Thomas's side, Staple screamed, "Where was he hit?"

"Left chest."

Rousing Thomas, Staple said, "Thomas, can you wiggle your toes and fingers?"

"Yeah."

"Do I look blurry?"

"No."

Staple opened Thomas's jacket and unbuttoned his shirt, revealing the armored vest. The slug stopped right above his heart.

"How is your breathing?"

Wincing, Thomas said in short quick breaths, "A-lot-of-pain."

Staple sprang up and said to Mack, "We go now."

Simion, showing monumental self-control, could contain himself no longer.

"Should I call an ambulance?"

While positioning his hands under Thomas's back Staple said, "No time. We are taking him to Georgetown Hospital. Call the cops." A moment later, Mack helped by sliding one arm under Thomas's pelvis and the other under his shoulders, lifting him effortlessly into the town car.

Mack rode in the back seat with Thomas's head in his lap while Staple and Jackie rode up front. Minutes later they pulled up to the emergency room.

In a trance, Mack followed every move as the aides got Thomas on a stretcher and rushed him into the ER hallway. Staple caught the intern's assessing eye and said, "Gunshot, an inch above the heart. The slug didn't penetrate the body armor. Sensation in feet and hands. Pulse elevated and erratic. Steady, forced breathing. Extreme pain. Possible internal bleeding. Requires MRI."

The doctor peered into Thomas's face while feeling for his pulse.

"Get me 20 CC's of diamorphine then get him to imaging. This is Thomas Quinn, people!"

A little surprised the doctor recognized Thomas so quickly, Staple said, "If it's okay with you, we would like to stay outside his door until the police arrive."

"Sure. Let's go, people!"

The MRI confirmed a clean break at the top of the third rib, the sharp end of which threatened to puncture the aorta, necessitating emergency surgery.

Thomas came to in the recovery room as an elderly woman with snow white hair smiled and said, "Everything's alright, Thomas. Your surgery went well. Everything's just fine. "

Smiling back Thomas wondered where do such angels come from before saying, "Can I see Jackie?"

"You need to rest here for an hour or so. Don't worry. Jackie knows you're fine. Try to sleep a bit. It'll make you feel better."

Thomas closed his eyes and drifted into a deep sleep. He dreamed he stood on a train platform in the middle of an eight-lane highway. The train tracks were unusual white porcelain disks spaced twenty feet apart. He saw a train gliding nearer and was greatly relieved because he very much needed to get on a train. Hovering to a stop, the train doors slid open and Thomas saw a man dressed in an Asian suit of iridescent burgundy who said, "If you want to ride this train, you need a ticket."

Realizing that he did not have a ticket, Thomas pleaded with the man to let him on, but the train pulled out, floating swiftly down the porcelain disks. Thomas bounded down the platform steps to the highway below. Instead of cars, the highway was packed with bicycles; hundreds of bicycles.

Thomas found himself riding one. Between their handle bars was a digital velocity display. As he peddled faster, the bicycle took to the air. He was flying. Looking around he saw small farms flow past and thought to himself how nice they looked. The flowing sound grew until, blinking his eyes, Thomas heard the respirator from the bed next to his.

Thomas stared at the curtain recalling his dream until the angelic nurse came back and said, "You're ready. We'll wheel you to your room where Jackie and your friends are waiting."

Still re-living his dream, Thomas watched the white speckled ceiling tiles pass one by one as a young man wheeled him to his room.

By the time the fourth speaker took the podium, Paul Harvey's head was pounding in shear agony. Willing his old creaking body up the steps of the capital building earlier that day, the pain had been no more than a faint discomfort. After an hour of mindless banter, a cold sweat passed over him and his head began to truly pound. Every word was like a lump of coal shoveled into the fiery stove of his mind, fueling his mental anguish until the migraine pain devoured his senses. Paul Harvey was sick. He was sick of it all. Sick of the deal-making; sick of spending day after day listening to the ranting; and most of all, sick of the protesters. He despised their presence. Gritting his teeth in pain and wishing it would all just go away, he became aware of a commotion in the room as a drowning man might see fish passing by.

The Speaker took the podium, grabbed the microphone and announced that Thomas Quinn had been shot. He was alive and no longer in critical condition. He called for a forty-five minute break.

Paul Harvey was in so much pain that he couldn't move to mingle with the other senators. Seeing him crouched over, the Majority Leader, Ely Baron, took a seat beside him and said, "We need you on this one, Paul."

Slowly focusing his eyes on Ely, Paul said, "You know what that will take, Ely. I need the Speaker's assurance that I will be the new Armed Services Committee Chair."

Ely grimaced.

"Damn it, Paul, this issue is more important than your political ambitions."

Paul folded his thin arms over his frail chest.

"Ely, I'm the last man. You know my terms. If you want this amendment passed, give me the Chair."

Standing abruptly, Ely swore under his breath as he walked in the direction of the Speaker, thinking, "This decrepit bastard will win this one, but I'll get him in the end."

Within the hour, Ely returned to assure Paul that he would get the Chair then he alerted the Speaker that Senator Harvey wanted to cast his vote, the final swing vote, to amend the constitution to prohibit the formation of hui corporations. Weakly raising his right hand in confirmation, Paul felt the pain in his head subside. His driver would come fetch him, Louise would have his ham and bean soup waiting for him and thanks to the proxy vote, he wouldn't have to return to this room for another six months, if not longer.

Standing in the solarium, President Dial looked out over the massive elliptical lawn and dreamed of taking a long walk. When was the last time he was able to take a simple walk? Trapped within the White House walls, President Dial called Larry Baker to the solarium.

Larry appeared within minutes and smiled at the President sitting with the sun on half his face.

"Funny how a room can affect you. When I'm in the Oval Office, my thoughts are much more rigid. Up here, surrounded by all of these plants, my mind feels more flexible."

"I know what you mean. Did you call me to discuss the cabinet meeting?"

"Partially, yes; but first, tell about James Carver."

"James Carver served three tours of duty in Iran before being dishonorably discharged for drug use; to be precise, crystal meth. His military record up until then had been admirable. His C.O. described him as valiant. But his record has three reports of disorderly conduct. For the past three years, James Carver has been an unemployed drifter."

"Do you think he acted alone?"

"The best we can tell, he is a disillusioned methamphetamine addict."

"I take it he has no ties whatsoever to the government?"

"None. As far as we can tell, James Carver acted alone."

"Any word from the Thomas Quinn camp about the shooting?"

"For once, they're on the same page as us. They believe Carver acted alone."

"How are they taking the passing of 28th Amendment?"

"That is a completely different matter. In step with their non-violence beliefs Thomas Quinn is asking the citizens of America simply not to acknowledge the law. Basically he is saying that if a democratic government defies the will of the people, it becomes a dictatorship and accordingly relinquishes its democratic authority to pass laws."

"He has a point."

"Apparently the vast majority of Americans couldn't agree more. The question is: what are we going to do about it?"

"That is the question of the day. Before we hear of what the cabinet members have to say what is their general consensus in enforcing the law?"

"They want us to act now. They say that postponing action will only complicate the matter. They want to close down Vorbine, now."

Getting up, the President shed his relaxed, contemplative self and grew stern.

"Anarchy is not an option. As much as I loathe the idea of using force to uphold the law, we are a nation governed by laws. Gather the Cabinet."

Chapter 16

In 1960, Chen Dong was born in the small rural village of Baojia in the northern province of Liaoning. When Chen Dong was six years old he had to walk two miles along a dusty road to the town's bus depot where his father toiled as a mechanic. Like most boys of his age he was particularly fond of mischief and on more than one occasion he ventured onto a farmer's field. One time a farmer who had a particular dislike for such boys caught Chen Dong whacking his pretend sward against one of his tomato plants. Ready to give Chen Dong a thorough thrashing, he was taken aback by Chen Dong insistence that the tomatoes will be destroyed soon any way and that he should plant long beans while he still had the chance.

Impressed by the boy's craftiness, the farmer relented and sent Chen Dong off with a stern warning to stay clear of his tomatoes or next time his backside would be blistered. Three weeks later, a storm destroyed the much of the farmer's crops, including the tomatoes. Having no idea how to find the little rascal, the farmer sat by the side of the road and waited for Chen Dong to pass. The next day, Chen Dong skipped along with his wooden sword in his hand and the farmer got his chance to ask the boy how he knew the tomatoes would be ruined.

"The ground told me."

Highly skeptical but fearing an empty stomach during the long winter, the farmer asked, "And what does the ground tell you I should plant now?"

"I told you, long beans."

The farmer planted long beans. After reaping a bumper crop of long beans, it wasn't long before news of Chen Dong's abilities reached the ears of the mayor in the neighboring city who hired the boy as his personal advisor.

Time and again, Chen Dong's predictions came true. He never erred. By the time he was eight, he had been whisked off to Beijing where he was kept under lock and key as a National Treasure.

Like any young boy torn away from those who loved him, Chen Dong was bitter and refused to speak to anyone. They tried pampering him then scolding him and finally punishing him, but he would not give in. Nearly two years passed this way until one day an old man came to visit him.

Shuffling over to sit on the edge of Chen Dong's bed, the old man asked to be left alone with the sullen ten year old. Chen Dong's room was narrow, with a high ceiling. The radiator's heat created a cold frost pattern on the single window at the back of the room. In front of the window was a small wooden desk and a flat back wooden chair. On the wall next to the desk hung a portrait of Chairman Mao. Chen Dong sat in the chair and stared down at his hands in complete disregard for the old man.

The old man unwound his scarf from his neck and took off his hat before placing his boney hand on top of Chen Dong's. Looking up with a frown on his face, Chen Dong stared into the smiling eyes of the old man. Like the jolt of a giant gong, Chen Dong felt the old man's words reverberate deep inside his being.

"Tell me: what is wrong, Chen Dong?"

Bravely holding back his tears, Chen Dong thought, "I want to see my parents."

The old man's smile revealed long, stained teeth as he thought in reply: "Okay, Chen Dong, I will take you to your home today."

Chen Dong jumped up from his chair and, with tears streaming down his cheeks, hugged the old man with all desperation he had held inside for the past two years.

The old man made no effort to stop Chen Dong's tears. When the boy calmed down, the old man peered into Chen Dong's eyes and thought, "Well, let's get packed and go!" And with that, Chen Dong walked away from his cold room, never to return.

Safely aboard the rocking steam train, Chen Dong fired off a thousand questions in his mind.

"How is it that you can speak to me without talking, and why does it only work when I look into your eyes? Who are you? Where did you come from? How long will the train ride take? Do my parents know I am coming?"

With his ever-present smile, the old man thought back, "Hold on! Hold on! One question at a time. I come from a small city called Aba, in Szechuan province. My name is Shal Gong. I am eighty three years old. It took me most of my life to master how we are communicating now. Do you know what we are doing, Chen Dong? We are speaking with our minds. No one can hear what we are saying. That makes us very special. There is only one other person in all of China who can speak with their mind."

Thinking only of his parents, Chen Dong thought, "How much longer till we get there? Will my parents be waiting for us at the station?"

"Five hours. And yes, they will be waiting."

For the next eight years, Chen Dong and Shal Gong were inseparable. Chen Dong agreed to go back to Beijing so long as he could live with the old man and return every two weeks to be with his parents for four days.

Shal Gong began the boy's education by teaching him the art of Qi Gong.

Chen Dong learned quickly as Shal Gong opened up a whole new world. Using telepathy, Shal Gong taught Chen Dong the secret techniques developed over thousands of years for harnessing the Qi energy flowing through all living things. Qi Gong turbo-charged Chen Dong's psychic abilities. Though thousands of practitioners claimed to be Masters only Shal Gong and Chen Dong were true Qi Gong Masters.

After mastering Qi Gong, the old man enlisted China's top physicians to teach Chen Dong Chinese medicine. But whereas these traditional Chinese doctors based their diagnoses on feeling the pulse, Chen Dong telepathically examined the patient.

By the time Chen Dong was twelve, he was treating People's Liberation Army generals. When Mao ZeDong was 79, he suffered a stroke. Even after a successful surgery, the nation's top physicians estimated that Mao had only months to live. With no one else to turn to, Chen Dong was sent to Zhongnanhai, the Center of the Northern Ocean. Zhongnanhai is a vast complex adjacent to the Forbidden City housing the Communist Party Central Committee, the State Council, and the glorious leader himself, Mao ZeDong.

Walking up the granite steps leading to the massive Zhongnanhai gate with Shal Gong at his side, Chen Dong intuited that their new home would be within these walls, at least for a while. Designated magistrates lead the pair through the compound to Mao's primary residence. True to his emperor-like status, Mao's bedroom was opulent. On the expansive walnut-paneled walls were huge liberation paintings of Mao ZeDong leading the masses. Purple and gold jacquard drapes were drawn across floor-to-ceiling windows reaching twenty feet high.

Huddled around Mao's gilded bed were doctors, nurses and the ever present Party Secretary. Bundled up in a blue padded jacket, still wearing his fur-lined hat with the ear flaps down, the adults smiled at this child as he made his way to Mao's bedside. But their smiles vanished when Chen Dong ordered them to remove the monitors and leave the room.

With a nod, the Party Secretary sent them scurrying away. Insisting on staying at Mao's bedside himself, he instructed his two most lethal body guards to stay right outside the door.

Chen Dong leaned over the bed and looked deep into the milky eyes of Mao ZeDong.

"Your vital essence is depleted. Your liver and kidneys are not working well so your blood is thick with toxins. I will pull the toxins from your blood and release them into your intestines. You are close to death, but I will help you keep Death at bay for three years."

Chen Dong calmly closed his eyes and gently rubbed his hands together then slowly passed them over Mao's body. After five minutes, Chen Dong opened his eyes and let his arms rest at his sides.

"I feel warm all over. What is that? I feel like…"

Before he could finish, Mao ZeDong pulled his knees toward his chest and, like mud flowing from a garden hose, defecated. For the first time in weeks, Mao hoisted himself up onto his elbows and smiled at Chen Dong, who began to laugh.

Late afternoon every day for three years, Chen Dong made his way to Mao's bedroom to reverse the emperor's bad habits of too many women, too much wine and too much rich food, until the day came when Mao's time was up.

Only the Party Secretary's inner circle knew that Chen Dong had kept Mao ZeDong alive. Of this group, Deng XiaoPing was most influential and soon ascended to the position Mao just vacated. Unlike Mao, Deng's intentions for the noble sixteen year old went far beyond medical concerns.

Cautiously descending a narrow flight of stairs leading deeper and deeper underground, Deng XiaoPing came to a large iron double door guarded by an armed soldier. Upon seeing the new Premier, the soldier snapped to attention.

"Comrade Deng, what an honor for you to conduct an inspection today."

Smiling with smoke stained teeth, Deng XiaoPing said "I understand that you have turned away many officials from these doors."

"Yes, Comrade. By the orders of the Illustrious Leader, no one was permitted to enter except Comrade Shal Gong."

"You did well serving your country. Today I will meet the men who live here, who also served our Leader faithfully."

The soldier swung the massive iron door open to reveal a small subway tunnel with lights extending as far as the eye could see. There was a twenty-foot streamlined carriage waiting on the tracks guarded by another soldier, who jumped forward to help Deng XiaoPing board. The soldier settled Deng in an over-stuffed reclining chair and moved to the controls in the front. He started the electric engine and they purred down the tunnel. The carriage swooshed through the tunnel, coming to rest minutes later in front of another massive iron double door guarded by a third soldier. This man nodded and threw open the door revealing a vast cavern at the end of which was a circle of lights, about a quarter of a mile away.

Deng XiaoPing was overwhelmed by the sheer magnitude of what he had seen so far. He was trying to accept that they were so deep under ground when out of the shadows stepped Chen Dong and Shal Gong.

Extending both hands, Deng grasped Chen Dong's hand.

"You cannot imagine how long I have waited for this day."

Chen Dong just smiled back, allowing Shal Gong to speak.

"It was wise of Mao to protect us. As Chen Dong's powers grow he becomes stronger, and yet, more vulnerable. But we have heard that you are also a wise leader. We are happy you have followed in Mao's footsteps."

Deng XiaoPing warmly shook Shal Gong's hand.

"Thank you, thank you. I will follow your recommendations as to safeguarding our National Treasure. Your sacrifices are commendable. Shall we go to your home now?"

Following a small path leading to the lights, Shal Gong said, "First Chen Dong lived in seclusion so he could not be kidnapped. Now, his powers have grown so much that people's thoughts bombard him, draining his Qi and troubling his mind. Imagine hearing the thoughts of every person within a twenty foot radius; it is very debilitating. Chen Dong must be isolated to maintain his sanity. "

Deng XiaoPing stopped and looked at Chen Dong and asked, "Would you mind telling me what I am thinking now?"

Chen Dong smiled: "You were just thinking about the pain coming from the corn on your left foot and wondering how far it is to our garden."

Astonished, Deng XiaoPing asked, "Is that all I am thinking?"

"Thoughts are like a flowing river. At times the river runs fast and there is only pure emotion, like hope, fear, pain, love or sorrow. At times the river runs slow and the water becomes clear. When this happens, I can read words that form ideas. When I first saw you, your mind was full of hope; as we began walking it shifted to your left foot, and now you are thinking of the cost of the lights surrounding our tree."

Laughing, Deng XiaoPing said, "It is a good thing you are not a politician." Off in the distance, Deng XiaoPing could just make out the trunk of a large tree.

"Tell me about these trees of yours."

"This Redwood tree came from the Jing Shan Monastery. It is a three hundred and thirty-eight year old bonsai. It is twenty three feet tall. Like the other trees here, it has great power. The most powerful tree is the Five Needle Pine. It is six hundred and twenty-two years old."

They reached a massive circular flagstone platform dotted with huge planters. In the center was Five Needle Pine. Standing a mere thirty inches tall, the Five Needle Pine looked as if it could make time stand still in a universe of its own making.

Looking at Deng XiaoPing and divining his thoughts, Chen Dong said, "Yes, you are correct, it is truly a treasure. I pull energy from all these trees every day in Qi meditation."

Taking in the magnificent trees, Deng XiaoPing thought: 'He's reading my thoughts. That could be dangerous.'

"I apologize for hearing your thoughts, but I cannot turn my mind off any more than you can turn your ears off."

Deng XiaoPing thought, "If only I had such powers, there's no telling what I could accomplish."

"My gifts come with a price. To keep from being overwhelmed I must be blindfolded and wear sound proof head phones whenever I leave this place. I can manage two to three people, but too many create an avalanche of thought. Everything becomes incoherent and I lose my strength."

"That is very similar to my problem. You see, Chen Dong, like you, I am given the ideas from the best minds in China. Each believes they know what is best for China. They all have a different focus, their recommendation are sometimes diametrically opposed. I need your help to know which ideas are best for China."

Chen Dong and Shal Gong sat patiently staring at Deng XiaoPing, hearing his words and his thoughts.

"For too long, China has been like a donkey lost in the desert. If we do not find our way to green pastures soon, we will perish. I want you to show us the way out of the desert."

Deng XiaoPing removed three reports from the satchel he carried and laid them on the stone table.

"Each of these reports is a Great Leap Forward plan to lead our donkey out of the desert. Tell me which one is best."

Without emotion Chen Dong said, "You place three reports in front of me asking me to choose, but I see that one of the reports is a test. You believe, like so many others, that the third report is absurd and if I was to choose that report, you would believe my service to the country without use."

Deng XiaoPing smiled.

"So much is at stake, we must be certain. To go down the wrong path could mean the end for China."

"There is nothing clear in these reports in and of themselves. If you give me three math equations, two being incorrect and one being correct, I see the correct answer in contrast to the other two. Faced with what you have given me, I can only feel the difference between the three. The feeling elucidates the emotional contrast: positive and negative, light and dark, yin and yang. To translate this emotion into the answer you seek, you must think of each plan individually in your mind. Based on your existing knowledge, I will be able to tell you which one will lead the donkey out of the desert."

For some time the three sat in silence until Chen Dong said, "You are mistaken; the path out of the desert requires foreign intervention."

Deng XiaoPing remembered when children turned their parents over to the Red Guard for simply owning a western book. After decades of denouncing the west, Deng XiaoPing wondered how he could get China to accept western ideas, let alone open its doors to westerner commerce.

Perceiving his concerns, Chen Dong said, "There is no mistaking it. The positive energy flow is like the sun clearing a dark sky. Denounce the Gang of Four, open the doors to the west, and prosperity will follow."

Over the course of many years, Deng XiaoPing frequently rode the underground train to sit with Chen Dong and receive his invaluable insight.

Following in Deng XiaoPing's footsteps, Li Ping earned the privilege to walk down the well-worn granite steps leading to the iron gate. Li Ping often wondered where China would be if it were not for Chen Dong, under whose influence the sleeping dragon awoke. In the blink of an eye, the nation transformed herself from rough rock to polished jade.

Now, the time had come for the sleeping dragon to awaken once again.

Like so many times before, Li Ping quickly walked through the rectangular tunnel. Activated by his weight, the floor started glowing green. Half way through the tunnel, the illuminated floor changed from green to red. Li Ping stopping as a glowing blue light completed an ultrasound of his organs, verifying his identity. The floor changed from red to green once again and Li Ping continued to the train platform.

If his identity had not been verified, two hundred and forty volts would have instantly killed him. The security system leading to Chen Dong was the safest ever devised.

At the end of the tunnel, a sliding door opened and Li Ping stepped into a small compartment containing four white calfskin swivel chairs. Traveling through darkness, the carriage seemed to glide motionlessly through the air. After an almost imperceptible shift in motion, the carriage's doors slid open. Li Ping stepped into one of China's greatest achievements, Chen Dong's tropical island thirty feet below ground.

Leaving the underground train Li Ping sighed to see it was raining. Choosing a green oiled-paper umbrella from the earthen pot next to a bench on the platform, Li Ping frowned, knowing his shoes would be muddied.

Glad for the exercise, Li Ping trudged into the windblown rain, carefully navigating the narrow path through the tropical jungle. Passing a thicket of elephant grass, Li Ping spotted a white egret and quietly snuck past. He did not wish to disturb anything, like the wild pigs he encountered on his last visit.

Ciphering the maze Li Ping finally came to a large body of water with a small island in the center. Walking along the shore in the fine white sand, Li Ping looked out over the windblown water. About sixty yards downwind Li Ping made out a person swimming with long, powerful strokes towards the beach. Li Ping hurried to the beach to meet Chen Dong as he labored up the sloping beach, exhausted.

Chen Dong's body was tan and muscular. Pulling off his mask and snorkel, Chen Dong smiled at his visitor.

"Feel like a swim?"

The very thought of getting into the water with white tipped reef sharks frightened Li Ping. If it wasn't for Chen Dong's insisting their absolute necessity, Li Ping would of never allowed such a lethal predator get close to Chen Dong.

"Ask all you like, but I'm not setting foot in your lagoon."

"You never know when you might change your mind. Things have a way of changing regardless of our desires."

"Ha! That is why I came. We need to talk."

Chen Dong draped the damp terrycloth towel he dried off on over his head and walked in silence along the shoreline with Li Ping until they came upon a structure that hovered two feet above the ground.

The rain dripped off the thatched roof. Glad to be out of the rain, Li Ping climbed the black oak steps leading to the veranda that wrapped around the building. Li Ping took off his muddy shoes and socks on a raw wooden bench as he listened to soft pipa music drifting from the interior.

Black walnut floorboards encased a sunken area where a young woman sat in a G-string bikini bottom. Hearing them enter she excitedly said, "Chen Dong! You are back! Did you bring a fish for our supper?"

Quite pleased with her joke she started to giggled as Chen Dong said, "May Hwa, I saw a mermaid who looked just like you, now make some tea for Li Ping while I rinse off."

Still snickering, May Hwa got up and climbed the marble steps, her firm tan breasts swaying with each step. May Hwa was more than comfortable with her nakedness: in fact, she reveled in it. She loved the power her body had over men.

As if nothing could be more important, she turned and asked Li Ping, "Would you like Lou Shan or Gi Long?"

"Lou Shan, please."

Li Ping willed himself not to stare at May Hwa's torso. Instead, he walked down the steps and sat on the white calf skin leather sofa. Left alone, Li Ping tried to recall how long May Hwa had been with Chen Dong. "She has lasted longer than most. It must be five or six months already. Oh well, she can't last much longer," he thought to himself.

None of them could. The women selected to live with Chen Dong never lasted long; some didn't last more than a day or two. Paradoxically, it wasn't the seclusion that drove them away; it was invasion of privacy. No one can endure another person continuously listening to every thought they have. Sooner or later the exposure is just too great and they leave only to be replaced with another.

As Chen Dong sat down next to Li Ping, Li Ping said, "May Hwa has been with you some time."

"Her comical personality is wonderful. Her mind thinks like a cartoon. May Hwa must be the happiest person I have ever met."

Holding a tray with her round breasts bouncing as she walked down the steps, May Hwa said, "What would make me happy is if my fisherman would bring me a nice big tasty fish!" Amused with herself, May Hwa's hands danced around the tea set. Like a conductor playing a well-rehearsed song, May Hwa gracefully transformed the small dark green tea buds into two tiny cups of tea. Knowing the two men needed privacy, May Hwa bowed with an impish grin and took her leave, the faint scent of her perfume lingering in the air.

Glad to get down to business, Li Ping said, "I believe the time is getting close."

"I feel your eagerness, but you need to realize time is an abstract prediction. I sense caution is needed."

"There are many who disagree. They say it must be done now. Allowing the Renminbi trade in the open market will strengthen China's economy. Li Ping sipped his tea. "Others believe the Renminbi should be backed by gold."

"I see the Renminbi needing a strong base, like the roots of a tree. But just as you cannot know how large the roots are or where they spread, we cannot define the Renminbi's value to an equal amount of gold. We know the roots are healthy because the tree is healthy. Gold is too definitive. The Renminbi should be backed by all forms of metal."

"Wouldn't platinum, gold and silver serve the same purpose? It would be easier to launch the Renminbi with a platform similar to other industrialized nations."

"It is not so simple. When you think of money you see luxury cars. You, like most people equate money with things they desire. When I look at currency I see only faith and a promise. I see the strength of the

Renminbi grow when it is backed by all forms of metal."

"But our mineral resources are insufficient. All we have left is coal."

"The world is vast. Start buying mines all over the world."

"That would mean we would need to sell off our US treasury bills. What will the US do when we sell off our holdings?"

Ever since Li Ping made his way along the beach holding his umbrella in the falling rain Chen Dong saw this thought dominating Li Ping's mind.

"The US dollar will be like leafs falling from maple trees, no longer serving its purpose. But you must realize there will be consequences."

"Military consequences?"

"I exhaust a great deal of my energy looking at war. War is a paradox of forces. Around the globe you have countries that hold great destructive power. None more so than the United States. On the other you have an infinitesimally small amount of world's population who desire war. Leaders of countries believe they can control their war machines. But they are mistaken. Governments controlling their vast armies is like a boy leading a water buffalo with a string threw its nose. At some time the water buffalo will become aware of its power and not listen to the boy.

"But back to your question: will the US use their vast military against China when we deliberately seek to destroy their economy? The answer to the question is most defiantly no.

"Will there be consequences? Most defiantly yes. I cannot tell you what they will be. But then again, I see that you already believe that you know what will happen. I will tell you this though, the entire world is metamorphosing. Turbulence will be followed by great prosperity."

Li Ping could not control the desire in his voice: "Will China become the next super power?"

"If you ask me if oil exists underground, or if the plans for a dam are sound, I can confidently tell you yes or no. The more variables a question has, the vaguer my answer becomes. I can tell you that a great upheaval is going to take place throughout the world. At first, China will endure some hardship, but this hardship will not last. We are on the verge of a new golden age in China."

Not caring that Chen Dong was watching, Li Ping allowed his mind to bloat on his vision of being the supreme one that will once again establish China as the world's new superpower.

Chapter 17

With Simion and Jackie at his bedside, Thomas said, "I feel fine. I'm sure the doctors will release me today."

Jackie puffed up indignantly. "Thomas, you are far from being fine, I can see it in your face. Why don't you take something for the pain? Why do you always have to be so stubborn?"

Thomas shot Jackie a smile. "I am fine. If I need more meds, I'll ask for them, I promise. But Simion, I don't see how staying in Washington is safer than going to Vorbine."

"It is not just your safety that's in question. Now that the amendment has passed, Peter and I believe you can get more done in Washington."

Thomas's cheery expression soured. As if waking up in a hospital at four am to have a lab tech draw his blood wasn't bad enough, receiving the news that congress passed the anti-hui amendment was the last straw.

"My work is with the people, not the government. If you want me to lock horns with politicians then I become one of them. They need me at Vorbine."

"I see your point, Thomas, but I also see Peter's point. We have the support of the people now. You've already won them over. If we can get enough congressmen and senators to support us, too, this ruling will be overturned. We don't want anarchy. This is the most peaceful path."

With increased tension Thomas replied defiantly, "I'm not going to be involved in politics."

Calming the waters Jackie looked into Thomas's eyes saying, "You know I want to leave, but Mack and Staple say they can protect you here better than at Vorbine. I don't care where we go as long as you are safe."

Wanting to put an end to the discussion Thomas said, "Let's get Cliff on the line to hear what he has to say." Reaching Cliff, Thomas put him on speaker phone.

"Cliff, I'm here with Jackie and Simion discussing if I should stay in Washington or stay at Vorbine. What are your thoughts?"

"Discussion? Seriously? It's a no brainer. You will do far more good at Vorbine than in Washington. When the shit hits the fan, you don't want to be a thousand miles away. You want that shit to hit you right in the face with the rest of us. And you better hurry, I smell shit on the horizon."

Wincing from laughing Thomas continued saying, "I'm with you there Cliff, now there is a second issue, Simion and Jackie are worried about my safety."

"Hell man, you are with your own people here. The only safety concern you need to have is if you insist on being the goalie again. I seriously doubt if you can withstand my awesome striking abilities."

"Thanks Cliff, that is just what we needed to hear. See you soon."

President Dial felt the lump in his throat grow. Glaring at Larry in frustration, he said, "What do you mean, 'he refuses to issue the order?'"

Larry knew when his long-time friend got that look in his eye, a storm was about to break.

"The Mayor of Boise is refusing to issue the order to have his Chief of Police close down Vorbine."

"Damn it. Well, we'll see about that. Some Podunk politician trying to buck the entire US government…get him on the line! Now!"

Knowing resistance was futile, Larry made some calls and had Manny Vargas on the line within minutes.

"Mayor Vargas, this is President Dial. It seems we have a problem."

"Mr. President, it's an honor. I voted for you. I'm a supporter."

Dial couldn't help but smile, until he remembered this man was thwarting his will.

"I thank you for that, but my associate informs me that you are unwilling to issue the Vorbine warrant. I need your support now more than ever. The nation needs you to abide by the law and shut down Vorbine."

"Oh no, Mr. President, I cannot do that."

"You do realize that the constitution has been amended to prohibit the formation of hui corporations, correct?"

"Yes, Mr. President."

"Then send in your Sheriff with a warrant to vacate Vorbine. Now."

"I am so sorry Mr. President, but this is a bad law."

"What exactly do you mean?"

"Before Vorbine came to Boise it was a sick town. We had no work. Many good men spent their days drinking. But now Boise is getting better. I'm sorry, but I don't want it to go back to the way it was before."

"Mayor Vargas, public servants are not required to interpret laws, we are only required to carry them out. It is your sworn duty to uphold the constitution of the United States and I expect you to take action immediately!"

Despite the fact that the President of the United States was screaming at him, Manny Vargas stood brave.

"Sorry Mr. President, but the Supreme Court has not ruled that the amendment is constitutional."

"Mayor Vargas, it is well known that the Supreme Court is in favor of the amendment."

"Yes, Mr. President. We may be simple people here in Boise, but we know the members of the Supreme Court always supports Big Business."

"So if it is inevitable that the Supreme Court will have a positive ruling, why wait? The law will be upheld despite your efforts to stop it."

"Yes, Mr. President. But lawyers and judges take time to make decisions. While they argue, it gets closer to election time. I think maybe the next election the people will change this bad law."

Holding his tongue, the president simply said, "Well at least I know where you stand on this matter, goodbye Mayor Vargus."

He slammed down the phone and ordered his assistant to get the Secretary of Defense on the line.

"Robert Chatsworth."

"Robert, I just got off the phone with the Manny Vargas, Mayor of Boise. He's sandbagging. He won't even send his Sheriff to issue a warrant to vacate. We'll need to handle this thing ourselves."

"I can have the National Guard there in the morning."

"Excellent. I don't want this turning into a Tien An Men situation. We can't give Quinn time to stage another protest. Give Vorbine twenty-four hours to move."

"And if they don't?"

"There are 5800 Vorbine members. Send in just enough men to secure the perimeter and remove the occupants."

"If we are using force, Mr. President, what response do you want if the members of Vorbine respond with violence?"

"Have your men stand down and surround the camp. Blockade Vorbine, but no violence. We just need to close them down. Hopefully in a few weeks the nation will forget about it."

Scott Burns used to loved to play football. As soon as school let out, Scott and his buddies would head out to the playground to play football until it was dusk. Scott loved running, catching and throwing the ball, but most of all he loved to huddle with his pals and call out brilliant plays. Scott's love of the game carried over into high school and by his senior year, Scott was the town's hero winning the state division two years in a row. Even as a young boy Scott dreamed of playing quarterback for the Kansas City Chiefs. When colleges passed him over on the account of his size, Scott did what many young men do when faced with defeat: he joined the army.

Three years in, Scott knew he had found a home. He fit right in with the regimentation and applied for Officer Candidate School when he was 21. But years of academic accommodation on account of his athletics left Scott with a poor education. Despite his best efforts, he failed the entrance exam three times. Even without a college degree, Scott's natural ability to lead along with success on the battle field, eventually resulted in Scott obtaining the rank of First Sergeant.

During a Thunder game, Scott got Major General Sandler's message, relayed by First Sargent McGillis.

"Sargent Scott, Major General Sandler will send a currier tomorrow at 0600 with a document you are to deliver to a Mr. Cliff Higgins at Vorbine by 0900."

"Yes Sir. May I inquire into the nature of the document?"

"It is a Cease and Desist Warrant issued by the Attorney General, and an order to vacate the premises. At 1300 you are to return to base to make your report via video conference."

"Yes sir. Is there anything else, sir?"

"That's all for now, sergeant."

Entering Vorbine eight hours later, Scott was amazed by the lack of security. A simple stucco sign was the only indicator that he had arrived at his destination. Following signs to the Visitor Center, Scott parked and entered, letting the attractive receptionist know that he was here to see Cliff Higgins.

Looking concerned by the Sargent's uniform, the pretty young woman called Cliff.

Hanging up the phone she took out a map of the facility and began speaking while highlighting at the same time.

"So, you're here, at the Visitor Center. To get out to the Finishing Plant, you'll want to take one of the Segues parked behind this building. Here we are at the visitor center, simply follow the highlighted line. See? Would you like a helmet? You don't need to wear one if you don't want to, but a lot of us do. You know, to be a good role model for the kids."

This was the last thing Sargent Scott expected from his potentially forceful shutdown of Vorbine. He didn't like to pull rank, but he couldn't help himself from snapping, "I'm not here for a tour, Mam. I have an important document issued by the Attorney General of the United States that I need to deliver in-person to Cliff Higgins."

In earnest, the receptionist nodded her head.

"I understand, sir. You're here to shut us down. Cliff has been notified of your visit. He is waiting for you at the Finishing Plant. Let me help you get a Segue."

Perplexed but utterly charmed, Scott followed the slim receptionist through the back door and saw about twenty Segues neatly lined up, each with a blue helmet balanced on the handle bars. Scott unbuttoned the top button of his uniform, slipped the official envelope inside and, opting not to wear the helmet, headed off in the direction of the finishing plant with a curt wave of thanks.

Winding the along the curving sidewalk, Scott marveled at the buildings on either side. Each mound-like structure emerged from the ground like an organic entity inhabiting its own space. Going up and over a small slope, a little stream appeared alongside the sidewalk. Scott could see the tiny streams flowing into an elongated lake settled at the center of the village flanked by trees and marathon grass.

As Scott maneuvered the Segue forward, dwelling units came into view, reminding Scott of large round tribal huts with sheltered terraces. The irregular hand-packed terra-cotta walls were nestled by lush green vegetation. Skirting the lake, Scott saw a group of kindergarten students dancing along in pairs wearing brightly colored jackets. Lead by their teacher, the troupe went from home to home, gathering students.

Leaving the dwelling units, the path widened as it approached a unique group of buildings. Passing through an archway, Scott was reminded of an amusement park. He stopped to study the map depicting a miniature town laced with pathways. Winding gracefully past restaurants, clothing stores, and a school, Scott couldn't help thinking how nice it would be to live in such a place.

Past the little town, Scott saw factories standing like massive circus tents about a half mile off. Letting go of the pleasure of the silent ride among fields of sage, Scott felt a growing remorse in having to serve the order to vacate.

With foreboding, Scott located building number six and walked up the steps to the entrance. He spotted Thomas Quinn standing next to a wiry man with big bushy hair and a nose that would make an Indian Chief proud. Wasting no time, Cliff stepped forward and shot out his arm to shake the stranger's.

"Welcome, Sergeant Scott Burns. I am Cliff Higgins." Smiling despite himself, Scott offered Cliff his hand, who grasped it with both his hands, staring into Scott's eyes while excitedly pumping his arm up and down as if nothing in the world was more important. Only after Scott peeled his eyes from Cliff and looked at Thomas Quinn did Cliff relinquish his grasp.

"Sergeant Scott Burns, let me introduce you to my good friend, Thomas Quinn."

With less vigor but no less warmth, Thomas shook Scott Burn's hand. Regaining his resolve, Scott said: "I'm pleased to meet you both but I'm here on official business." He pulled the warrant from his inner pocket.

Cliff unbuttoned the cuffs of his shirtsleeves and started rolling them up, saying, "Yes, we know. We've been expecting you, or someone like you, but we thought it'd take longer. What's that you got for us?"

Accepting the envelope, Cliff turned to Thomas.

"Oh my, this does look official." Removing the packet of papers a Cliff looked admiringly at the handmade cotton paper cover letter. "Look Thomas it even has a gold embossed presidential seal and it is signed by the Attorney General." Glancing at it for a fraction of second Cliff continued saying, "They want us out of here in twenty-four hours." Smiling as if the document had no meaning what so ever Cliff continued saying, "Why that hardly gives us time to pack a tooth brush."

Scott stood at attention, anticipating a cascade of admonitions but Thomas, looking just as unperturbed as Cliff, said, "What time do you need to be back to base?"

Relieved by the two men's gracious acceptance, Scott let his shoulders drop and replied, "I have a meeting with my commanding officer at one o'clock."

Thomas put his arm on Scott's shoulder. "That's good. Cliff and I would like to give you a little tour of the place and send you on your way by 11:00. That gives you three hours before your meeting starts. We'll have a box lunch prepared for you to take. Sound good?"

Rationalizing his desire to see more of this amazing place by telling himself he would gain a tactical advantage if he saw more of Vorbine, Scott didn't hesitate to accept their invitation. With childlike excitement, Cliff and Thomas showed Scott the foundry, the generator assembly plant, the spinning and weaving plants, the cut and sew factory and the metal fabrication plant. Circling back to the finishing plant where Scott's Segue awaited, none of them wanted their time together to end.

"It took us two months to make the first Vorbine. Within four months, we were producing a Vorbine a day. Now we produce and install two Vorbines a day. Just think: one Vorbine produces 10.6 megawatts of power, enough to power 1800 homes. At this rate, we'll replace US coal-fired electric plants with clean wind energy before the decade is over."

Thomas turned to Scott. "Do you know how we doubled production in just four months?"

Venturing a guess Scott ventured, "You expanded?"

"That's true, in part. We did expand the forge, and we also brought in more textile equipment. But those steps were taken just to keep up with production. The fact is you're looking at the world's most efficient factory in the world's most sustainable town. It's not the machinery that makes these factories so efficient: it's the workers."

Cliff chimed in: "About three months ago we began cross training. Most workers are certified to work multiple positions now so they switch up to make it interesting, and it's good if anyone gets sick or needs to leave for a while. About half of the work force switches jobs on a daily basis. This is just one example of how workers become more productive. The bottom line is this: empowered employees are encouraged to take ownership of their work and become very productive. And when their home life is easy and fulfilling, employees go to work happy."

Leading Scott down a ramp Thomas said, "Now that you've had a chance to see how Vorbines are made, you need to see one up close." Approaching a four passenger electric all-terrain vehicle, Cliff motioned for the other two to climb in and said, "I'll drive. Scott, sit up here next to me, you'll get a better view. Wait until you see Vorbines in action."

They held onto the ATV's roll bar as Cliff steered it up the side of a hill. Rounding the top Scott gasped to see a valley filled with Vorbines. The sheer scale of the project was awe inspiring. Scott counted a total of 128 Vorbines. They towered 625 feet in the air. They stood in eight rows spaced one mile apart. Scott thought it looked like a vast whirling alien city.

Cutting the engine, Cliff jumped out and with zeal stretched out both of his arms as if he were embracing the grandness below.

"Have you ever seen anything more amazing?"

Scott thought for a moment. Even the massive military instillation for the second battle of Fallujah couldn't compare.

Cliff stepped over to Scott and asked, "What do you see before you?"

Scott hesitated a moment before venturing, "A Ferris wheel fanatic's wet dream."

Cliff looked at Thomas and cracked up. Their laughter spread and despite his serious appearance, Scott couldn't help himself. He burst out laughing.

Catching his breath Cliff said, "Yes, that's it exactly. But the truly amazing thing is what you can't see: the absence of 141 tons of carbon dioxide spewed into the sky every single hour. Because that's what it would take to produce the same amount of energy by burning coal. One hundred and forty-one tons of carbon is hard to wrap your head around. Just imagine 3400 one-ton pickup trucks filling the sky above us at the end of every day.

"Did you know the inhabitants of China's major cities haven't seen a blue sky in twenty years? Soon the smog blanket over China will spread to all corners of the globe, and then it'll be lights out for you and me. What do you think will happen to America when land west of the Mississippi dries up and lands north of Tennessee become permafrost?"

Feeling like he'd been transported to another dimension, Scott let all of his inhibitions go.

"People in my line of work will be in high demand."

Cliff laughed loudly and slapped his thigh. Turning to Thomas, he said, "See, I told you! This is the guy!" Turning to Scott he said, "I had a feeling about you, I told Thomas yesterday. I told him you are the one."

Scott thought maybe Cliff and Thomas were making fun of him and said defensively, "What do you mean, 'the one?'"

Thomas put his hand softly on Scott's shoulder and said, "We believe you are the person who will change the course of history."

Suspecting that Thomas and Cliff were not of sound mind Scott stood stiff and looked at them with apprehension.

Easing the tension Thomas said, "We know little of the power each of us posses. We are taught to believe that others have power over us. That we must do another's bidding. That is wrong. Inside each of us is more power than what we can imagine."

Thomas stepped closer.

"Scott within you is more power than all the generals and president combined. You can forever change the course of history."

If it was not for the deadly serious expression of Cliff and Thomas, Scott would have tried to make light of the matter, but instead he asked, "What am I to do?"

Thomas put both hands on Scott's shoulders and looked him dead in the eye.

"You know what to do. You have the strength. Do it, or forever fall into a pit of regret and self despise."

With that, Thomas climbed into the back seat of the ATV and Cliff drove them back to the entrance in silence. Getting out of the ATV Scott smiled and held out his hand and started to say something, but before he could form words Thomas grabbed him up in a hug and, firmly pounding him on the back, said, "I love you, brother."

An odd sensation came over Scott; a feeling he did not have since he was a teen. With tears in his eyes, Scott looked into the eyes of Thomas. Quickly turning, he dug his hand into his pocket to pull out his keys, and without looking back, headed down the road.

Scott felt like he was in some kind of hypnotic trance. He rolled down his window in an attempt to clear his head, but he kept drifting in and out of lucidity.

Driving through the base's gate a strange sensation came over Scott. Up until that very moment Scott had the feeling that his life was just a long, elaborate play. All the people he ever knew and everything he ever did had been scripted. Passing the soldier sitting at the desk outside his office, Scott felt compelled to tell him, 'the play is over; you can stop playing your part and leave.' Restraining himself, Scott entered his office and sat at his desk. He stared at the photographs on the walls, at his books and awards, knowing they were merely props in a play that was over.

The ringing phone startled him from his trance. He slowly picked it up.

"Yes?"

"Major General Sandler is on the video line for you."

Switching on his monitor, he was face to face with the General, who wasted no time asking, "Did Higgins agree to vacate?"

Without replying Scott stared at the monitor, stone faced.

"Sergeant Burns, did you hear me? Turn up the volume! Did Higgins agree to vacate?"

"Sorry sir. No sir, Mr. Higgins did not agree to leave the compound."

"I figured. Look, you need to get those people out of Vorbine. Do it peacefully, but if they refuse to leave, carry them out if you have to. Based on what we know about the inhabitants, we don't anticipate any violence, but if there is, you are to sit tight and wait for further instructions."

"Yes sir."

"Deploy 1200 men. I know that sounds like a lot, but there are 5800 people at Vorbine and we want them to know we mean business. Your men are to enter the compound unarmed."

"Yes sir."

"The schematics are ready to download. Memorize every detail of this operation. Your performance in Fallujah was flawless, so I have complete confidence in you. But the hui group can be very persuasive. Don't let them undermine your mission."

"Yes sir."

"Your men are not to know of the mission until 0500. This is a need-to-know operation from this point forward. The last thing we need is a leak to the press. Questions?"

Scott's chiseled expression went through several iterations before he asked calmly, "What will happen to the people of Vorbine?"

"We're chartering 13 Greyhound buses. They'll be lined up outside the Vorbine compound at 0800. You are to transport all who don't leave on their own to Amarillo. It's all in the report. Any other questions?"

"No sir."

"Good. A lot of people are counting on you."

"Yes sir."

Signing off, Scott downloaded the reports and, sitting at his gray metal desk with a blank expression on his face, watched his printer spit out page after page, mesmerized by the methodical whirring. Any other day, he would have dove into the data, memorizing every last detail, but not today. Today, Scott sensed a dry putrid odor blanketing the room. It was as if the room and everything in it, down to the last speck of dust, was sucking the life out of him. With the printer still running, Scott got up and left without a word to anyone.

Without knowing where he was going, Scott instinctively drove his truck home. Pulling up to the modest brick-facade house, he felt like he was seeing it for the first time. The rectangular side hedges and the neatly trimmed grass along the walkway leading to the front door looked ridiculous. In fact, everything, including the mailbox, looked absurd.

Feeling faint, Scott threw himself into his brown vinyl recliner and lay back, staring up at the ceiling. The fading light made strange shapes appear on the ceiling; when it was totally dark, Scott fell into a deep sleep.

Scott dreamed he was in the dessert outside Fallujah. It was twilight; a silvery full moon illuminated the barren landscape. Looking up at the starry sky, he heard a tiger roar. All of a sudden the tiger began to run towards him. Scott franticly tried to grab his riffle lying on the ground, but it was too late, the tiger leaped into the air and knocked Scott to the ground. Ready to face his death Scott looked up into the face of the massive tiger hovering above him.

Suddenly the ground below Scott turned into quicksand. Scott frantically pulled at the sand trying to get a firm grip, but the more he struggled the swifter he sank. Buried up to his shoulders Scott called out to the tiger to help him. As if the tiger was waiting all along to be summoned, it bit down Scott's collar and pulled him to safety.

After catching his breath a moment Scott looked lovingly into the tiger's eyes. They began to run. Scott never ran so fast. The ground below his feet whizzed by just as Scott leaped into the air and began to fly. Flying high above ground the sun was just rising over an emerald island with lush green palms encircling a deep blue pool.

Scott dove into the pool. He climbed out and walked along the powdery white sand, feeling happier than he had ever felt before.

Scott woke up at 0430, reveling in the wave of peace that cleansed his soul. Completely at ease, he took a long, hot shower, dressed in fresh fatigues and made a sandwich of two raw hot dogs and peanut butter before heading out to the base.

At 0445 Scott called the Corporal on duty.

"Sorry to wake you so early Eugene, but I received notification from Major General Sandler yesterday afternoon that we are to conduct a military operation this morning in Boise."

"Yes sir."

"As you've probably guessed, it involves Vorbine. I cannot divulge the details until we arrive at 0800 hours. We are to mobilize the entire squadron, all 1200 soldiers. This will be an unarmed mission. We don't have a time-line so pack enough food and supplies to last two weeks in the field. I estimate we'll need all eight MK28s. Start immediately. I want to be ready to roll at 0730. Inform Carpenter and Walbash that this operation involves Vorbine and no one else. Do you understand? No one. I will personally address the men at Vorbine as to our mission. Understood?"

"Yes sir."

As planned, the military caravan pulled off right outside Vorbine's entrance shortly before 8 AM. Scott saw off in the distance the members of Vorbine began to fill Vorbine's entrance. Scott stopped his Humvee and had his Corporals call the men to attention.

Scott had addressed much larger assemblies of men before, but never had he been so calm and confident. With a warrior's energy, he jumped on top of his Humvee and addressed his men.

"I've known most of you for years. We've fought side by side in Fallujah; some of you were even with me in Kandahar. We fought bravely, we conquered, and unlike many of our fallen brothers, we survived. Like our fathers before us who fought in the Vietnam and Korean wars, we weren't always sure of why we went to war. It's still not clear why we fought in Iraq and Afghanistan."

Scott saw that the members of Vorbine began to link hands forming a long human chain.

"We followed the commands of our senior officers because we believed in duty and honor, and we felt pride in following the orders of our senior officers. We took pride in protecting the life and liberty of Americans."

The men, women and children of Vorbine were close now, gathering around the soldiers. A bearded man with a large camcorder on his shoulder was filming.

"Even after no weapons of mas destruction were discovered, we followed our orders. Even after being hated by the very people we were trying to protect in Iraq and Afghanistan, we followed orders. Many of our brothers died. Still we placed our trust in our leaders.

"Yesterday Major General Sandler asked for our trust once again. Our orders are clear. For the sake of national security, we have been asked to physically remove the citizens of Vorbine from their homes.

"Take a good look around. Do the people standing next to you threaten you? Are the Vorbines you see in the distance a threat to national security? Instead of our government supporting the only viable clean energy solution that is keeping mankind from almost certain destruction, your government has asked you to imprison its members and close down its factories. Despite the over whelming support by the citizens of America, our government has asked us to close down Vorbine.

"Today I choose to uphold my sworn duty to protect American citizens. Join me in protecting the rights of the citizens of Vorbine."

General Sandler stared in disbelief at the large screen inside the National Military Command Center as he watched the troops join in celebration with the members of Vorbine.

As the other Joint Chiefs of Staff looked on, General Sandler barked out a command to his staff lieutenant.

"Get Sergeant Scott Burns on the line. NOW!"

Before the lieutenant could respond the vice chairman announced, "Vorbine's streaming a time-delayed video. It's on screen."

They were watching Scott tell 1200 men that their orders were unethical for the third time when Vice Chairman Olsen came on the screen.

The joint chiefs of staff watched in disbelief as they watched Scott openly defy their orders with the support of 1200 troupes. As general Sandler began to bark out another command, the Vice Chairman Olsen announced over the intercom.

"I have heard enough breaking of command with this operation today. The next person who orders a command without my approval will be facing court martial along with Sergeant Burns."

The room fell silent as Olsen controlled his fury.

"Who can tell me where is the closest military base to Boise?"

"We have 4800 men at Fort Sill in Lawton, Oklahoma, three hours south of Boise."

"How soon can they be mobilized with armored transport?"

The men looked at each other, shaking their heads with trepidation. Vice Chairman Olsen didn't wait for a reply.

"Very well. Ready the chopper and contact Boling. I want to be in the air in fifteen minutes."

Getting up the surrounding generals stood at attention as Vice Chairman Olsen left the command center. On the way to the heliport Olsen dialed he president.

"Mr. President it's Olsen calling about the Vorbine incident."

"You call this an incident? It's a disaster. Every single American has seen the video. Your incompetence has rendered the nation defenseless! What the hell happened?"

"I'm on my way to remedy the situation now. By tomorrow morning this will all be over."

"The damage is irrevocable."

"Mr. President, may I suggest we take up the finer points of this discussion at a later date? The longer we engage in discussion, the longer the mission is delayed."

"And just what is your mission, General Olsen?"

"To arrest and detain Sergeant Burns, along with the men who conspired with him, and to ensure Vorbine is vacated."

"And just how do you propose to 'arrest and detain' 1200 trained American soldiers?"

"We have verified that Burns and his men are unarmed. Non-lethal riot control methods should suffice."

"General Olsen. I need you to listen carefully. I am giving you a direct order. Not a single shot will be fired. There will be no teargas or physical violence of any kind. Do I make myself clear?"

"Yes sir."

"The cameras will be running, Olsen. The success or failure of your operation will be televised."

"Understood, Sir."

"What's the ETA to Boise?"

"4 PM."

"Very well. You are to personally report me at 4:15."

Li Ping received the call at 3 AM. Still feeling the effects of too much to drink from the night before, Li Ping sat up, trying to get his bearings. His head swayed as he realized the voice-activated emergency intercom was on and the Party Secretary was speaking.

"I am sorry to disturb you, Premiere, but as you requested I am informing you of the unprecedented events unfolding in America."

"What events?"

"The American military sent in troops to close down Vorbine, but instead of carrying out their mission, they have setup camp pledging to protect the members of Vorbine."

With a chuckle Li Ping ran his tongue over his dry lips.

"Very good, very good. Bring the Minister of Economy to my home immediately. We have work to do."

Traveling in a F14 Tomcat, at speeds exceeding 1600 miles per hour, General Olsen felt his stomach harden. It wasn't the confined space, or even the speed turned his guts. It was the video clip of Sergeant Burns deserting his duty three hours ago with the support of 1200 men. Desertion was rampant. The General recalled his aide's statistics that over 40,000 men have deserted the military since 2000.

Hate welled up in General Olsen. Deserters! Weak-kneed, yellow-bellied, immoral pieces of shit. If he had his way he'd personally put a bullet into the heads of every single one. With an avalanche of hate cascading through his mind, Olsen sat clenching his teeth. If only there were real officers, officers like himself, who understood what it meant to be a man.

Arriving in Lawton in just under an hour, General Olsen saw a caravan of military combat vehicles stretching from Fort Sill's gate to the barracks. Not stopping to greet the commanding officer, he walked directly into the mess hall to address the men. Looking as mean and ugly as a man can, he strode up to the podium and grabbed the mike.

"A monumental tragedy occurred this morning. Disobeying direct orders from our Commander in Chief, Sergeant Burns along with his original company of 1200 men have committed treason, mutiny and desertion.

"For those who don't know, under the uniform code of military justice, these crimes are punishable by death."

With hate running through his veins General Olson leaned into his podium.

"These men deserve death for the crime they have committed."

Catching hold of himself, General Olsen backed down a notch.

"But we are not gathered here to deliberate the punishment of the 1200 men under sergeant Burn's command. We are here to carry out the President's orders and remove Sergeant Burns, his men, along with the residents of Vorbine, today. I hope you understand how momentous our task is.

"The men under Burn's command are not armed, but they're trained in physical combat. They're not likely to change their minds once we arrive. Be prepared to engage in hand to hand combat to remove Sergeant Burns and his 1200 troops.

"I am fully confident that twelve hundred men from Fort Sills could easily remove the cowards at Vorbine, but the world is watching our operation. We want a quick, decisive battle. We will deploy 3600 men with 1200 standing by.

"The eyes of America and the world are watching. It is time to restore America's dignity. Now let's go kick some butt."

Raising his fist, expecting cheers of support, General Olsen's neck turned beet red as he was met with silence. No one made eye contact with him. Someone coughed toward the back and someone said something under their breath. He climbed down from the podium steaming. He glared at the commanding officer, Major General Mark McKenzie, who finally snapped to and barked out orders for the men to board their vehicles.

Arriving just after four pm it was just as General Olsen expected. Several thousand Vorbine residents stood with Sergeant Burns and his men in front of the military camp they erected.

Calling the battalion officers to his Humvee, General Olsen gave the final assault instructions.

"General McKenzie, you are to approach first with twenty Bradley tanks spaced ten yards apart. On each tank I want one man on a machine gun mount and one man on a grenade launcher. Once in position, you are to use a loudspeaker to inform Sergeant Burns that he and his men are to vacate Vorbine immediately."

General McKenzie said, "Do you honestly believe Sergeant Burns will surrender because of this show of force?"

"No I do not. That is why the 100th and the 168th Brigade Battalion are to position their MTVR's directly behind the Strykers. Once deployed, I want the men to form groups of three and to physically load Burn's men onto the MTVRs."

"What's the contingency plan if any of Burn's men fight?"

"Subdue them through any non-lethal means necessary. Do I make myself clear?"

"Yes sir."

"Good. Move out."

General Olsen tried to find McKenzie with his field binoculars in the cloud of red dust the Bradley tanks raised as they flattened everything in their path.

"McKenzie, any response from Burns or his men?"

"No sir. They're not responding and they're not budging."

"No matter. They're going to get the beating they deserve."

Looking out over the prairie grass, Vorbines spinning in the setting sun, General Olsen thought back on his victories in the Gulf War and a great sense of pride washed over him.

Just as the MTVRs were making their final approach General Olsen watched in disbelief as the Bradley tanks turned their guns in the opposite direction of Vorbine. General Olsen ground his teeth as he watch the men disembark from the MTVRs to join Sergeant Scott Burn's troupes.

Crazed with anger General Olsen shook his head in fury and let out a low breathy repressed yell. Seeing red General Olsen ran to his Humvee. Driving sixty miles an hour over rough terrain General Olsen was just barely able to hold on before he skidded to a stop in front of a tank.

Shaking from head to toe, General Olsen yelled in fury.

"McKenzie, where the fuck are you?"

Totally losing it, Olsen took out his 9mm and popped off three shots in the air, screaming, "General McKenzie, front and center!"

Cutting a path through the swarm of men, General McKenzie and Sergeant Burns made their way over to General Olsen. Seeing them together, General Olsen felt like he was about to explode.

"Have you totally lost your fucking mind? You WILL follow my orders."

Stepping forward with authority, General McKenzie said, "It's over, General Olsen. No one's getting arrested today and the people of Vorbine will continue their work."

Raising the pistol to General McKenzie's head, General Olsen said, "Order your men to detain the traitors or so help me God I will put a bullet in your head."

As if admonishing a disobedient child, General McKenzie said, "No one is going to kill anyone. Now put the gun down."

Wild-eyed and trembling, General Olsen looked at General McKenzie then at the men encircling them and frantically pointed his gun at the crowd. As if pushed by an invisible force the men backed away from the muzzle. He spun around, pointing the gun to the opposite side, and the circle around them widened as the threatened men pulled back. Swinging his arm around a third time he stopped it at his own head, gasped in desperation and pulled the trigger.

Hundreds of miles away, the men gathered in the President's Situation Room fell silent. Staring at the screen in horror, the President's voice cracked.

"Call them back."

Robert Chatsworth, the Secretary of Defense said, "Do you mean the air support that's standing by?"

"Yes Robert: air support, ground support, and all military actions dealing with Vorbine are to cease immediately."

"But sir, these men need to be court marshaled. We can't just tell them to return to base! They've all committed treason. That's a crime!"

"What about the crimes we committed Robert? How are we going to pay for our crimes? We were sworn into office to uphold the will of the people of the United States. We violated that trust and now we are paying the consequences. Now call the men back before we have a civil war on our hands."

Without another word, the President left the Situation Room. He walked the long way around to the north face of the White House, ascended the three flights of stairs leading to the Blue Room, closed the door and like before when deeply depressed, laid down to sleep.

Chapter 18

The next morning while walking with Larry Baker along the West Terrace, a White House aide approached the two men and said apprehensively, "I'm sorry to disturb you but Ross Hamilton has arrived."

President Dial turned to Larry.

"Was I supposed to meet with the Chairman of the Federal Reserve today?" Larry shook his head 'no,' and Dial turned back to the aide.

"What's this about?"

Unsure of herself, the aide said, "China is cashing in their treasury bills."

Without hesitating, President Dial replied, "Tell him to meet me in the oval office."

Ross Hamilton was ghostly pale when the President opened the door. Shaking his sweaty hand, President Dial wondered if Ross wasn't having a heart attack. He guided him to the sofa and called for his secretary to get some fruit juice and coffee.

"I understand China is cashing in their treasury bills. How much are we talking about?"

Ross Hamilton's leg began bouncing with anxiety.

"All of it, basically: one point two trillion, to be exact, and they'll take another two hundred billion when it matures in a month."

"They can't do that. We have an understanding! What are they doing?"

"From what we can tell, China is buying mines all across the globe, even here in the United States, from iron ore in northern Minnesota to copper mines in southern Arizona. Australia, India, Brazil… China is buying every mine they can get their hands on."

"Did China's T bills mature all at once?"

"They have been mature for several months. It's not unusual for China. In the past they would hold mature bills before renewing them again. We always expected China to honor their promise."

Knowing the answer but wanting to hear it from the Chairman, Dial asked, "What will be the result of selling off one point two trillion dollars?"

"With no other country to carry our debt, our double A rating will be shattered. If we don't take action, within a day or two, the US dollar will be worth five times less than what it is now."

"So China is converting its American treasury bills into metal investments…unbelievable."

"Yes. I believe China intends to wait until the US dollar is crushed before announcing that the Renminbi is going to be offered in world markets. Instead of pegging the Renminbi to the US dollar, China plans to back the Renminbi to their metal holdings."

"So overnight the dollar will plummet while the Renminbi becomes the world's new super power currency."

"Exactly. Even if the Renminbi is not backed by a specific amount of metal, the very idea that it's backed by more than just the good faith of the government will skyrocket its value."

The President calmly poured a small glass of pomegranate juice and handed it to Ross, who admired the President's composure after receiving such devastating news. He was too sick to drink anything but he took the ruby liquid from the President and waited patiently as president Dial stood up and walked over to the oval windows behind his desk.

Like so many times before, President Dial stared out the window at the garden below and allowed his mind to go blank. Just as a runner prepares for a race by stretching, the President cleared his mind to seek answers. He enjoyed letting the landscape go in and out of focus, emptying his mind to induce meditation.

Relived by the break, Ross reviewed what they could do to avoid the looming catastrophe, or at least minimize the destruction. For some time the two men remained silent.

At last, the President turned and, as if addressing a large gathering, said, "If we have the courage, overwhelming hardship can be transformed into overwhelming reward. What steps do you believe we need to take?"

"We must restore confidence in the dollar or our economy will collapse. We must immediately cut one trillion from our budget. Today."

"I was hoping you would say that. Where would you cut?"

"Medicare, social security, infrastructure, military. I wish there was another way but our hands are tied. If we don't act now, before world markets open tomorrow, we won't have an economy to save. It will be too late."

"We will slash the budget and restore confidence in the dollar, but we will not hurt the people of America."

"But what other option do we have?"

"There is another option, one we should have taken long ago."

Walking over to the phone on his desk, President Dial hit the intercom to his secretary.

"Call the Joint Chiefs of Staff, and get all the Cabinet members to the Cabinet Room for an emergency meeting. Then get Li Ping on the phone. They can deliberate while I'm on the phone with Li Ping."

Turning to Ross, the President asked him to brief the assembly until he gets off the phone. Ross hurried away and moments later Present Dial was addressing Li Ping.

"Thank you, Premiere Li Ping, for taking my call."

"Of course. It is no bother."

"Under the circumstances, I was concerned that you might not."

"Although it is a bit late, China has always had an open door policy with our American friends."

"Friends' is a strange choice of words. From where we stand, China has just committed an act of war against the people of the United States."

"War? We have done no such thing. Our troops are stationary. You are misinformed."

"You know exactly what I'm referring to. You have launched an economic war against the United States. I hope you realize the consequences for your actions."

"Indeed I do. Since the US government no longer has control of either your stock market or your military, our government no longer has confidence in the America dollar. We are bound as world leaders to protect our investment. If we don't, the suffering of our people will be monumental."

"But the US still has an excellent rating by Standard & Poor's. You are purposefully trying to destroy the value of the American dollar. You have forced my hand. I will issue tariffs on Chinese imports before the day is over."

"Such a short sighted move will devastate your economy. America is a country of big box stores filled with Chinese products. What will happen to all the millions of Americans who work for these mega giants? You have no choice but continue importing China products."

"You are undermining the resiliency of the American public."

"America is addicted to consuming. There is nothing you can do to stop this addiction. The world has only one China. If you stop China imports millions of unemployed Americans will rise up in revolt. You need China."

"Twenty years ago, China was a poor backward country. Your wealth came from America's buying power. Without America, China would still be a poor third world country."

"You bend reality to fit your purpose. Capitalistic greed fueled China's economy and capitalistic greed will be the destruction of the American economy. China did not force America to sell off all of its factories. Now you will suffer the consequences and China will emerge as the world's new super power."

"Li Ping, enjoy your fantasy while you can. Before the day is over you will see your plot has backfired."

Hanging up the phone, President Dial asked the secretary, "Did you record it?"

"Yes sir. I have the entire conversation."

"Good. I want you to play it for the members in the Cabinet Room. But first, get the Prime Minister of Japan on the line."

Catching his breath, Dial picked up the handset when it started flashing.

"Prime Minister Mishima, no doubt you have heard that China has sold one point two trillion dollars in US treasury bills. Are you going to liquidate your investment as well?"

"We are trying to honor our agreement, but even the strongest anchor line will snap in a strong storm."

"Meaning you're cashing in, too?"

"We can try to hold on, but we cannot afford to lose one trillion dollars. You must correct the problem, or we will be forced to sell off our holdings before the Asian markets open in the morning."

"You have a little less than 500 billion that is able to be converted at this time."

"Five hundred billion is still five hundred billion."

"I thank for you holding fast in these turbulent times. I am confident we can restore confidence in the American dollar before the day is out."

For some time President Dial sat in silence with a peaceful expression on his face before getting up and heading for the cabinet room. Voices in conflict were audible even before he reached the door. Stepping inside, the assembly immediately stood at attention as the President solemnly made his way to his seat at the head of the table. He let the silence linger a moment so that all present could focus.

"Ladies and gentlemen the events that unfolded over the past several weeks have brought our nation to the edge. The grim reality is that our economy is in shambles. Those Americans who are fortunate enough to have some money put away for retirement watched their investments be cut nearly in half with the recent stock market crash. To weather the crisis, companies have responded by slashing their workforce. Today, nearly fifty percent of our youth are out of work.

"Long before the stock market crash, the vast majority of Americans have demanded change. They want what the employees of Vorbine, Kimball Industries and P&G have. But, most of us in this room, including myself, turned their back on the citizens of this nation and made it illegal to work for a hui corporation.

"When Vorbine refused to close it doors, we sent in the National Guard followed by the military. When 6000 men and women of our military refused to obey a command, a crime punishable by death, we were attacked. China believes we no longer have control of our military and has choose to attack us when we are most venerable.

"As you have just heard, there is no mistaking Li Ping's intention to destroy the American economy. If successful, China will render the US dollar worthless while establishing China as the world's new super power. As we speak, China is using a trillion US dollars to buy every type of metal they can get their hands on. And they are not stopping at just buying metal; they're buying mines all over the world, including mines in America.

"Our time is running out. Prime Minister Mishima informed us that Japan will give us until 3:00 PM today to restore the confidence in the dollar, or they will begin to liquidate 500 billion in US treasury bills.

"If we fail to act we will find ourselves at the bottom of the cliff. America will plunge into a depression that will send our nation back 100 years. But there is hope. We can act with bold confidence to restore the faith and the future of this nation."

President Dial turned to the Chairman of the Federal Reserve.

"Mr. Hamilton, what needs to happen to restore confidence in the dollar?"

"There needs to be a dollar for dollar exchange. For every dollar taken out of the treasury, we must reduce spending by one dollar."

The Secretary of Defense stood up and said, "We can curtail military equipment purchases, reducing defense spending by nearly three hundred billion. This, along with the staggered elimination of social security, should be enough to restore confidence in the dollar."

The President looked at the members seated at the table and asked, "Curtail military spending and end social security; are there any other viable solutions?"

Secretary of Defense answered. "The only other alternative is to cut Medicare."

"Yesterday I turned my back on the people of the United States. That, will never happen again. No. The solution is staring us in the face. We must cut all military spending."

The Secretary of Defense shot up and shouted, "Preposterous! We have 739 bases spread throughout the world. Dismantling the military will leave us completely defenseless."

President Dial retorted, "On the contrary, our military spending has left us completely defenseless. Are we to take our multi-trillion dollar military to China's shores and demand that they assume our debt? We have fallen victim to years of neglectful military spending. Now, with our backs against the wall, we can finally put a stop to military spending."

General Jorgensen, the newly appointed Joint Chief of Staff

Chairman, rose and addressed the President.

"What do you propose to do with the one point five million military personnel on active duty? Add them to our already bloated ranks of the unemployed?"

Several voices rose up in agreement, causing the President to once again stand.

"We can choose 'business as usual' and continue down the same destructive path that brought us to this desperate pass, or choose innovation and cooperation. And no, I am not just talking about eliminating the jobs of one point four million American military personnel. I am also including two-hundred and thirty thousand members of Home Land Security."

Jorgensen sputtered, "You'll be leaving the doors wide open for another 9/11 attack!"

"We bankrupted the country because of the 9/11 attack. We spent three trillion to catch Osama Bin Laden. We've been at war for over a decade. For what? The time to stop the madness is now."

General Jorgensen stood.

"I will hear no more of this. I will not sit by idly and listen to this lunacy."

As Jorgensen walked to the door, President Dial called out, "General Jorgensen, this meeting is not adjourned. I am giving you a direct order to take your seat."

Looking scornfully at the President, General Jorgensen reluctantly took his seat.

"The days of American military colonialism are over. The world no longer desires, nor can we afford a US military presence scattered throughout the world. World peace is not threatened by rogue nations, but rather by threats from global warming, squandering natural resources, poverty and unbalanced distribution of wealth. Our inability to solve these core issues leads to world instability. Over the past 70 years the money we spent building our massive war machine could have been used to solve so many of the problems we face. Now, after being pushed to the brink of economic catastrophe we are forced to shut down the military. It is time to begin again and solve the problems of the world before it is too late."

The members of the cabinet were quiet for a moment then someone began to applaud. The applause spread across the room except for a few hardliners like General Jorgensen, who sat with disgusted looks on their faces.

Sitting down the President continued.

"I'm glad that we agree. Now, we need to come to a consensus concerning our stance toward China. Ross Hamilton and two of his colleagues at the Federal Reserve have been working on this problem. Mr. Hamilton."

"As most of you are aware, we have an unofficial agreement with China and Japan that we will not impose import tariffs and we sell grain at subsidized prices as long as they finance our debt.

"In retaliation to China's action, the US will impose an export tax on agricultural products to equal China's current luxury tax on American made goods of 135%. In addition, like Myanmar, the US will place a 100% band on all China imports. Finally, the US will freeze all of China's assets."

Dorothy Hendricks, the Secretary of Home Land Security retorts, "China will counter attack. American companies doing business in China will get hurt."

Hamilton answered, "True, but keep in mind any American company doing business in China has less than 50% ownership. Also, as Li Ping so graciously pointed out, big box retailers will suffer, but like any sweeping economic change there were be causalities."

The Secretary of Commerce interjected. "Eliminating one point two million military jobs will create rampant unemployment."

Normally more reserved, Ross Hamelton spoke up.

"The military will be re-employed in government sponsored industries. When the government spends money on the military there's a zero return on investment. But when the government takes on a project like FDR's Hoover damn, it provides employment and receives a return on its investment. It is the only solution to save the dollar."

Robert O'Neil interjected, "Like the auto bailout."

"Yes, something like the auto bailout. Gentlemen, for decades America has been loosing an economic battle with countries like South Korea, Japan and China."

To everyone's surprise Ross Hamelton slammed his fist on the table and shouted.

"We must act now, or there will be no economy worth protecting tomorrow."

The room grew icy cold. In a calming voice the President spoke.

"Thank you Mr. Hamilton. To restore confidence in the dollar we will divert all military and Homeland Security funds to be used to establish new American corporations. These corporations will be built by the men and women comprising the military and Homeland Security. These new companies will be the most profitable, fastest growing companies in existence. Like Vorbine, these new entities will be hui corporations.

"The government of America will answer the call to action by not only supporting the formation of hui companies, we will instigate the largest industrial investment of hui corporations the world has ever seen. Soon our nation's unemployment problem will be a thing of the past. Non-polluting sustainable hui corporations will dominate the landscape and global warming will no longer be a threat. As America prospers, this new found wealth will spread to the corners of the globe. Within our lifetime economic equality is feasible not for just the citizens of America, but for all of mankind."

Epilogue

Thomas stood on the balcony watching the Vorbines spin in the distance when Jackie opened the sliding glass door.

"Thomas, we're going to be late. Let's get going."

"I can't find my glasses. Help me look for them. I'm not leaving without my glasses."

"I don't see why you don't have your eyes fixed. It only takes an afternoon."

Coming in from the balcony Thomas said, "Now don't start with that, old lady. I like my eyes just the way they are, thank you."

Jackie let out a peel of laughter. Even at eighty-two, Jackie retained her spontaneous ability to crack up. Pointing at Thomas, she stopped laughing long enough to say, "Call off the search party, the antiquated treasure is hiding in your shirt pocket."

"Ha! A devious hiding place. The only antiquated treasure around here is you."

Speeding in the mag train over 600 miles per hour, Thomas couldn't curb his excitement at seeing his grandson perform at the Kennedy Center. He tapped out various rhythms he had heard Martin create when he was a young boy. Now, at the age of twenty-six, he is the youngest percussionist in the New York Philharmonic.

Sitting in one of four side balcony boxes, Jackie held Thomas's hand. The conductor stood and announced, "Today we are going to perform a new piece in honor of someone here with us today. The piece calls to mind what our world was like forty-five years ago. It is titled: A World With No Boundaries."

The lights went down and thunderous music accompanied images appearing on a screen behind the orchestra. Mountains of garbage heaped under smog filled skies filled the screen. Building in ascending emotion came a barrage of images of starving men, women and children interlaced with images of opulent wealth.

As the music grew more thunderous images of smoke stacks spewing out tons of black smoke turned to images of polluted oceans and rivers drifting onto the shores of cities encircled with shanty town ghettos shifted to images of highways with miles of parked cars. Leading on, oil fields a blaze cascaded with images of rolling tanks firing rockets as jets dropped bombs on soldiers battling below. Building in sound and emotion the screen went red and the orchestra suddenly was silent. The screen went from red to dark red to black all the while the faintest music from a single flute became to float up.

As the flute played softly in the darkness, other instruments gently joined in as the screen gradually changed from black to gray. Soon the entire orchestra joined in, playing more and more joyously until the screen became bright white.

The brilliant white slowly changed into the billowy soft veins of a feather. The music danced on as the image of the feather slowly began to float down from a clear blue sky into the hands of a smiling child. Laughing the child threw the feather back up into the sky and it changed into a large white sea bird that flew upward against a sea cliff.

When the bird was high, it turned and dove. The bird plunged into the ocean where a group of dolphins played with a piece of seaweed and mother whale swam with her calf below. As the music gained momentum, the bird lifted up out of the water, taking flight over New York. In and out of the skyscrapers it flew. Down below people were walking or riding bikes in the streets as trams calmly moved along.

Passing over the converted magtrain highways, up and up the bird flew before plunging into the Tigris River where fish darted in and out of graceful stands of coontail. Rising out of the water, the bird circled Baghdad and floated down to a small community outside the city where children were playing soccer.

Catching the ball, the goalie kicked it into the air. As if floating on the wings of the violin, the ball rose up against the blue sky and dropped back to earth on a South African soccer field where a young boy kicked it into the air to where a young Brazilian girl headed it over to another field where a Chinese boy kicked it. On into the blue sky the ball floated up and up until it slowly changed into shape of the world fading out among the stars.